Laotian Daughters

IN THE SERIES **Asian American History and Culture,**
edited by Sucheng Chang, David Palumbo-Liu, Michael Omi,
K. Scott Wong, and Linda Trinh Võ

ALSO IN THIS SERIES:

Cherstin M. Lyon, *Prisons and Patriots: Japanese American Wartime Citizenship, Civil Disobedience, and Historical Memory*

Shelley Sang-Hee Lee, *Claiming the Oriental Gateway: Prewar Seattle and Japanese America*

Isabelle Thuy Pelaud, *This Is All I Choose to Tell: History and Hybridity in Vietnamese American Literature*

Christian Collet and Pei-te Lien, eds., *The Transnational Politics of Asian Americans*

Min Zhou, *Contemporary Chinese America: Immigration, Ethnicity, and Community Transformation*

Kathleen S. Yep, *Outside the Paint: When Basketball Ruled at the Chinese Playground*

Benito M. Vergara, Jr., *Pinoy Capital: The Filipino Nation in Daly City*

Jonathan Y. Okamura, *Ethnicity and Inequality in Hawai'i*

Sucheng Chan and Madeline Y. Hsu, eds., *Chinese Americans and the Politics of Race and Culture*

K. Scott Wong, *Americans First: Chinese Americans and the Second World War*

Lisa Yun, *The Coolie Speaks: Chinese Indentured Laborers and African Slaves in Cuba*

Estella Habal, *San Francisco's International Hotel: Mobilizing the Filipino American Community in the Anti-Eviction Movement*

Thomas P. Kim, *The Racial Logic of Politics: Asian Americans and Party Competition*

Laotian Daughters

Working toward Community, Belonging, and Environmental Justice

BINDI V. SHAH

TEMPLE UNIVERSITY PRESS
Philadelphia

TEMPLE UNIVERSITY PRESS
Philadelphia, Pennsylvania 19122
www.temple.edu/tempress

Copyright © 2012 by Temple University
All rights reserved
Published 2012

Library of Congress Cataloging-in-Publication Data
Shah, Bindi V., 1960–
  Laotian daughters : working toward community, belonging, and environmental justice / Bindi V. Shah.
    p. cm. — (Asian American history and culture)
  Includes bibliographical references and index.
  ISBN 978-1-4399-0813-6 (cloth : alk. paper)
  ISBN 978-1-4399-0815-0 (pbk. : alk. paper)
  ISBN 978-1-4399-0814-3 (e-book)
  1. Laotian Americans—California—Contra Costa County. 2. Teenage girls—California—Contra Costa County. 3. Children of immigrants—California—Contra Costa County. 4. Environmental justice—California—Contra Costa County. 5. Contra Costa County (Calif.)—Race relations—Case studies. 6. Asian Pacific Environmental Network. I. Title. II. Series: Asian American history and culture.

  F870.L27S53 2012
  305.895'073079463—dc22   2011016214

2 4 6 8 9 7 5 3 1

*For all the young Laotian women involved in
Asian Youth Advocates from 1997 to 1999—
they demonstrated spirit, perseverance, and commitment
to social justice in the face of adversity*

*And for my children,
Anirudh and Apurva*

*Each has taught me what is important
and what it means to be the new second generation*

CONTENTS

	Acknowledgments	ix
1	"Where We Live, Where We Work, Where We Play, Where We Learn": The Asian Pacific Environmental Network	1
2	From Agent Orange to Superfund Sites to Anti-immigrant Sentiments: Multiple Voyages, Ongoing Challenges	22
3	New Immigration and the American Nation: A Framework for Citizenship and Belonging	37
4	The Politics of Race: Political Identity and the Struggle for Social Rights	52
5	Negotiating Racial Hierarchies: Critical Incorporation, Immigrant Ideology, and Interminority Relations	82
6	Family, Culture, Gender: Narratives of Ethnic Reconstruction	106
7	Building Community, Crafting Belonging in Multiple Homes	130
8	Becoming "American": Remaking American National Identity through Environmental Justice Activism	153
APPENDIX	Socio-demographic Information on Second-Generation Laotians Who Participated in the Study	167
	Notes	169
	References	181
	Index	197

ACKNOWLEDGMENTS

So many people have touched my life and work over the years that this book is profoundly the result of a collective effort. First and foremost I owe immeasurable thanks to all the teens and staff at Asian Youth Advocates, the Laotian Organizing Project, and the Asian Pacific Environmental Network. In addition to being open and honest, they were extremely generous throughout the research phase and years later, providing me with information and resources and welcoming me into the "APEN family." They were extraordinarily willing to tolerate my scrutiny and questions even when they sometimes felt unsure about my motives. I hope that they find something of value in my portrayal of them.

The research for this project was funded by a University of California–Davis Graduate Fellowship, a University of California–Davis Humanities Graduate Research Award, and a research award from the Consortium for Women and Research at the University of California–Davis. Participation in a dissertation workshop organized by the University of California–Davis Center for History, Society, and Culture and a workshop on youth and immigration organized by the University of California's Humanities Institute helped shape some of my early writing on the project. Generous financial support from the Economic and Social Research Council, U.K., gave me valuable time for the writing of this book.

At the University of California–Davis I benefited from the inspiration, support, and encouragement of various educators, colleagues, and mentors. I am especially grateful to Diane Wolf, Ming-cheng Lo, and Yen Le Espiritu, who saw an earlier version of this project. Without their comments, critical insights, and constant urgings to be aware of contexts and nuances, that version would have not achieved the clarity it had. Diane Wolf is a valuable friend and mentor. And Fred Block, Ruth Frankenberg, Suad Joseph, Lata Mani, Judith Stacey, and John Walton were all instrumental in developing my skills for critical inquiry. I was fortunate to participate in a graduate reading group, and I thank Estee Neuwirth,

Eileen Otis, Preston Rudy, and Eva Skuratowicz for their camaraderie and emotional support, and for taking time to read earlier versions of this project.

Many thanks go to colleagues in the United Kingdom who provided intellectual enrichment and encouragement or shared their comments on previous versions of this project: Avtar Brah, Claire Dwyer, Umut Erel, Tariq Modood, John Salt, and Miri Song. At Roehampton University, where I was an Economic and Social Research Council Research Fellow, I greatly benefited from support and intellectual exchanges with Floya Anthias, John Eade, Aisha Gill, and Pathik Pathak.

I wish to thank my editor at Temple University Press, Janet Francendese, who supported this project through all its stages. I especially appreciate series editor Linda Võ's unwavering belief in this book. Linda Võ and the two anonymous reviewers at the Press devoted a great deal of time and effort to reading and commenting on the manuscript. There is no question that this is a vastly improved book because of their critical insights. My thanks to Charles H. E. Ault and Amanda Steele at Temple University Press, as well as Kimberley Vivier and Lynne Frost, who moved production along smoothly.

I owe an enormous debt of gratitude to my parents, Pramila and Velji Shah. Their early support for my education and their encouragement to follow my heart and interests gave me the confidence and desire to embark on an academic career in sociology. While I was conducting the research for this book and writing the earlier versions, they traveled from the United Kingdom to California several times to help care for my children and feed us all. My siblings, Urmi and Ameet, and my brother-in-law, Mukie, have provided much love and support. I am also indebted to Farm Saephan and Patricia Robles. My children thrived under their warm and loving care during the early phases of this project. And simple words of thanks cannot express my deep appreciation for Rajen Shah, my partner in life, my companion, and my emotional mainstay. Without the countless meals, relief from my share of household chores and care for our children, and his willingness to listen to my frustrations and milestones, without his constant love and support, I could not have completed all the phases of this book. Our two children, Anirudh and Apurva, bring tremendous joy and laughter. They help me keep balance and purpose in my life.

Sections of some chapters have been published previously. I thank the publishers for permission to use the material here.

> Material from portions of Chapter 4 appeared in "The Politics of Race and Education: Second-Generation Laotian Women Campaign for Improved Educational Services." *Social Justice: Special Issue on Asian American Activism*, Vol. 35, No. 2 (2008): 100–118. Copyright © by Social Justice.

> Material from portions of Chapters 4 and 5 appeared in "'Is Yellow Black or White?' Inter-minority Relations and the Prospects for Cross-racial

Coalitions between Laotians and African Americans in the San Francisco Bay Area." *Ethnicities*, Vol. 8, No. 4 (2008): 463–491. Copyright © by Sage Publications Ltd. UK.

Material from portions of Chapters 4, 6, and 7 appeared in "Gender, Family, Community: Cultural Reconstruction among Teenage Laotian Girls in Northern California." In *Asian American Children: A Historical Handbook and Guide*, ed. Benson Tong, pp. 101–121. Westport, CT: Greenwood Press, 2004.

An earlier version of material presented in portions of Chapter 6 appeared in "'Being Young, Female and Laotian': Ethnicity as Social Capital at the Intersection of Gender, Generation, Race and Age." *Ethnic and Racial Studies*, Vol. 30, No. 1 (2007): 28–50. Copyright © by Routledge, Taylor and Francis Group.

Laotian Daughters

1

"Where We Live, Where We Work, Where We Play, Where We Learn"

The Asian Pacific Environmental Network

Ethnographic Moments

Seventeen thirteen- and fourteen-year-old girls, three Asian Youth Advocates (AYA) staff, reporter Joe Garofoli from the *West County Times,* and I clamber onto a yellow school bus, hired to take us on a "toxic tour" of Richmond and San Pablo, California, in July 1998. The teens in AYA's Group 3 are leading the tour for the benefit of those in Group 4. Before we set off from Grace Lutheran Church, Lai and Fiey give us a brief overview of the level of contaminants present in the air, water, and land each year in both cities. The most shocking fact is that workers and residents in Contra Costa County are exposed to contaminants from chemical accidents every two and a half months. As we begin our tour, the excitement among the girls is palpable in the cacophony of noise. This trip is a change from sitting in a room at Grace Lutheran. Our first stop is the Electro Forming Chrome Plating Company, situated in a mixed residential-industrial zone. As the bus stops, Tsiet comes to the front and tells us that nitric acid leaked from one of the tanks and spread over a twenty-block area in August 1992. More than one hundred people were hospitalized. Following this incident, the people in the neighborhood organized to file a class-action suit against the company. The company not only changed its name to avoid the lawsuit but also went as far as laying the blame for the leak on a bullet fired into the tank by someone in the community. The police never found the bullet and concluded that rusting caused a hole in the tank. However, the city and the county claimed that their hands were tied because the company had been located at this spot long before the residential area that developed around it.

We continue along the streets of Richmond and come to a halt outside Peres Elementary School. Everybody jumps off the bus, and we assemble by the wire mesh fence that marks the school boundary. It is a stark and desolate place, with asphalt-covered grounds surrounding the one-story brown buildings. There is not a tree in sight, but the Chevron refinery looms over it. Pham, who attended Peres, informs us that instead of doing fire drills or earthquake drills, they constantly practiced evacuation drills. Whenever there was a toxic leak, "the principal would tell us over the intercom to get into a line and put a paper napkin or tissue over our mouths and nose so that we wouldn't breathe in the toxins. We would get into a bus and ride around town for a few minutes, maybe an hour, so that the spills or leaks would be cleaned up and it was safe for us to return to school." Pham ends her story by stating that test scores for students at Peres have been in the lowest 1 percent of the state.

From Peres we drive past the three oil tanks, painted brown so as to blend in with the surrounding hills, and the Chevron refinery. Pham informs us that according to the Environmental Protection Agency (EPA), this facility produces over 20 million pounds of toxic emissions per year. Since October 1991 the facility has had ten serious chemical spills, including a 40-ton dust blizzard that spread over a 16-square-mile area. Such toxic emissions have caused health problems such as cancers and brain damage. We continue on our "toxic tour" through north Richmond, where the only store in sight is a liquor store. Our fourth stop is the Drew Scrap Metals Superfund site, where the company operated until 1976. We get off the bus and walk around this empty overgrown lot with a chain-link fence around it. Tracy recounts the history of this site, now dubbed "Laotian Gardens." Drew Scrap Metals had released heavy metals such as lead and cadmium into the soil, all of which can cause learning disabilities and brain damage. After the company had stopped operations, an African American family moved in to the house adjacent to this lot. They experienced health problems, and some died of cancer. The African American family eventually moved out, but several Laotian families replaced them, growing herbs and vegetables in the toxic soil to supplement their diet. They were completely unaware of the dangers until a public health nurse, concerned about the level of lead in their children, discovered where their food was grown. The primary source was the contaminated soil and the lead-based paint chips from the house. Although there were warning signs at the facility, they were in only English and Spanish. The Laotians were relocated, and the house was torn down. Twelve years after the company shut down, the area became a Superfund site, or one of the worst toxic sites in the United States identified by the EPA. The government attempted to clean up the area by mixing clean soil with the contaminated soil and paving over the land. Tracy points out the EPA warning sign tied to the fence and the white meter in a corner, which the EPA uses to check the level of contaminants. Next to "Laotian Gardens" is what looks like the remains of a factory. Across the lot are a mom-and-pop grocery store and a few single-story houses. Though some are boarded up, others have well-kept gardens. The only people in sight are a few middle-aged African Americans and three younger Latino men.

The next site on the tour is the Chevron Ortho Pesticide Plant and Incinerator, now closed down. Paeng comes to the front of the bus to give us the history of this site. Chevron had operated this plant since 1967 on a temporary permit and had repeatedly tried to get a permanent permit but without success. The company hid the fact that it was manufacturing a chemical called methylene chloride, a known cause of cancer. In 1997 the plant was finally shut down after a campaign led by the West County Toxics Coalition, Communities for a Better Environment, and Greenpeace, showing how the community organized to solve its worst problem. As Paeng makes this statement, there are cheers and claps. The sixth stop is General Chemical, still in north Richmond. Alison comes to the front of the bus and reminds us that in July 1993 there was a chemical disaster here. Workers were unloading a railcar filled with the chemical oleum for Chevron's use. It became overheated, and a cloud of sulfuric acid escaped through a hole and covered an area three by seventeen miles. More than 20,000 people visited local hospitals with symptoms of burning throats and eyes. As Alison mentions this, several of the Group 4 girls utter "uh-huh" and tell us that they remember the sulfuric acid spill and having to go to the hospital. "One good thing came of this spill," Alison informs us. "Chevron spent $1.8 million to build a warning system and fund the North Richmond Center for Health."

The final stop on this "toxic tour" of Richmond and San Pablo is the United Heckathorn Superfund site at Richmond harbor. We all get off the bus to look around. I notice that the EPA warning sign telling people not to fish in the San Francisco Bay is in English. Up ahead several men are fishing! I can't tell whether they are Asian or Latino. The wind has picked up now, and we huddle around Maya so we can hear what she has to say about this site. The EPA has put United Heckathorn on the Superfund site list because the company discarded pesticides, including DDT, into the harbor between 1947 and 1966. Once the EPA closed the site, the original plan was to dig up the mud and dump it in a landfill in the small Arizona community of Mobile, where about one hundred Latinos and African Americans lived. The company developed these plans without consultation with or permission from the communities in Richmond and Mobile. Eventually, after strong community pressure in both places, these plans were changed. "But even though they don't dump it here, they'll dump it somewhere else, which is not a solution," asserts Maya. Finally, she reminds us that the toxic dumping, though now ceased, continues to impact Laotians and other local communities that fish in the harbor. Warning signs are ineffective because many Laotians cannot read or understand English. In any case, fishing is an important source of food, as more than 50 percent of Laotians live below the poverty level and about 60 percent are on public assistance, compared with only 17 percent of the general population. I overhear Joe Garofoli say, "I learned a lot today," but the girls in Group 4 do not exhibit surprise at these facts. Perhaps for them these are all too familiar facts of life.

We climb back onto the bus and head back to Grace Lutheran Church. There is a contemplative silence as the teens mull over this "toxic tour" of Richmond and San Pablo.

It's a warm August evening in Richmond in 1999. Several of the AYA youth and I are sitting around a couple of long tables in the Laotian Organizing Project's offices. Over pizzas, soda, and fruit, we are having a wide-ranging conversation about Laotian culture, what it means to be an American, living in Richmond, experiences of racism, how they would envision their dream community, and what kind of image of Laotian teenagers they would want a reporter to portray. On these last two themes the overwhelming desire among the young women is not to be stereotyped. Gabriela recounts the following incident when she took her mom to the local public hospital when she was having health problems. When Gabriela asked the attending nurse for the diagnosis, the nurse, instead of responding to Gabriela, turned to another nurse nearby and said, "Why can't they just take it and go somewhere else? They are getting it off for free." Understandably angry, Gabriela retorted, "My mom didn't get off for free; we pay for half of the stuff." In response to my question about how they would want a reporter to represent them, Tsiet also recalled how nurses had stereotyped her: "Like in a hospital they go 'Oh! It's good that you're not having sex yet, not having kids, 'cause I just have two twelve-year-old girls in here,' and then, like, 'She's pregnant.' They will say stuff to me like that when I go to the hospital so I'll be mad." Tsiet acknowledged that many young Laotian girls do have children, but she wanted a reporter to show that some "have their own mind, they have goals in their life, and they wanna achieve it."

The U.S. Environmental Justice Movement and the Asian Pacific Environmental Network

These two ethnographic moments, the first based on field notes recorded during a "toxic tour" of Richmond and San Pablo, California, given by a group of fourteen-year-old Laotian girls and the second drawing from focus group discussions with sixteen-year-old Laotian girls, illustrate how they are simultaneously cast as racialized minority, immigrants, refugees, young people of color, poor, and teenage girls and how they challenge dominant understandings of social formations in the United States through participation in Asian Youth Advocates (AYA), a leadership development project established by the Asian Pacific Environmental Network (APEN) in the Laotian community in Richmond, California. Founded in 1993, APEN has roots in the environmental justice movement in the United States. Two reports published in the 1980s, one by the U.S. General Accounting Office (GAO 1983) and a second by the United Church of Christ Commission for Racial Justice, titled *Toxic Wastes and Race in the United States* (1987), found that African Americans and people of color were more likely to be exposed to environmental hazards than white people. These seminal studies and the First National People of Color Environmental Leadership Summit, held in Washington D.C., in October 1991,[1] popularized the notion of "environmental racism" and "environmental justice." The Principles of Environmental Justice,[2] adopted at the summit, galvanized the environmental justice movement (Sze 2007), and activists in communities of color had a new language to understand their work. The summit mobilized regional environmental justice networks in the late 1980s and early 1990s (Chang and Hwang 2000), propelling the reconceptualization of the environment in the United States as "where we live, where we work, where we play, where we learn" (Cole and Foster 2001:16).[3] With the creation of an Office of Environmental Equity within the Environmental Protection Agency and President Bill Clinton's executive order on environmental justice in 1994, all federal offices and agencies were directed to create policies to address the environmental inequities experienced by communities of color, further institutionalizing the environmental justice framework into U.S. laws (Sze 2007).

In contrast to more traditional environmental groups, the environmental justice movement adopts a civil rights discourse, providing a social justice framework for understanding environmental problems and risks and the uneven distribution of the effects of such risks in terms of race and class. As Cole and Foster (2001:33) point out, it thus offers a broader perspective on environmental activism through its goals (fighting for health, homes, and community), strategies (direct action), and political orientation (linking environmental problems to wider social justice issues). APEN, as part of the environmental justice movement, presents a radical perspective on integration and incorporation into American society to Laotians, a new immigrant community:

> All people have the right to a clean and healthy environment in which their communities can live, work, learn, play and thrive. Towards that vision, the Asian Pacific Environmental Network was founded in 1993 to unify, empower, and strengthen the capacities of our diverse Asian and Pacific Islander communities to build a broad movement for environmental, social and economic justice. (Mission statement in APEN's 5th Anniversary Celebration Program, 1998)

One of the central philosophical elements of the environmental justice movement is the concept of self-determination, translated into the credo "We speak for ourselves" (Cole and Foster 2001:27). The staff at APEN has sought to stay true to this principle and do "base building work" (Peggy Saika, then APEN executive director, interview, 21 October 1998), or build community organizations from the bottom up, in communities that have few formalized structures for creating social change. With this goal, in 1995 APEN created the Laotian Organizing Project (LOP) in the city of Richmond, located in west Contra Costa County, California. From the beginning, LOP has focused on a leadership development program for teenage Laotian girls, aiming to raise a political consciousness about environmental and social justice issues as well as address issues pertinent to adolescents, such as self-esteem and identity. APEN hoped to both empower and engage this bilingual second generation in community activism, and through these girls to nurture social capital and political efficacy in this new immigrant community, with the ultimate goal of challenging existing racial hierarchies and related structures and processes of racial inequality (Shah 2007, 2008).

During the time I was in the field, 1997–1999, thirty-one girls ranging from thirteen to seventeen years of age participated in the program. Once accepted, the teens were expected to make a four-year commitment to AYA. They participated in an intensive six-week summer program, meeting four hours a day, four days a week, during which time they earned a stipend. The curriculum for the first summer session for each new group included reproductive health, sexuality and sexual orientation, body image and cultural identity, gender roles, team-building exercises, and an introduction to the principles of environmental justice. In the second and subsequent summers the curriculum for each group varied but included a stronger emphasis on environmental justice as well as elements of Asian Pacific Island histories and community organizing strategies, Laotian history, and the development of organizing skills among the girls. AYA staff delivered these themes through popular education and experiential learning methods. The summer sessions ended with a graduation, to which the girls' families and other community members were invited. Each group continued to meet several times a month during the school year, under the leadership of young Asian American and Laotian counselors, to carry out specific projects, partake in training (developing skills in, for example, popular theater), and attend conferences, workshops, and exchanges with other youth groups. In these ways AYA staff encouraged the young women to actively participate in developing their leadership and community organizing skills. Another important component of the youth program was emotional support through peer counseling.

During the first three years of AYA the staff primarily focused on building capacity among the teens so they could become active in decisions that affect their lives. In September 1998, with four cohorts of teenage girls in the program, APEN staff decided to shift from what they called "youth programming" to "youth organizing" (Peggy Saika, interview, 21 October 1998), reflecting a desire to harness the energy and leadership skills of the youth to help build LOP as an organization that can eventually form part of an Asian American face in the environmental justice movement in the United States. As I note in Chapter 8, APEN no longer runs a youth program for teenage Laotian girls. Thus this book marks a particular historical moment in APEN's organizing work in the Laotian community in Richmond, California, and captures a specific stage in the lives of these second-generation Laotian girls.

Why write a book about a small youth leadership development project? *Laotian Daughters* offers an ethnographic account of the strategies and practices of APEN's Asian Youth Advocates and second-generation Laotian girls' engagement with community politics and environmental justice activism in order to investigate the process of becoming "American" among the children of one the newest immigrant groups. But it is not a story framed in the dominant paradigm of assimilation and incorporation. It is a story that casts immigration as a generative site for critiquing and transforming American national identity. In other words, this story does not just tell us about the children of immigrants; it also addresses what the experiences of adaptation and incorporation reveal about the contemporary United States, particularly how racialization processes and understandings of national identity and membership play a role in the integration of Laotian immigrants and their children and in the formulation of their claims for citizenship and belonging. These immigrants draw attention to the politics of belonging, the nature of citizenship, and national identity in the United States in the twenty-first century. As Lisa Lowe reminds us,

Asian immigrants and Asian Americans have not only been "subject to" immigration exclusion and restriction but have also been "subjects of" the immigration process and are agents of political change, cultural expression, and social transformation. (Lowe 1996:9)

Contemporary social justice organizations such as APEN acknowledge the intersectionality and simultaneity of processes of racialization, class exploitation, and subordination based on gender, age, and other axes that shape individual and collective experiences in the United States. In addition to race and class, gender has been integral to APEN's vision of a youth leadership development program in the Laotian community in Richmond. APEN staff was increasingly aware of the link between women's reproductive health and the environmental health of the community, as well as the need for access to adequate and timely health care. In a community that is linguistically isolated, bilingual girls play a key role as disseminators of information about reproductive and environmental health to members of their families and community. At the same time, there were barriers to the young women's participation in a leadership development program, including teenage pregnancy. While motherhood confers high status on women within the Laotian community, and parents encouraged girls to marry and have children at a young age, the APEN staff, adopting a feminist and middle-class ethos, believed that the high number of teen births among Laotian girls placed enormous emotional, financial, and educational burdens on them and prevented them from leading stable and productive adult lives. In early conversations with Laotian girls, the staff also heard complaints of gender discrimination from parents and a sense of schizophrenia as the girls navigated different cultures at home, at school, and among peers. The APEN staff thus viewed Laotian girls as the most marginalized sector in the community. A leadership development project aimed at these girls would not only address their specific needs and strengthen their cultural identity but also nurture a new generation of women leaders, in a community where authority is traditionally vested in elderly Laotian males, to act as advocates for the health of their community and to organize around environmental justice, reproductive health, and broader community issues. Few studies focus on immigrant women in the context of politics and civic life.[4] Through rich ethnographic detail, including the four profiles presented later in this chapter, this book makes visible teenage Laotian girls' political development and their engagement with political activism and community building.

The case of AYA also demonstrates that citizenship is not just an adult experience. Such a characterization ignores both the social/cultural context of young people's lives and their efforts to achieve social change (France 1998:99–100). For Asian American young people, the "model minority" stereotype obfuscates the complexity of their lives. Moreover, popular culture and subcultural sites such as underground magazines, alternative music and style, and computer hacker clubs are not the only arenas for oppositional politics among young people (Giroux 1998:24). *Laotian Daughters* illustrates the teenagers' resistance and struggle in relation to issues of class and race, as well as gender and intergenerational relations, and the construction of substantive citizenship among young people through organized activism. I argue that through Asian Youth Advocates, APEN exposes young Laotians to dominant cultural values of freedom, autonomy, and security, as well as to the more critical discourses of race and gender equality and justice. In so doing, it engages in the cultural politics of *critical incorporation,* or a set of practices in the cultural political realm that challenge, accommodate, or transform power relations within the nation, civil society, and the Laotian family. It is at the level of everyday life that "the interests of the dominant culture are negotiated and contested" (Escobar 1992:75). The cultural work done by APEN allowed the young Laotian women to understand how systems of domination permeate everyday life, to produce meaning in relation to complex relations of power, and to construct collective identities and collective capacities for change. At the same time, in this process of learning to belong and to become subjects through AYA, second-generation Laotian women also resisted specific agendas, modified meanings and practices, and inserted critiques, suggesting active participation in shaping the meaning of what it means to be "American."

A primary theoretical goal of this book is to analyze multiple spatial scales—the nation, civil society institutions, and the family—to illustrate the ways in which the teenage daughters of Laotian immigrants are negotiating the contradictions between the liberal ideology of universal citizenship and the collective boundaries of race, class, nationality, gender, and life stage that define substantive citizenship. Here I want to distinguish between legal or formal citizenship as a status that confers rights and duties, and substantive citizenship, or citizenship as social practice, which is actively constructed through forging a sense of belonging, political participation in its broadest sense, and equal access to rights and opportunities (Glenn 2004; Ehrkamp and Leitner 2003; Isin and Wood 1999).

The practice of citizenship encompasses the local as well as the national level. The United States has a laissez-faire approach to immigrant political incorporation (Bloemraad 2006). Government policy and resources remain focused on managing the entry of immigrants into the country. Beyond entry there is little official involvement with later processes of integration and incorporation, the exception being federal government support in the form of settlement aid to legal refugees. However, as Aihwa Ong (2003) reminds us, refugees and immigrants experience everyday processes of making and self-making in official and public arenas, such as refugee camps, the welfare state, the court system, community hospitals, local churches, and civic organizations, as they become subjects of dominant norms, rules, values, and systems (see also Glenn 2004). Such daily encounters shape their ideas about what being American might mean and provide the resources to contest exclusion and make claims at local, state, and national levels. In other words, they undergo a process of sociopolitical incorporation. In this book I focus on micropolitics to examine the nature of incorporation enacted through a youth leadership development program by a contemporary social justice organization, APEN.

The Study

In 1995 APEN established the Laotian Organizing Project in the city of Richmond, California. The Laotian community here is invisible: it has no representation in local government structures (Lochner 1997). Moreover, as I discuss in detail in Chapter 2, Richmond is a critical site for APEN's environmental justice work. The city of Richmond's industrial history has left local residents disproportionately prone to environmental toxins emitted from 350 industrial plants. Nearly all the studies that have investigated the distribution of environmental hazards during the 1980s and 1990s have found race and income to be significant factors. Where it has been possible to assess the relative importance of these factors, race has tended to be the better predictor of the location of environmental hazards (Mohai and Bryant 1992). These trends are also evident in Richmond, where the population is overwhelmingly constituted by communities of color—79 percent in 2000 (U.S. Census Bureau 2000b)—and experiences high levels of unemployment and welfare dependency. In the last two decades of the twentieth century the city of Richmond and surrounding areas witnessed a dramatic transformation in the racial landscape. There has been tremendous growth of Latino and Asian communities, though African Americans still represent the largest majority. This socioeconomic milieu creates the potential for interracial tension as well as opportunities for cross-race coalitions and common struggle for a new immigrant and refugee community.

Since 1995 LOP had been focused on creating a leadership development program for teenage Laotian girls. An opportunity to realize such a project arose when the University of California–San Francisco's Center for Reproductive Health Research and Policy (CRHRP) received funding from the California Wellness Foundation to conduct research on teen pregnancy prevention in Asian and Pacific Islander communities. CRHRP sought to implement this grant through community partners and selected Asian Pacific Islanders for Reproductive Health (APIRH), based in Oakland, California, as one such partner. Peggy Saika (then APEN's executive director) and Ming Chang[5] (then a staff member at APEN) were also members of APIRH's board, enabling APIRH and APEN to work together to initiate a youth program for Laotian girls in Richmond. The California Wellness Foundation grant supported AYA for one year; in the second year, funding was more precarious and APEN subsidized the program through its other project budgets. Asian Youth Advocates gained a firm footing in 1997 when the Ms. Foundation for Women awarded APEN a three-year grant through its Healthy Girls/Healthy Women Collaborative Fund. In 2000 the Ms. Foundation renewed this grant for one year, and the California Wellness Foundation awarded APEN a two-year grant to continue health education in the Laotian community through AYA.

Beginning in 1995, the AYA staff recruited young Laotian girls from a local middle school attended by most of the Laotian children who live in Richmond or the adjoining city of San Pablo (Grace Kong, interview, 9 October 1998). An informal agreement with the principal at the school allowed AYA staff to present the program to all the Laotian girls in the seventh grade. Fliers posted at the school promoted the summer program as a chance for the girls to work with other exciting Laotian girls; develop leadership skills; organize a campaign; learn about their health, their community, and their environment; build a community; take field trips; and earn money. In early June AYA staff and one or two youth members already involved in AYA visited the school to present the summer program and meet with the girls. Those who were interested completed an application form that asked why they wanted to join the program, what they thought of their community and environment, and what they would do to change it; they were asked as well to describe the experiences they had had at school, work, church, or in other settings that would help them in the program. The staff also gave them a consent form and an information packet to take home to their parents. After reviewing the applications and interviewing potential recruits, the staff selected ten to twelve girls to join the program each summer based on their interest and their willingness to make a four-year commitment to help build the Laotian Organizing Project and work for social change in the community (Grace Kong, interview, 9 October 1998). Executive Director Peggy Saika suggested that the Asian Youth Advocates is unlike other youth programs:

> We were not talking about creating a summer experience for young people, you know. But we were really talking about a four-year program, a four-year experience that would be really at its core about building the community. (Interview, 21 October 1998)

Asian Youth Advocates began in the summer of 1995 with a group of twelve Laotian girls aged thirteen and fourteen.[6] Recalling the very first meeting with these teenagers, Saika remembered "how withdrawn and shy they were. How they hadn't found their own voice." But Saika also observed that "they were so streetwise because of their exposure to gangs, and drugs and poverty . . . and yet had so few opportunities for personal growth" (interview, 21 October 1998). In the summer of 1996 a second group of nine girls joined the program, in 1997 a third group of eleven girls enrolled, and in the summer of 1998 a fourth group of ten girls was recruited. While I was in the field, the retention rate for the first group was 50 percent. For the second group, it was 50 percent until the girls in that group reached the end of their third year, when it dropped to 40 percent. Retention rates for the third and fourth groups were approximately 80 percent. These high rates attest to the intensity of staff-youth interactions as well as peer support relationships, which I discuss further in Chapter 7. The following profiles of four girls, each belonging to one of the groups in AYA, provide a portrayal of their social, cultural, and economic experiences and community activism.

Seng

Seng, seventeen years old, was a member of Group 1, the first group of girls to be recruited into AYA. She was born in Thailand and arrived in the United States at age two and a half with her mother and younger brother. Seng's mother worked in a factory that made candles. Being the oldest child and being bicultural and bilingual in Mien and English, Seng helped her mother navigate American institutions. Her mother placed high expectations on Seng, urging her to succeed in school and go to college, and most of all not to become a teenage mother. Seng herself was an ambitious young woman and aspired to graduate with honors from Richmond High School and to attend the University of California–Berkeley. Financial constraints within Laotian families are one of the key factors preventing young Laotians from attending four-year colleges. Teachers at Richmond High School had nominated Seng for a full scholarship to U.C. Berkeley, which would go some way in paying for college. Eventually, she hoped to acquire a teaching certificate, and toward that end she was working in a tutoring program at her church and had taken on the role of youth counselor during her final summer in AYA. Initially, Seng had joined AYA because it was an opportunity to make new friends. Three years later, at the time of this study, she described it as a "sense of belonging to a family" and as having gained a lot of sisters. Seng had been an active member of AYA, participating in events to inform other young people in the Bay Area about environmental justice work, becoming a precinct leader in the campaign against Proposition 209 (to abolish affirmative action in California), and campaigning against Proposition 227 (to dismantle bilingual education in California schools). Seng attributed not only her self-confidence and high level of motivation to her involvement in AYA but also her awareness about environmental issues in west Contra Costa County and the racial discrimination that young people like her faced. In her junior year Seng drew on her growing political consciousness and her organizing experiences to found ACTION (All Colors Together in One Nation), a multiracial student club aimed at helping students and teachers address issues of race and learning at Richmond High School. For her leadership roles at school and her community work through APEN, Seng won a teen magazine's Take Action Award in 1997 and in the same year was featured in *Time* magazine.

Leah

What I most remember about sixteen-year-old Leah is that she was vocal and confident and had a dry sense of humor. Born in the United States, Leah was bilingual in Lao and English, as were her parents and three siblings, and she had a strong desire to remain a Buddhist and maintain the traditions and ceremonies practiced by her family. Leah's father was a chef, and her mother was a homemaker and attended school. Leah was attending Middle College High School, an "early college" high school that offered underserved students with academic potential the opportunity for dual enrollment in high school and college courses. She hoped to attend a two-year community college before transferring to U.C. Berkeley, which had links with U.C. San Francisco for courses related to medicine. She aspired to be a pediatrician. Leah was part of Group 2, having decided to join AYA after hearing from her older sister in Group 1 that she not only would have opportunities to do interesting activities but also would learn about the community and the environmental issues affecting Richmond residents. Through AYA she had protested against welfare reform; worked precincts and the phone bank to campaign against Proposition 227; participated in one of Ms. Foundation's annual training conferences; acted as the emcee at the Environmental Health Festival in Richmond, organized by AYA youth and APEN staff; acquired organizing skills through her role in the AYA planning committee, helping the staff plan and facilitate the school-year meetings; and worked as a youth counselor for Group 5 in the summer of 1999. Leah had a strong sense of community and believed it was important for Group 2 to make a contribution to LOP's goals of building a voice among Laotians in west Contra Costa County. To that end she had used her leadership skills to try to persuade four of her fellow Group 2 members to remain in AYA for the fourth and final year and to take on greater responsibilities. She believed she would be working in some way to help the Laotian community in west Contra Costa County in the future.

Pham

During my time in the field, fifteen-year-old Pham of Group 3 transformed from a shy teenager to a confident young woman who aspired to study business and law at college and then become a successful businesswoman before marriage. Pham was determined to shatter dominant stereotypes of young Laotian women. She had arrived from Thailand when she was six months old with her parents, three brothers, and two sisters. Both her parents worked as jewelry assemblers. She was bilingual in Mien and English but had no interest in participating in the Mien traditions and ceremonies performed by her parents and other family members. As the oldest daughter, she was expected to help her mother with cooking and chores. Pham often resisted, preferring to spend time on school work so she could maintain her grades at Richmond High School, which her parents also expected, and participate in AYA activities. Pham, along with a few other members of Groups 2 and 3, volunteered to give a "toxic tour" to a multiracial youth group from Oakland and was one of the first to sign up to walk precincts and work the phone bank during the campaign against Proposition 227. Pham was acquiring organizing skills in her role as a member of the Planning Committee in AYA, which gave her responsibility to help plan and facilitate Group 3 meetings during the school year. She was also an active member of the intergenerational committee in LOP and campaigned to improve counseling services at Richmond High School during summer 1999 sessions. In all these ways she was proud to be involved in a program that allowed her to both create awareness within the Laotian community and advocate for its health and well-being in the wider society.

Bryanna

Fourteen-year-old Bryanna, a member of Group 4, described herself as a feminist and identified strong women in popular culture as her role models. Born in the United States, she lived with her parents, grandmother, and four brothers. Her mother worked at two jobs, one involving jewelry assembling and the other making relaxation bath products. Her father worked in a factory that assembled exercise machines. Bryanna was bilingual in Mien and English and enjoyed the occasions when family came together to perform ceremonies. In her freshman year at Richmond High School, Bryanna made a great effort to keep her grades from dropping. After graduating, she hoped to attend a community college for a couple of years, if her family could afford it, before training to become a chef. For Bryanna, AYA provided a welcome respite from the gender expectations she experienced at home as the only daughter and the tense relations between one of her brothers and the rest of the family. She and her cousin Lisa were unique in that they had become involved in LOP's campaign against Proposition 227 even before they officially joined AYA in the summer of 1998. Once she became an AYA member, Bryanna soaked up everything that she was learning, was an active participant, and took every opportunity to volunteer for roles that required learning leadership and organizing skills, such as in the campaign for the multilingual emergency warning system discussed in Chapter 4. Though diffident about the role she could play in the Laotian community, Bryanna expected to remain committed to AYA until she graduated from Richmond High.

Methodology

I describe the participants in this study as Laotian, for reasons discussed in Chapter 3, and the young women understand that AYA is a program of the Laotian Organizing Project. However, when asked how they would identify themselves, sixteen self-identified as Mien, ten as Lao, three as Khmu, and one each as Lue and Hmong. Of this group, twenty-three were born in the United States, six had migrated with their parents before the age of three, and two had arrived at age six. In recent literature on the children of immigrants there is no consensus on how to define them in demographic terms. Scholars such as Danico (2004) and Chan (2006) denote American-born children of immigrants as second-generation and those who were born abroad but migrated at a young age as 1.5-generation. Those falling into the 1.5 generation are said to be bicultural, able to shift between various generational identities and ethnic identities depending on contexts, and able to "code-switch," speaking in both their ancestral language and English in the same situation (Danico 2004:7–8). All the young women in this book perceived themselves as bicultural and were able to code-switch between one of the Laotian languages and English even though they did not all read and write their ancestral language. Moreover, those who had migrated at a young age had similar experiences and outlooks as those born in the United States and perceived their parents as the immigrant generation. Given this lack of distinctive characteristics between those born in the United States and those who arrived at a young age, I follow Portes and Rumbaut (1996) and Zhou (1997a) in adopting the term "second-generation," defined as children of foreign-born parents who are either born in the United States or born abroad and brought to the United States by about age six, to demographically identify the participants in the AYA program.

At the time of this research, the principal staff members at APEN and LOP were second- and third-generation Asian American women community activists from outside the Laotian community. Peggy Saika, the executive director, described herself as the product of the 1960s and the 1970s, during which time she developed an Asian American consciousness within the ethnic movement and a feminist perspective. Other key people who worked with LOP and its various programs were all Asian American women activists under thirty years of age. LOP also employed as counselors young, 1.5-generation Laotian women who had arrived in the United States after age six and who were still in college or had recently graduated. The APEN staff viewed these 1.5-generation Laotian women as role models for the teenage girls as well as potential staff members for the Laotian Organizing Project. In addition, a male Laotian community organizer, who had been instrumental in the resettlement process of Laotians in west Contra Costa County throughout the 1980s, was a member of the LOP staff. His main role was to work with and organize Laotian adults and elders.

The findings from this case study of APEN as a site for sociopolitical incorporation are not generalizable to other sites. Yet I believe that the ethnographic approach adopted in this book has yielded distinct stories about the role of political organizations in the incorporation of new immigrants and their children. This case study demonstrates how second-generation Laotian girls' adaptation and incorporation experiences are shaped by the historical and contemporary politics of race in the United States, and how they negotiate and contest multiple levels of exclusion through their engagement with community politics and Asian American activism. The information gathered here reveals the tensions and struggles, negotiations and accommodation that emerge within family relations, APEN, and specifically AYA, as well as in relation to other racial groups. An ethnographic approach also allows for a critical analysis of APEN's role in the incorporation of second-generation Laotian girls. In the concluding chapter I critically revisit the role of a social justice organization in the sociopolitical incorporation of immigrants and draw attention to the interethnic and gendered power relations within the Laotian Organizing Project and how they shape power and resistance in a marginalized community.

I conducted ethnographic research at the APEN youth program during a two-year span from September 1997 to August 1999.[7] I implemented a triangulation of methods in order to avoid making unwarranted assumptions and essentializing the young women. I conducted intensive, semistructured interviews with all youth members in the four different cohorts (a total of thirty-one, ranging in age from thirteen to seventeen years; socio-demographic data for these individuals appear in the Appendix) and eleven adult staff members who were working or had worked with the youth program. I held interviews with the girls, either in pairs or individually, at a local fast-food restaurant or coffee shops. I interviewed staff members individually at the APEN and LOP offices. In addition, I facilitated four focus groups, one with each of the different cohorts of girls in the program. All the interviews and focus groups were recorded, transcribed, and coded using a grounded theory approach. Throughout the book, quotations from the girls come from these interviews and focus groups as well as other written material they produced.

I participated in and/or observed all games, projects, discussions, trainings, field trips, protests, media events, and end-of-summer graduations, as well as a workshop for Asian and Pacific Islander teens in the San Francisco Bay Area and APEN's fifth anniversary celebration. I attended all event planning meetings, staff meetings, planning committee meetings (which involved staff and youth representatives from each cohort), as well as regular meetings with the girls, though I did not participate in or observe peer counseling sessions during this time. I also participated in a retreat in April 1998 on the San Francisco Peninsula and a three-day retreat in Marin County for all the girls and youth program staff members at the beginning of the 1998 summer program. At this retreat I administered a survey that asked questions about racial/ethnic identity (self-identified), family demographics, immigration history, the social problems the girls identify and/or encounter, and reasons for joining the APEN youth program. My role as documenter of the program allowed me to take full notes openly and collect any materials produced for activities and events. In addition, in the tradition of ethnography, my presence as a researcher at these events and activities involved countless interactions and observations that gave me a sense of the important issues facing the young women in their everyday lives and allowed me to build relationships with them and the staff and to observe how the girls interpreted, reacted, and/or responded to the material presented to them or to the situations in which they found themselves.

During the summer of 1998 and the subsequent year, I often had opportunity to drive small groups of girls to activities or drop them at home after meetings or interviews. Informal conversations during these times provided me with knowledge about family life and relationships, school, and their interests in music, as well as a chance to note the environments they lived in. I also had informal conversations with one dean and five teachers at Richmond High School, as well as four social workers and one community organizer who worked with Laotian young people in Richmond and San Pablo. These conversations with adults working with Laotians in the community gave me a sense of the social/psychological and school-related issues that Laotian young people were experiencing. Finally,

I carried out ongoing archival research of written and print material produced by APEN for the youth project, cultural products created by the girls, reports by other relevant organizations, and print and other media reports on the Laotian community.

Fieldwork as Critical Social Practice

Since the late 1980s, scholarship in feminist theory and critical ethnography has urged us to view the research process as a critical field of social practice (Wolf 1996b; Võ 2000; Hesse-Biber and Yaiser 2004; Thapar-Bjorkert and Henry 2004; Haraway 1991; Clifford 1986; Stacey 1988; Mohanty 1991b; Ong 1995). Here I take up this call for greater reflexivity in social science research and writing. I initially became interested in studying APEN's youth program because it was unique in its goal of developing leadership among teenage Laotian girls. Before beginning my graduate studies, I had been involved in feminist organizations in the United Kingdom and United States and in supporting the women's movement in Asia, particularly the Philippines. Within the United States it was rare to find organizations aimed at mobilizing Asian immigrant women around broad social justice issues, an exception being Asian Immigrant Women's Advocates in the San Francisco Bay Area. However, Asian Youth Advocates was also unique in that it aimed to organize Asian immigrant women who were in their teens. I believed that it was important to make this program visible and that it would also yield significant theoretical contributions to scholarship in sociology, in Asian American studies, in youth studies, and in environmental justice studies.

As a condition of entry into the field and access to AYA girls, APEN staff asked me to help document the youth program. While filling the dual role of researcher-cum-documenter of AYA activities, I experienced a great deal of anxiety as I negotiated being an "insider/outsider/both/neither" (Wolf 1996a:15) along multiple planes. As Linda Võ (2000) has noted, the process of negotiating "difference" not only is ongoing but also is not confined to a rigid and simplistic insider/outsider dichotomy. My role as documenter of the youth program was confined within specific parameters and could not be expanded unless I was willing and able to take on more of a staff role. In other words, I remained primarily a researcher. However, in practice my role became ambiguous. During program activities and events both staff members and the girls invited me to do "check-ins,"[8] evaluate the meetings, and participate in ice-breaker games, exercises, peer counseling sessions, and other activities. Almost immediately, I developed a good rapport with the staff members and came to identify with them and the goals of the program. Moreover, I had access to all meetings, including staff meetings, and events organized by the staff.

While I was allowed some "situational flexibility" in my roles (Võ 2000:22), as a participant-observer I was constantly struggling to balance the fine line between insider and outsider (see Wolf 1996b). I found that from an academic perspective the optimal position was on neither extreme of this divide (Burawoy 1991), but I was constantly frustrated at not having a "useful" role in meetings and activities and at not knowing whether the girls perceived me as one of the staff or an outsider. On occasion I felt like an outsider who often appeared in "insider" spaces. I found myself constantly evaluating whether or not I was present in a space where I did not belong, especially in the case of adult staff meetings during the summer of 1998. These meetings sometimes became quite emotional as staff members, particularly new ones, discussed the challenges of working with each other in the fast-paced, intense environment of the summer program.

Even more emotionally strenuous for me were negotiations of insider/outsider status along lines of my social identities vis-à-vis the girls in the program. When I first entered the field, I had a profound sense of social distance from them. The most striking was their use of standard English mingled with Black English. I had great difficulty understanding what they were saying, and I worried that I would never be able to communicate with them. As a South Asian in her late thirties with a middle-class upbringing and education in standard British and American English, I found that their clothing styles, music, and American high school culture, as well as use of Black English, were markers of my distance and outsidership from this group of second-generation girls. I had no desire to become an adolescent, which in any case would have been disingenuous. Espiritu (2003:226) has called attention to the gendered nature of fieldwork and the constraints imposed on women's efforts to conduct ethnographic research "systematically." In my case, while being a working mother with young children certainly circumscribed my fieldwork, these gendered commitments also aided the fieldwork, especially in the early stages. My then three-month-old son "broke the ice" during my first foray into the field. He helped to establish my status as a parent, a valued position in the Laotian community. I took him to the very first meeting with the girls, despite my nervousness. During a short break in the meeting several of them came over to play with him. I did not take him to subsequent meetings, but I took both my children to holiday parties and end-of-summer graduations. Even so, many of the girls frequently asked about them.

Difficulties in reducing the social distance were exacerbated because my relationship with the girls was formed solely within the context of APEN-organized events and meetings. There were no spontaneous opportunities to interact with them outside these occasions, and my own family constraints prevented me from organizing social outings with them. However, participation in meetings, activities, and peer counseling sessions allowed me to reveal some of my social background, particularly my experiences of growing up as a 1.5-generation Asian immigrant in the United Kingdom. As I got to know my teenage respondents, I came to identify with them in their struggles with issues of intergenerational differences and adaptation/acculturation. Other scholars (Kibria 1993) who have studied ethnic groups other than their own discuss how they have managed to create a rapport and racial insidership with their research participants through common experiences of immigration, adaptation, and discrimination. While creating rapport, my immigrant experiences as a South Asian did not lead to designations of racial belonging. As I came to understand later, the girls defined Asian in specific ways that excluded South Asians and for the most part referred to Laotians, Cambodians, Vietnamese, and Chinese. Unlike most of the staff working at APEN, they did not categorize me as an Asian American, highlighting the different understandings and ongoing debates in the United States over which groups belong to this racial category. They perceived me as an outsider on both racial and ethnic grounds. It was in my capacity as a mother and a graduate student that I was afforded some social status and was positioned as a role model in the eyes of those who were high-achieving students with aspirations to go to college. Over time they identified me as a nonofficial adult with several roles: older sister, researcher, friend, counselor. This allowed me to draw on aspects of my roles and identities flexibly to negotiate interactions in the field.

Despite the constant discomfort that emerged from the balancing act between participant and observer, negotiating outsider/insider status on "shifting and competing similarities and differences" (Võ 2000:19) in the APEN youth program (even if my position was marginal and temporary) brought with it a rich and deep understanding of APEN, the youth program and its staff, and the experiences of the young participants. I hope I have been able to reciprocate in some way. Comments from Gain, of Group 2, and several other girls, who believed that through this study others will learn about second-generation Laotian women, their experiences of growing up in Richmond and of being involved in APEN, provide some reassurance. Peggy Saika, APEN's executive director, thanked me for spending two years with the girls, believing that such relationships with concerned adults were important for the young women's self-esteem and well-being.

Power relations are inherent in any social research (Wolf 1996a). Yasmin Gunaratnam (2003:170–171) argues that researchers attempt to manage and formally organize the psychosocial spaces of research interaction to regulate the use, meaning, and nature of these spaces. Moreover, researchers assume that if they practice fieldwork skillfully and ethically, participants will be fully cooperative. However, as several scholars have argued (see Bhavnani 2004; Gunaratnam 2003; Thapar-Bjorkert and Henry 2004), power hierarchies are not stable and the circulation of power is not unidirectional; research participants, including children and young people (Davis et al. 2000:210; Fine and Sandstrom 1988), can challenge the dominant coding of space or act to subvert dominant spatial practices to assert their own concerns or agendas. Our respondents are the final gatekeepers to their social worlds: they have the ability to withhold access to their world and to decide when to let us in. I developed a particular closeness with girls from the third cohort and a good rapport with most of the others. As Julia, of Group 4, said: "I feel special because nobody ever did this [write about them], you know." Alison of Group 3 expressed surprise that "somebody actually wants to know what we have to say." I decided to take the approach in interviews, and in my research generally, of asking the girls to become my teachers and to help me understand their lives and involvement in APEN. While I exhibited some degree of knowledge about the Laotian community, at the same time I adopted an attitude of willingness to learn and to understand the meanings of their experience. However, there were at least five or six girls who distrusted me and who were unclear about my role at APEN. I did not facilitate any activities like other staff members, nor did I offer support and advice unless asked, unlike the staff. Moreover, my presence there was temporary. Even though they had consented to participate in the study, it appeared that they did not think it worth investing the time and energy to build a relationship with me. My attempts to develop rapport with them became increasingly awkward and sometimes pushed me to withdraw from them. I note these moments not to claim powerlessness or that such resistance subverts hierarchies of power (Wolf 1996a:22) but to argue that researchers cannot overcome these challenges simply through "better" or different methodological procedures. Instead, we need to eschew rigid binaries of researched/powerless and researcher/powerful and acknowledge the power and subjectivity of our research participants. Moreover, my experiences underscore the challenges of maintaining emotional detachment and marginality (Võ 2000:23) in ethnographic research.

In this book I have taken the position that my respondents, both the girls and the adult staff, have knowledge of their own lives and involvements. Still, my use of the words of APEN youth participants and staff in the process of writing, interpreting, and representing is under my control and I present them as "situated knowledge" (Haraway 1991), shaped by my own life experiences and academic and political interests. I treat the words of the Laotian teenagers and APEN staff members as neither representative of second-generation Laotian girls and Asian American activists, respectively, nor representative of themselves; rather, I use their words as representations of my own understanding and interpretation of these specific women's lives and work in a particular social justice organization. Moreover, in an effort to challenge essentialized representations of second-generation Laotians, I emphasize the internal diversity in this group.

I chose to do research at APEN's youth program primarily because it was a productive site to explore identity based on politics rather than politics based on identity (Angela Davis in Lowe 1997:318). As I discuss in the following chapters, while the youth program represents an ethnic-specific organization, its political work engages with issues arising from the prevalent material conditions and the intersecting systems of gender, generation, race, class, and immigration. The particular events and people are unique to this organization and program at a particular historical moment, but the questions and concerns raised by the data speak beyond this case study. My goal is to shed some explanatory light on processes of racial and ethnic identity formation in societies organized around racial hierarchies, and how they simultaneously shape and are shaped by the critical and organized efforts of resistance on part of the most marginalized.

Looking Ahead

Organized around the concept of "critical incorporation" and processes of ethnic identity formation, this book focuses on APEN as a site for incorporation and integrates the analysis of experiences, narratives, and social practices at the micro level with discourses on nation and citizenship and wider economic, political, and cultural contexts at the macro level. Chapter 2 describes the historical background and the sociopolitical context of this case study on second-generation Laotian girls. The migration of Laotians to the United States is intimately linked to U.S. foreign policy and the deep entanglement of Laotians in the Vietnam War. Their marginal position in the United States reflects their arrival as refugees at the end of the Vietnam War as well as the local, state, and national contexts within which Laotians in northern California are creating a new life. Chapter 3 presents trends and issues in immigration patterns and the questions of belonging, citizenship, and American national identity that these patterns stir up. I delineate an analytical framework for the study and explain the importance of a focus on sociopolitical incorporation among the children of immigrants. After an overview of contemporary scholarship on the new second generation, I turn to critical theories of race and feminist theories to frame this research, emphasizing the broader historical, social, and political contexts in which sociopolitical incorporation takes place. I then develop the notion of "critical incorporation" as a concept that best represents the complex and contradictory experiences of sociopolitical incorporation among second-generation Laotian girls participating in APEN's youth project in northern California. Threaded throughout this chapter is an argument for an intersectional approach to the study of the new second generation that recognizes its heterogeneous and diverse experiences and identities, and acknowledges structures of power and agency that shape the children of immigrants.

Chapter 4 focuses on the community activism and political practices that second-generation Laotian girls engage in through APEN. I delineate their political responses to experiences of exclusion at the local, county, and state levels. Specifically, I examine APEN's goals and strategies and the young women's roles in these campaigns to understand the kind of political subjects that are produced and the impact on groups differentiated by race, ethnicity, gender, and generation. I argue that APEN is enacting new forms of politics in immigrant communities and mobilizing shifting ethnic and racial identities in collective contexts. Chapter 5 examines discursive understandings of race and racial hierarchies and how second-generation Laotian girls make sense of the complex racial politics in the United States. I argue that racial and ethnic identities intersect with gender and class and are formed relationally through interaction with other groups. These interactions are imbued with complicated experiences of cooperation and conflict, intermingling and social distancing. I analyze how these contradictory positions contribute to and shape APEN's attempts to create cross-race and cross-ethnic solidarities. Focusing on the family as a site where struggles over the gendered meaning of Laotian ethnicity in the United States are taking place, Chapter 6 analyzes the narratives and social practices of the young women to understand the intricate negotiations involved in navigating multiple and overlapping discourses on gender, sexuality, intergenerational relations, independence, and individualism. I argue that while APEN's youth program provides a space for the young women to navigate these differing socio-ideological points of view, APEN also plays a role in transforming cultural norms and practices within the Laotian community and in the construction of new gendered subjects. Chapter 7 addresses the varied manifestations of the notion of "home" and discusses the notion of belonging in both its emotional and identificatory senses. Through an exploration of the multiple contestations that teenage Laotian girls experience regarding the spaces that are perceived as home, the chapter asks whether experiences of exclusion in the nation lead to home only in the family or ethnic-specific community organization. Does a localized and an ethnic identity preclude home in the nation? Or does the safety and security of home in the family or community organization provide a means to assert and negotiate one's culture *and* one's right to a place in the nation? In Chapter 8 I summarize the book's main arguments and critically revisit the notion of a social justice organization as a site of incorporation. Specifically, I highlight the challenges posed by stronger assimilative forces in the broader society to the notion of critical incorporation and analyze the power relations within such organizations. In all, these chapters tell us how second-generation Laotians are challenging what it means to be American and are becoming American in the process.

2

From Agent Orange to Superfund Sites to Anti-immigrant Sentiments

Multiple Voyages, Ongoing Challenges

Laotian Migration to the United States

Laos is a small, landlocked country located between Vietnam and Thailand. It is ethnically, linguistically, and culturally diverse, comprising more than sixty ethnic groups (Chan 1994:3), including ethnic Lao, Iu Mien, Hmong, Khmu, Lahu, and Thaidam. In the mid-1970s, highland groups such as the Iu Mien constituted 20 percent of the population and the Hmong accounted for another 10 percent. The Lao-Theung, the original inhabitants of Laos and living in the low hills, represented another 20 percent of the population, while the ethnic Lao, living in valleys and plains, numbered 50 percent of the country's population. These lowland Lao predominantly resided in urban areas and controlled the government, operated the school system, had centralized religious institutions, and controlled markets, thus giving them a position of dominance far beyond their numbers (Hein 2006:63).

The migration of Laotians to the United States is intimately linked to U.S. foreign policy and the deep entanglement of Laotians in the Vietnam War. In the late 1950s and early 1960s the Central Intelligence Agency (CIA) recruited clans from the Hmong, Lao, Mien, Khmu, and other, smaller ethnic groups as part of an irregular force to resist the Pathet Lao (Communist) forces and support the Royal Lao Army (Tayanin and Vang 1992; Dao 1992; Crystal and Saepharn 1992). From 1961 to 1973 thousands of Hmong, Khmu, and Iu Mien were involved directly or indirectly in the secret war in Laos, which was financed and equipped by the CIA. The United States recruited young men to join Hmong general Vang Pao's army to fight the Pathet Lao, prevent North Vietnamese troops and military supplies from reaching South Vietnam, and help rescue U.S. pilots whose planes were shot down on bombing raids over northern Laos and North Vietnam. Other Mien and Hmong households were encouraged to continuing growing poppies and produce opium for sale as part of a CIA plan to support its anticommunist activities. Thousands more Hmong, Khmu, and Mien farmers and their families fled their highland villages to escape the heavy bombings and extreme violence of the secret war. In addition to the toxic defoliant Agent Orange, millions of tons of bombs were dropped on Laos by the U.S. government, destroying large areas of agricultural lands and forests and poisoning water sources (APEN 2002). These villagers lived in jungles or in temporary villages built by the U.S. Agency for International Development (USAID) and depended on the Royal Lao government and USAID for food and other essentials (Dao 1992; Crystal and Saepharn 1992; Smith and Tarallo 1993:95).

The war years not only uprooted thousands of Laotians but also disrupted the maintenance of traditional social relations. Men and women in Laos had well-defined roles. Women shouldered the responsibility for sustaining their families on a day-to-day basis, and men oversaw the welfare of the family over time and within the wider community. Men were also responsible for religious affairs (Crystal and Saepharn 1992:344; DeVoe 1997:120). In addition to clear-cut roles and responsibilities, all adult men had special status in the household. Women served food to men first, and wives were expected to remain subservient and deferential toward their husbands (Moore-Howard 1989:25; DeVoe 1997: 120). The asymmetrical nature of gender relationships was intended to create an ordered, interdependent, and cooperative social order (Crystal and Saepharn 1992). However, as more and more able-bodied men were drafted into the military, often as young as fifteen as the war progressed, women became responsible for all family affairs (Smith and Tarallo 1993:99).

The collapse of the U.S.-supported regime in South Vietnam, followed by Communist takeovers in Cambodia and Laos, triggered a massive outflow of refugees. In 1975 the Vietnamese-allied Communist Pathet Lao assumed control and established the Lao People's Democratic Republic, prompting an exodus of Hmong, Iu Mien, and a sizable population of ethnic Lao, as well as other, smaller tribes that had supported the United States and the Royal Lao Army. Additional numbers of ethnic Lao fled Laos in 1977, when the Pathet Lao sent those who had been part of the old government, even at lower ranks, to "reeducation" camps in northern Laos (Waters 1990; Anderson 2005). In all, the U.S. "secret war" in Laos pushed more than 400,000 Lao, Hmong, Khmu, Iu Mien, and smaller ethnic groups, or 10 percent of the country's population, to seek refuge across the border in Thailand (Dao 1992; Yang 2001:165), as the United States did almost nothing to assist them in Laos (Hein 2006:72).

The escape route for the survivors—soldiers, elderly, women, and children—already saddled by their belongings, was a long and strenuous trek over mountains and through the jungle. Crossing the perilous Mekong River, usually under the cover of darkness, was a frightening and unforgettable experience. Many individuals and sometimes entire families were overcome by illness and exhaustion, drowned, injured, or killed by Pathet Lao soldiers in the bid to flee communist rule (Crystal and Saepharn 1992). Those who survived often spent years of temporary asylum in refugee camps along Thailand's northeastern border while awaiting acceptance as legal refugees in countries such as the United States, France, Australia, and Canada (Moore-Howard 1989:75). The U.S. government assumed responsibility for this consequence of the Vietnam War and greatly expanded the domestic refugee program, which allowed many Laotian refugees to come to the United States in the early 1980s (Rumbaut 2000).[1]

The U.S. Department of State delegated the process of resettlement of Laotians to numerous voluntary agencies, such as the American Council for Nationalities Services, International Rescue Committee, United States Catholic Conference, and World Relief Resettlement Agency. Close relatives also sponsored some Laotians (Trueba et al. 1990; Knoll 1982:147–148). While the Laotians waited in the refugee camps, they did not receive any special orientation, educational courses, or job training that would help them resettle in a new country (Crystal and Saepharn 1992; Knoll 1982:245). Yet as Crystal and Saepharn point out:

> No people so traditional, so lacking in educational background or economically relevant skills, from so geographically and cognitively remote a homeland had ever been brought *en masse* as refugees to the United States. (Crystal and Saepharn 1992:375)

Given the numbers, background, and conditions of the Laotian refugees, U.S. officials and the voluntary agencies had three primary goals in their efforts to resettle Laotians: dispersal, economic self-sufficiency, and medical attention for those suffering from acute diseases (Trueba et al. 1990). State and voluntary agencies scattered refugees around the country in the hope that no particular geographic area would be overburdened and the potential for conflicts with members of the host community would be minimized. The goal of economic self-sufficiency was to prevent long-term reliance on welfare. The majority of Laotians coming to the United States, 80 percent, were laborers, farmers, or other manual workers (Chang 2001a). Thus they possessed few skills that were transferable or even readily adaptable to employment in the United States. And while the ethnic Lao had lived in urban centers, the majority of Iu Mien, Hmong, Khmu, and other ethnic groups were from rural, highland Laos and therefore had little exposure to life in an urban industrial country. For those refugees unable to obtain jobs immediately, vocational training programs and English instruction were established (Trueba et al. 1990).

While the government's policy was to disperse refugees around the country, many Laotians relocated after arriving in the United States to be close to family and friends. Henry Trueba et al. (1990:39–40) note that inconsistencies in the interpretation and implementation of resettlement policies by the multitude of voluntary agencies resulted in resentment and competition among refugees. Many Laotians responded by participating in secondary migrations, bringing them to areas of highly developed services and unification with family and friends. Secondary migration among Laotians is consistent with Roger Waldinger's (2001:2) observation that immigration is "a network driven phenomenon": newcomers are attracted to places where family, friends, and community members can provide resources to get them started in a new country.

Laotians in the United States: Socio-Demographic Patterns

The 2000 census enumerated 384,516 Laotians (including 186,310 Hmong) living in the United States, a 60 percent increase over the 1990 census figure (U.S. Census 1990, 2000a). Immigration records indicate that the flow of Laotian refugees to the United States may have ended. From a peak of 55,500 in 1980, the numbers of Laotian refugees had dwindled to just 64 in 2000 (Niedzwiecki and Duong 2004:10). However, Laotians, like other Southeast Asian groups, are a young population compared with other Asian American groups and the U.S. population in general. Correspondingly, fertility levels are high and will contribute to rapid natural increase in the Laotian population (Rumbaut 2000:187).

Patterns of settlement reveal that despite the initial government placement policy of refugee dispersal, California has emerged as the favored state; it is the home of 33 percent of the Laotians and 39 percent of the Hmong in the United States.[2] The 2000 census indicates that 136,799 Laotians (including 71,741 Hmong) reside in California, of whom 4,585 live in the northern county of Contra Costa (U.S. Census 2000a). This is a 25 percent increase over the 1990 census figures. However, community leaders argue that this figure represents a serious undercount; they estimate that the community actually numbered around 10,000 individuals in 2002, with the Iu Mien community representing the largest of the six Laotian ethnic groups in the county, followed by Lao, Khmu, Thaidam, Lue, and Hmong (APEN 2002). Nearly 30 percent of Contra Costa's Laotian community lives in a two-square-mile area in San Pablo and Richmond, part of west Contra Costa County and the location of the Laotian Organizing Project. This area is also the focal point of Laotian-run markets, shops, and restaurants (Chang 2001b). Richmond and San Pablo, together with West and East Oakland and San Francisco's Tenderloin, are poverty-stricken and marginal housing areas in which Laotian refugees were placed and continue to make their home (Walker and the Bay Area Study Group 1990; Crystal and Saepharn 1992).

Along with other Southeast Asians, Laotians have the highest rates of poverty and reliance on public assistance of any Asian American group and in the United States in general (Rumbaut 2000:188; Niedzwiecki and Duong 2004; Sakamoto and Woo 2007). An examination of per capita incomes in 1999 reveals that at $6,613 and $11,454, respectively, the Hmong and Laotians had lower average per person incomes than any other racial and ethnic group in the United States. Almost 30 percent of Hmong households and 14 percent of Laotian households relied on public assistance in 1999, compared with 4 percent of Asian Americans households overall and 9.5 percent of households in the United States overall (Niedzwiecki and Duong 2004:21–24). This is not surprising given that Laotians have made a leap from village life and agricultural self-sufficiency to a complex market economy with thousands of occupational roles that require competency in both the English language and vocational skills. In addition, many Laotian adults who grew up during the war never experienced the self-sufficiency of village life but instead survived on air-drops of food and essentials by USAID or rations provided in refugee camps (Dao 1992; Crystal and Saepharn 1992). In west Contra Costa County, of the adult Laotian population 25 years old and older, 40 percent live below the poverty level,[3] and 46 percent have less than a fifth-grade education (APEN 2002). Nationally, Laotian parents have the lowest education of any Asian immigrant parents (Rumbaut 1994; Niedzwiecki and Duong 2004:15). As Sakamoto and Woo (2007:46–47) observe, in the 1970s the school system in Laos did not offer education beyond the twelfth grade, and it was mainly available to the small proportion of the population living in urban areas, primarily ethnic Lao. Groups like the Hmong, who lived in rural highland areas, were mostly illiterate and met their subsistence needs through hunting, raising animals, and engaging in traditional slash-and-burn agriculture (Hein 2006:65). In the United States almost 44 percent of Laotians of working age are employed in production, transportation, and material moving occupations, compared with 13 percent of Asians as a whole and 15 percent in the United States in general (Niedzwiecki and Duong 2004:23).

According to Rumbaut (1995:248), in the 1990 census over 50 percent of Laotians lived in linguistically isolated households, meaning that no one over the age of fourteen in that household spoke only English or spoke it very well. While these figures were reduced to 35.1 percent of Hmong and 31.8 percent of Laotians in the 2000 census (Niedzwiecki and Duong 2004:18), they indicate that large numbers of Laotian families are effectively cut off from most major forms of mass communication, which has serious implications for this community's understanding of how institutions in U.S. society operate.

In addition to growing up in disadvantaged socioeconomic circumstances, second-generation Laotians face gang violence in Contra Costa County. Almost all my respondents mentioned that their brothers and male cousins and friends were in gangs or had become victims of the violence that pervades parts of Richmond. In 1996, 208 Laotian young people were in California Youth Authority (CYA) institutions.[4] This figure represents 16.6 percent of the total Asian commitments and contract cases with the CYA for that year, second to the number of Vietnamese youth commitments. The actual number of Laotian young people in CYA facilities remained stable over the years, but proportionally, Laotians thirteen to eighteen years old represented 25.4 percent of all Asian youth commitments and contracts in 2000, outstripping Vietnamese teens in CYA facilities (CYA Information Systems Bureau, personal communication, 6 March 2002).[5] In west Contra Costa County, media reports documented the presence of Asian gangs, made up of teenage boys and young men, in the cities of Richmond and San Pablo (see Bulwa 1999; Giordani 1999).[6] The prevalence of gang involvement among young Laotian males may be due to the inability of parents to provide critical support structures needed during adolescence. Both early and more recent studies on Southeast Asian refugee teenagers suggest that parental authority was weak among Laotian teens but peer group influence was strong (Rumbaut and Ima 1988; Peters 1988, cited in Hein 1995; Jeung 2002).

Other scholars have argued that gang membership may be a reaction to racialization processes and widespread violence in schools and urban multicultural environments, which have limited the refugees' opportunities (Walker-Moffat 1995:111) and led to marginalization and mistrust among Southeast Asian young people (Jeung 2002).

In addition, according to data collected from 1989 to 1998, Laotian high-school girls had the highest teenage pregnancy rate in California of any racial-ethnic group (almost 19 percent) and the highest number of teen births (9 percent). Moreover, 60 percent of the Laotian teenage mothers were married (Weitz et al. 2001). Scholars such as Mike Males (1996) have explained teenage pregnancy as a result of poverty, but in the Laotian community parenthood conveys status and thus teenage motherhood continues to be an accepted practice.

School data on English learners provide an indication of the group size and location of new immigrants and the degree of hardship that students in a particular language group may experience. English learner (EL) students (formerly known as limited English proficient, or LEP) are those students whose primary language is other than English and who have been determined to lack clearly defined English-language skills necessary to succeed in the school's regular instructional program. EL students represent the closest approximation to the number of most recently arrived immigrant children (Rumbaut 1995:50). In 1995, 990 English learners (16.2 percent) in the West Contra Costa Unified School District were Laotian. In 2000 this number dropped dramatically in percentage terms to 9.3 percent but still represented 810 students. The proportion of Laotian English learners at Richmond High School, where the majority of the teenagers in this book went to school, was 19.7 percent, or 145 students, in 1995. While this percentage dropped to 12 percent in 2000 for Richmond High School, it still represented 104 students, second only to Spanish-speaking students (California Department of Education 2002a). Rumbaut (1995) observes that refugee students' educational attainment is related to both parents' class origins as well as to size of household and length of time spent in U.S. schools.

At the same time, Asian American and white students continually outscore African American and Latino students in general achievement tests in west Contra Costa County schools (Shire 2001).[7] Data on English learners suggest that in 1998 over 70 percent of Asian students at Richmond High School were Laotian (California Department of Education 2002b). However, at Richmond High a greater proportion of students categorized as Asian complete all courses required for entrance to the University of California and California State Universities than any other racial-ethnic group except Filipino students (California Department of Education 2002c). In June 1998 the majority of thirty or so students on the California Scholarship Fund roll were Iu Mien, as inferred from their last names. These data on gang involvement, teenage pregnancy rates, large numbers of English learners, yet high achievement at school among some Laotians paint a complicated picture of the socioeconomic adaptation of young Laotians in west Contra Costa County.

West Contra Costa County: Socioeconomic Transformations

The vista from the El Cerrito hills across Richmond to the San Francisco Bay and Mount Tamalpais beyond it belies west Contra Costa County's deeply ingrained industrial character. From this vantage point in El Cerrito, the only clues are the shipping port, the Chevron refinery, and the oil storage tanks on the ridge behind it, painted brown so they blend in with the surrounding landscape. The Chevron installations rise above Richmond's gritty Iron Triangle neighborhood, flanked by the railroad tracks that gave it its name. Chevron's oil refinery has been Richmond's most visible landmark for more than a century.

The city of Richmond's industrial history over the past century captures growth and change in the Bay Area economy as a whole.[8] Early in the twentieth century, Richmond, the county's principal city, had a heavy industrial base made up of companies in the chemical, automobile assembly, and food processing sectors. During World War II the Kaiser Richmond shipyards represented one of the biggest wartime shipbuilding operations, which drew a large-scale in-migration of workers, both white and black, from the South and Southwest. At the height of the war effort "56 different war industries, more than any other city of its size in the United States," were located in Richmond, highlighting the city's significant role during the Home Front years, from 1940 to 1946.[9] Paralleling this growth, the city's industrial labor force increased from approximately 6,000 workers in 1940 to more than 100,000 by 1943. Richmond's African American population rose from 270 (1 percent) in 1940 to 13,780 (14 percent) in 1947 (Wenkert et al. 1967, cited in Schafran and Feldstein 2009). Among these newly arrived workers were large numbers of women who worked as unskilled laborers in assembly lines, welding ships and tanks together. Richmond is one of the main birthplaces of the national icon Rosie the Riveter, representing the hundreds of thousands of women who contributed to the Home Front during the Second World War.[10]

At the war's end the shipyards closed, along with plant closures in other older industries such as Pullman shops and Ford Motor assembly plants, leading to a concomitant decline in population.[11] New manufacturing, chemical processing and research facilities, petroleum refining and waste disposal, and warehousing operations moved into the vacated shipyard structures, together with plant nurseries, metal recycling plants, and equipment yards. The Chevron refinery, built in 1902, is one of Richmond's largest tax contributors and biggest employers. More than 3,000 people work at Chevron's refinery and technology center, and almost 20 percent of those people are west Contra Costa County residents (Metinko 2001). Thus Chevron continues to play a significant role in the city's economic landscape (APEN 2008).

This industrial past and present not only shaped the county's economic fortunes but also had extensive environmental impact on the region, as described in Chapter 1. The California Department of Toxic Substances and Control has listed 65 of the 350 industrial sites in Richmond, including one active and one former

Superfund site and four facilities with current hazardous waste permits, where there is known contamination or where cleanup action has been planned or completed (Schafran and Feldstein 2009). More than two decades ago the Communities for a Better Environment (CBE) reported that at least 210 different hazardous chemicals had been stored and/or released into the Richmond environment (Communities for a Better Environment 1989). Between 1989 and 1995 more than 1,900 incidents were reported in Contra Costa County, and 35 of them were major accidents.[12] These industries generated 800,000 pounds of toxic air contaminants, nearly 18,000 pounds of toxic pollutants in waste water, and about 179,000 tons of hazardous waste annually (field notes, Toxic Tour by Group 3, 7 July 1998). Chevron, with its 2,900-acre refinery, is one of the major polluters in the San Francisco Bay Area, according to Greg Karras (2000). It is one of the largest refineries in the United States, with a capacity to process nearly 243,000 barrels of crude oil per day.[13] More than 11 million pounds of toxic, explosive, and corrosive chemicals are stored at the refinery. According to long-time environmental justice activist Henry Clark, who grew up in Richmond, the Chevron refinery has had a long history of fires and accidents.[14] During the period 1989 to 1995 Chevron alone was responsible for 304 industrial accidents.[15]

These toxic emissions, along with high levels of flaring, have continued into the twenty-first century, and in 2005 Chevron Products Company, along with two other refineries, accounted for 80 percent of toxic releases in Contra Costa County (Pontecorvo 2008). The Environmental Protection Agency reported almost three hundred highly toxic spills from Chevron's Richmond refinery between 2001 and 2003 and identified the refinery as in "significant noncompliance" for air pollution standards (APEN 2008). Such pollution disproportionately affects the health of African Americans, Latinos, and Asian and Pacific Islanders. Morello-Frosch (2008, cited in Communities for a Better Environment 2009) reports that 79 percent of the people who live within one mile of the Chevron refinery are people of color and over 25 percent are below the national poverty line. Industrial pollutants can cause a range of health problems, such as respiratory allergies, headaches, and nausea, as well as chronic conditions such as developmental issues and cancer (Communities for a Better Environment 2009). In fact, Richmond's cancer and child-asthma rates exceed area, state, and national averages (Pontecorvo 2008; APEN 2008).

Since the late 1980s Richmond has sought to attract biotechnology, other high technology, light industrial firms, and retail chains to its new business parks and commercial development areas.[16] This shift in Richmond's employment and industrial landscape is reflective of wider changes brought about by global economic restructuring. Waldinger and Lee (2001:66) identify three economic trends for the San Francisco Bay Area. First, the area is increasingly dependent on its service sectors, particularly business services. Second, the economy comprises a new manufacturing base in which deindustrialization in traditional "smokestack" durable goods is offset by the growth in high-technology manufacturing in computers, electronics, instruments, and defense. Third, these changes have produced a unique economic structure in San Francisco; high levels of manufacturing employment persist, but highly skilled and educated workers outnumber their less-skilled cohorts.

The shift away from basic manufacturing and toward high-technology, nondurable industries and petrochemical processing has meant substantial job losses and significant changes in the kinds of employment and working conditions available (Teitz and Shapira 1989). While employment in the Richmond area grew from 34,244 jobs to 52,390 jobs between 1980 and 2005, 62 percent of these new jobs were in the service sector (health care, security services, food preparation, janitorial work, and personal care) and were less likely to pay family-supporting wages than basic manufacturing (Lin and Greenwich 2007:6, 19). Richmond's reputation in the first half of the twentieth century as a prime industrial zone has not been regained. New immigrants from Asia and Latin America, who often come with low skill levels and education, have joined African American workers displaced by deindustrialization. While the expanding high-tech and biotech industries in the last two decades of the twentieth century provided jobs for new, highly educated immigrants, Southeast Asians (and Central Americans), groups with the lowest human capital, have not participated in the overall gains that have occurred over this period. In fact, during the 1990s, while the rest of the Bay Area experienced an economic boom and consequently a tight labor market, especially in the high-technology sector, Richmond's jobless rate was much greater than the unemployment rate in the eastern part of the Bay Area. Richmond residents faced double-digit unemployment rates from 1992 to 1995, at a time when the East Bay had well under a 10 percent rate. From 1991 through 1996 the average unemployment rate in Richmond was at least 85 percent higher than that experienced in the East Bay overall (Avalos 2001). These trends have continued in the twenty-first century; while the East Bay experienced an unemployment rate of 5.2 percent in 2005, the figure for Richmond was 7.7 percent for the same period (Lin and Greenwich 2007:7).

Paralleling these economic transformations has been a socio-demographic transformation in west Contra Costa County. Richmond's overall population has ebbed and flowed since the 1960s, shaped by deindustrialization, immigration, and the construction of new homes that were relatively affordable in comparison with the rest of the Bay Area. Immigration, in particular, has brought with it dramatic racial and ethnic changes. In 1980 persons of Hispanic origin constituted 10.3 percent of the city's population. This share increased to 14.5 percent in 1990 and 27 percent in 2000. At the same time, the Asian and Pacific Islander population increased from 4.9 percent in 1980 to 11 percent in 1990 and 13 percent in 2000. The African American population has decreased from 48 percent in 1980 to 44 percent in 1990 and 36 percent in 2000. The white population has decreased from 36 percent in 1980 to 31 percent in 1990 and 21 percent in 2000 (U.S. Census 1990, 2000b; Voderbrueggen 2001).[17] New immigration patterns have transformed whole neighborhoods and shopping strips along the 23rd Street corridor from once mainly African American to Latino and Spanish-speaking. The numbers and percentages of English learners in Richmond and other west Contra Costa County schools, discussed earlier, reflect these demographic changes in local schools.

Such socio-demographic transformations have often sparked interracial tension and gang violence. It has also created challenges for community activists and church and civic leaders as they work to form coalitions between groups with such different racial and immigration histories and limited English facility, especially among the first generation of immigrants (Chang 2001b; Lochner 2001). In the mid-1990s Laotian leaders developed relations and established alliances with African American and Latino leaders to address gang activity and curb gang violence, an issue that has affected all three communities (Schafran and Feldstein 2009). However, these alliances did not lead to a critical racial solidarity with other young people of color among second-generation Laotians, as I note in Chapter 5, and it was not until the first decade of the twenty-first century that these relations were consolidated into significant cross-racial coalition work, as I discuss in Chapter 8.

This is the socioeconomic context in which Laotians in west Contra Costa County, one of the most recent refugee populations in the United States, find themselves. The history of war, emotional trauma, and hardship, together with these socioeconomic realities, lack of access to adequate and regular health care, few job opportunities, and interracial tension, shape the quality of life and adaptation experiences of Laotians in Contra Costa County. And a rising tide of anti-immigrant sentiment in California and the nation has further exacerbated the pressures for Laotians as they build a new home.

Anti-immigrant Legislation in the Late Twentieth and Early Twenty-First Centuries

In the contemporary era the 1996 campaign finance scandal prompted by the so-called Asian connection (Wang 2000) and the U.S. government spy case against scientist Wen Ho Lee that erupted in 2000 suggest that Asian Americans continue to be racialized.[18] Although there is not currently a forced Americanization program in place, minority communities with immigrant histories, such as Asians and Latinos, face persistent pressure to conform.[19] In the last decade of the twentieth century and at the beginning of the twenty-first century racialized nativistic attitudes toward both documented and undocumented immigrants have appeared in three distinct forms: the fear of linguistic differences and the promotion of English-only regulations; the fear that multiculturalism and affirmative action policies will encourage ethnic retention; and the fear of a drain on public resources such as welfare, education, and health care by both illegal and legal immigrants (Sanchez 1997:1020).[20]

Deep-seated fears about changes in U.S. society and culture have led to a political backlash in California and the nation at large. Political initiatives in California, such as Propositions 187, 209, and 227 (concerning public benefits, affirmative action, and bilingual education, respectively), signal extensive retrenchment of the social and civil rights of new immigrants and their children (Cornelius 1995). In November 1994 California voters approved Proposition 187, the so-called Save Our State (SOS) initiative. A year later, in November 1995, a federal judge ruled large sections of Proposition 187 unconstitutional (Takacs 1999:611). If implemented, Proposition 187 would have created a state-mandated screening system to verify the legal status of all persons seeking public health, education, and other benefits (Martin 1995:255).

Martin (1995) observes that many of the grassroots supporters of Proposition 187 became vocal supporters of Proposition 209, the California Civil Rights Initiative (CCRI), which would

> prohibit the state or any of its political subdivisions from using race, sex, color, ethnicity, or national origin as a criterion for either discriminating against, or granting preferential treatment to, any individual or group in the operation of the state's system of public employment, public education, or public contracting. (Quoted in Martin 1995:262–263)

Proposition 209 was approved by voters in November 1996. This ballot was preceded by a vote by the University of California Board of Regents to abolish affirmative action preferences in the University of California system because the regents deemed them to be "unfair," "divisive," and a cause of "racial tension" (Taylor 1999:95). The abolition of affirmative action was an attempt to roll back the gains achieved during the civil rights movement in the 1960s, negatively affecting those groups that have historically suffered discrimination and also restricting access to educational and work opportunities for more recent arrivals such as Laotians.

California was in the vanguard of abolishing another right enshrined in the civil rights reforms. On 2 June 1998, Californians decisively rejected bilingual education by approving Proposition 227, the so-called English for the Children initiative.[21] By the late 1990s nearly half of all states had followed California's lead and implemented rules making English the official language (Agrawal 2008:662). Ron Unz, the creator and sponsor of Proposition 227, upheld the proposition as an immigrant's ticket to "the American Dream of economic and social advancement" (English Language in Public School 1998, cited in Crawford 1999). However, like the California Civil Rights Initiative, Unz's attempt to dismantle bilingual education also represented a wider neoconservative agenda of rolling back social programs and language legislation encoded during the civil rights movement of the 1960s; at the same time, the action cast him as "pro-immigrant" and "pro-assimilation" (Crawford 1999).

Legislation passed at the national level has also constructed immigrants as criminals and threats to the nation through the creation of what Susanne Jonas (2006:9) calls a "national security regime for immigrants," which reversed immigrant family reunification norms in operation since 1965 and stripped both legal and undocumented immigrants of numerous due process rights and entitlements.[22] In 1996 President Clinton vowed to "end welfare as we know it" when he signed into law the Personal Responsibility Work Opportunity Reconciliation Act (PRWORA). Before this Welfare Reform Act, as it is also known, U.S. citizens, legal immigrants, and refugees were all eligible for means-tested public benefits. PRWORA introduced a hierarchical system in which citizenship status determined access to welfare programs, in the following order: U.S. citizens retained the widest access, followed by refugees and asylum seekers, and finally legal immigrants, who have limited access. Illegal immigrants are ineligible.

The reduction in benefits caused hardships to refugees who had already lived in the United States for more than five years and poorer legal immigrants who lacked an extensive work history (Espenshade et al. 1997:778). Under PRWORA, refugees would be eligible for SSI (Supplemental Security Income) and food stamps for only their first five years in the United States, Medicaid would also be available for the first five years and thereafter at the state's discretion, and TANF (Temporary Assistance for Needy Families), which replaced AFDC (Aid to Families with Dependent Children), was reduced to a lifetime limit of five years and required recipients to participate in work or work-related activities such as English classes, job training, and job search. These changes in welfare and the discourse employed in congressional documents emphasized the principle of self-sufficiency and the notion that immigrants should not rely on public resources (Agrawal 2008:663; Truong 2007).

The Welfare Reform Act has had a unique impact on Southeast Asians, who mostly arrived as refugees in the late 1970s and early 1980s (Truong 2007; Fujiwara 2005; Lee 2005). As noted earlier, Laotians and other Southeast Asians have the highest rates of poverty and government aid, and more than one-third of Laotians live in households where no one over the age of fourteen speaks English well. This raises some pertinent questions about individuals who are simply unfit to become economically independent (Truong 2007). Due to limited English proficiency, disability, or age, many Southeast Asians were unable to navigate the new rules and regulations and comply with the arcane requirements, leading to their removal from public assistance rolls. They were also unable to take advantage of job training and search services, leaving them vulnerable to assignment to demeaning jobs (Truong 2007:266). One year after the passage of PRWORA there were reports of refugees and immigrants from Asia committing suicide in the face of losing their SSI benefits (Fujiwara 2005:79, 81).

Racializing and gendered politics permeated the popular and congressional discourse that surrounded the far-reaching welfare reform, characterizing immigrants as "undeserving foreigners, abusing the system and taking resources from hard-working Americans" (Fujiwara 2005:79). As Truong (2007:262) notes, in discussions of Southeast Asians on public assistance there is a collective national amnesia about the fact that their poverty was not of their own making and about the U.S. government's role and responsibility in creating and sustaining their "refugee conditions." Truong describes the contemporary relationship between the American welfare state and Southeast Asians as one of gross neglect and points out that Southeast Asian refugees are no longer useful to ease the national pain of the Vietnam War. Given that a high proportion of Southeast Asians would have lost SSI benefits, immigrant rights groups mobilized to revive the image of the "refugee," along with other discourses of aging, disability, and frailty, and successfully appealed to the moral consciousness of politicians to recognize the impact of the Welfare Reform Act on those who were innocent victims of America's role in Southeast Asia. A few weeks before PRWORA became law, legislators in the House and Senate partially restored benefits to elderly and disabled noncitizens (Fujiwara 2005:82–90).

Immigration continues to remain a major political and social concern in the first decade of the twenty-first century.[23] Agrawal (2008) views the exclusionary measures implemented at state and national levels as part of a broader social discourse prevalent during the late 1980s and 1990s, which challenged and redefined the meanings of immigration and citizenship in the United States. Anti-immigrant sentiments and legislation have targeted both legal and undocumented immigrants, representing a broader wave of concern about the integrity and identity of the American nation. Specifically, such legislation emphasized political citizenship prior to social integration, thus privileging legal citizenship, which confers unique benefits and opportunities and for which legal immigrants are deemed ineligible. Jonas (2006:13) reminds us that "it is important to emphasize the distinction between assimilation and immigrant incorporation with political rights." The multiple movements and challenges described in this chapter underscore the fact that Laotians as a group have been both included in and excluded from the nation, thus exacerbating the barriers to incorporation with full social, civil, and political rights. The social, economic, and political contexts that Laotians confront in west Contra Costa County also shape their engagement with environmental justice issues. This book's case study of second-generation Laotian girls participating in APEN's youth program demonstrates that environmental justice work in new immigrant communities must link environmental issues to concerns arising from race/ethnicity, immigration histories, class, gender, and generation to foster citizenship and belonging and thereby facilitate "speaking for ourselves," a central concern of the environmental justice movement.

APEN's Role in West Contra Costa County

APEN is not the first social justice organization to address the environmental concerns of residents in west Contra Costa County. The West County Toxics Coalition (WCTC), an organization with a multiracial membership of low- and moderate-income residents, has campaigned against the toxic threat posed by petrochemical and hazardous waste facilities in the Richmond area since 1986. WCTC has been particularly successful in mobilizing thousands of local residents and drawing in scientific experts and legal advocacy organizations to maintain pressure on the Chevron Oil Refinery and General Chemical Plant to provide compensation, prevent future accidents, and make improvements in systems and equipment. One of its major achievements was the closure of a Chevron waste incinerator that had been releasing carcinogens such as methylene chloride and dioxins in the north Richmond area, including Peres Elementary School, for almost three decades. The waste incinerator was shut down in 1997 after a six-year battle led by WCTC and Communities for a Better Environment (CBE) and supported by LOP/AYA teens and staff. In 1999 a new health center opened in north Richmond, where it serves three thousand residents. Funding for the $1.8 million facility was secured through a settlement with General Chemical after a toxic spill in 1993 affected more than 20,000 local residents. In 2006 WCTC and CBE were successful in forcing the Bay Area Air Quality Management District to adopt a flare control rule to curb unnecessary flaring activity at the Chevron refinery.[24]

The Laotian community in west Contra Costa County has certainly benefited from these victories. However, they face toxic exposure from additional sources. Laotian families consume fish from San Francisco Bay to supplement their diets. Local health officials warn that fish from this source contains PCBs, mercury, dioxins, and pesticides and recommend that fish from the Bay be eaten no more than twice a month. But efforts to notify the Laotian community are ineffective since few Laotians are literate in their own language or in English (Kong 2001:13). Another source of contamination unique to the Laotian community is the consumption of vegetables and herbs grown in toxic soil in backyards and communal gardens.

As a new immigrant community, Laotians are not only affected by the environmental and economic issues of west Contra Costa County but further marginalized as a result of linguistic and cultural isolation and lack of access to information, services, and decision makers (Kong 2001:7). Limited English facility among elderly and adult Laotians, and the presence of more than 62 Laotian dialects (Kong 2001:13), complicate efforts by state agencies and social service providers to address the needs of all residents in Contra Costa County. Within the county's Laotian community there are a number of informal community organizations, representing Lao, Iu Mien, Khmu, Hmong, and Thaidam groups, which aim to help the community adjust to American life; such organizations seek to preserve the groups' own culture, language, and customs and form a link between the community, government, and voluntary agencies that provide assistance to refugees. MacDonald (1997:136–137) notes that since village councils, the traditional form of political organization made up of community leaders, has no legal authority in the United States, most Iu-Mien communities here have adopted a new type of community-based nonprofit political organization known as a mutual assistance association (MAA). While MAAs cut across clan and lineage structures (MacDonald 1997:137), they are still sub-ethnic specific, such as the Lao Family Community Development, Inc. Lily, a 1.5-generation Laotian woman who had worked as a counselor with the APEN youth project in the summers of 1995 and 1996, noted that there had been "confrontations over turf, rather than working together," among these organizations (interview, 24 September 1998).

APEN's Laotian Organizing Project addresses environmental health concerns that are unique to the Laotian community in west Contra Costa County but also works in coalition with other environmental justice groups such as WCTC and CBE to mitigate toxic threats common to all the communities in the county. At the same time, LOP's goal is to move beyond refugee resettlement issues that are the primary concern of the MAAs in the Laotian community and focus on a broad array of environmental, social, and economic justice issues facing the Laotians. Moreover, by adopting a community organizing strategy that develops leadership among young women and adult women as well as elders, LOP challenges traditional sub-ethnic conflicts and divisions and unites all Laotians to create greater visibility for the community. Through LOP, APEN also aims to build a desire, and a sense of efficacy, among Laotians that as citizens they should be involved in improving "this imperfect democracy that is the United States," according to Peggy Saika (interview, 21 October 1998). In this way APEN is engaging in a process of critical incorporation of Laotians into the American polity.

The Laotian Organizing Project is one element in APEN's three-pronged strategy to give an Asian Pacific American face to the environmental justice movement in the United States. The Asian American activists present at the First National People of Color Environmental Leadership Summit, the majority of whom were from the San Francisco Bay Area, realized "that if it's about race, economics, and environmental exposure . . . what a powerful context that could be to build an Asian American face as a part of a broader social justice movement," especially in light of the fact that few Asian Pacific American organizations describe themselves as working within an environmental justice framework (Peggy Saika, interview, 21 October 1998). To further this goal, in 2002 APEN launched a second direct organizing project, Power in Asians Organizing (PAO), in the city of Oakland. This pan–Asian American project brings together the diverse Asian ethnic communities of Oakland—Vietnamese, Chinese, Laotians, Cambodians, and Filipinos. PAO has campaigned for affordable housing as well as environmental and occupational health issues for those working in the semiconductor manufacturing industries. The second part of APEN's strategy is to develop a network of Asian Pacific Islander organizations addressing environmental justice issues in the San Francisco Bay Area. APEN's goal is to expand this network throughout California and eventually the nation. The third goal is to create strategic multiracial alliances with other environmental networks around the country, such as the Farmworker Network for Economic and Environmental Justice, the Indigenous Environmental Network, and the Southwest Network for Environmental and Economic Justice. Asian American staff members implement this program of work under the guidance of the Board of Directors, made up of individuals who identify themselves as Asian American activists.[25]

3

New Immigration and the American Nation

A Framework for Citizenship and Belonging

New Immigration: Trends and Issues

Demographic changes in the late-twentieth-century United States indicate that immigration is once again transforming America. Almost one in four Americans, or more than 67 million people, are first- and second-generation immigrants (Portes and Rumbaut 2006:246). Historical relationships between the United States and the sending countries, especially U.S. military, political, economic, and cultural involvement and intervention, together with the passage of the Hart-Celler Act in 1965, have resulted in unprecedented growth in new immigration. Of the post-1965 immigrants, most have come from Latin America and the Caribbean, with Mexico alone accounting for 28 percent of the total. Another 29 percent have come from Asia and the Middle East (Rumbaut, Foner, and Gold 1999:1259). Newspaper headlines that appeared in the San Francisco Bay Area as the U.S. Census Bureau released data from the 2000 census reflect how these racial and ethnic shifts were transforming the state.[1]

Like past immigrants, today's immigrants are more likely to live in metropolitan than rural areas. The foreign-born are concentrated in key urban regions, such as California's southern corridor from Los Angeles to San Diego; in south Florida and particularly Miami; in the northeastern coastal corridor, including New York City, Boston, Philadelphia, and Washington, D.C.; and in the metropolitan areas of San Francisco, Chicago, Detroit, Houston, Dallas–Fort Worth, Phoenix, Atlanta, Minneapolis–St. Paul, and Seattle (Portes and Rumbaut 2006:43). Nearly 30 percent of the 31.1 million foreign-born population enumerated in the 2000 census made their home in California. The other five states with large concentrations of immigrants were New York, Texas, Florida, Illinois, and New Jersey (Portes and Rumbaut 2006:43–47). Places of settlement are initially more dispersed for refugees, whose original destinations in the United States are usually determined by government officials and sponsoring agencies; secondary migration, however, tends to bring about greater ethnic concentration, as exemplified by the Vietnamese in Orange County, California, and the Hmong in the Central Valley area of California.

What is unique about current immigration trends is that more than 44 percent of today's foreign-born population arrived after 1980, with that number reaching 50 percent among those of non-European origin (Zhou 2001:300). Consequently, the "new second generation" is an overwhelmingly youthful population, consisting mostly of children and adolescents (Zhou 2001:273). In fact, immigrant children and U.S.-born children of immigrants are the fastest-growing segment of the country's total population of children under eighteen years of age. By 1997 they accounted for one out of every five American children (Portes and Rumbaut 2001:19).

These trends in contemporary immigration patterns stir up a number of concerns among academics as well as the public. One key topic of interest among scholars is adaptation outcomes, that is, understanding differences in educational attainment, occupations, and income between different ethnic groups. Given the sheer numbers of immigrants and their concentration in a few metropolitan regions, immigration scholars are concerned with their socioeconomic integration into dominant American society:

> Whether this new ethnic mosaic reinvigorates the nation or catalyzes a quantum leap in its social problems depends on the forms of social and economic adaptation experienced by this still young population. (Portes and Rumbaut 2001:xvii)

The new second generation is also the site of ethnogenesis, however, where cultural and ethnic reconstruction, and the consequent reshaping of what it means to be an "American," is taking place. The rise in nativism in the United States during the 1990s and first decade of the twenty-first century is an acknowledgment of this social process. What the public, and particularly the white public, really wants to know is "whether or not the new immigrants will assimilate into the Euro-American society of the United States, and how that society and culture might change as a result of this incorporation" (Massey 1995:632). Anti-immigrant hysteria is not simply focused on the economic and social implications of large numbers of immigrants; such sentiments also express concern about symbolic and cultural issues, especially those related to language, loyalty, and national identity (Rumbaut 1994:752). Despite the popular belief that "America is a nation of immigrants," concerns about assimilation are often directed at immigrants from Latin America and Asia and center on the perceived tendency of people of color to place ethnicity above individuality and thus thwart the process of assimilation into a homogenous, monolithic, and fixed national culture (see, for example, Schlesinger 1992; Brimelow 1995). New immigrants, and particularly immigrants of color, have stirred up ideological questions about "American" identity: "who are we?" and "who belongs to the 'American' family?" (Shohat 1998). These newcomers are viewed as "space invaders," as Nirmal Puar

(2004) put it, whose presence challenges the perpetuation of national myths of essentialized singular cultures and racial histories. An understanding of the experiences of sociopolitical incorporation among the new second generation can teach us about broader processes of change in American society and politics and how new immigrants and their children contribute to new racial formations in the United States. The aim of this book, then, is to comprehend the ways in which contemporary immigration is changing the social meanings of race and ethnicity, of American identity, and of citizenship. In particular, I focus on how members of the new second generation associate, claim their rights, build community, and create a sense of belonging in the nation that is the United States.

Toward a Critical Study of the New Second Generation

Assimilation continues to be the master paradigm both in the popular imagination and in sociological writing on immigration. For example, on the cover of the Fall 1993 special issue of *Time* magazine was a computer-generated image of a woman said to represent "a symbol of the future, multiethnic face of America," according to James R. Gaines, *Time* managing editor (*Time* 1993:2). This cyber-image, which is 15 percent Anglo-Saxon, 17.5 percent Middle Eastern, 17.5 percent African, 7.5 percent Asian, 35 percent southern European, and 7.5 percent Hispanic, is said to dramatize the "melting pot" notion of the United States. In the eyes of the *Time* editors (1993:3), the face illustrates not only America's future physiognomy but also its unparalleled diversity in "peoples, cultures, languages and attitudes that make up the great national pool." However, no explanation is given for the percentages used by *Time*, and the face still looks remarkably white (Hsu 1996:47).

This issue of *Time* is titled "The New Face of America: How Immigrants Are Shaping the World's First Multicultural Society." The words and images ask us to appreciate the diversity and the "universal humanity which supposedly binds us all" (Hsu 1996:47). But the overall message is unmistakably one of assimilation. A "true" American will display a commitment to the political values "embodied in such seminal documents as the *Federalist* papers and the Constitution," "respect for the rule of law," the freedom to succeed or fail, and "the English language," and will share "a cultural idiom that ranges from Bugs Bunny to baseball's seventh-inning stretch" (*Time* 1993:7). In other words, as Ruth Hsu (1996:48) writes, America is portrayed as the "Promised Land wherein hard work and loyalty to 'vital' cultural tenets are rewarded." And I would add that adherence to these values is seen as the only path to full citizenship.

The dominant paradigm in historical and sociological studies of immigrants in the United States incorporates the language of assimilation, adaptation, and acculturation. Developed to explain generational change among European immigrants, the classical assimilation model predicts that over generations there will be a reduction of cultural heterogeneity and convergence in patterns of language, religion, thinking, feeling, and behavior. This process is seen as an inexorable linear progression as diverse immigrant groups become more similar to the "core society" and culture and meld as non-ethnic, or "Americans," through structural assimilation (Gordon 1964; see also Thomas and Znaniecki 1927; Warner and Srole 1945; Park 1950).

In recent years the experiences of new immigrant groups and their descendants have induced a reevaluation and, in some cases, a revival of the classical assimilation paradigm (Zhou 1997b). Alba and Nee (2003) adopt the new institutionalism approach and issue a fervent defense of the classical assimilation paradigm. Based on their review of factors shaping socioeconomic mobility and spatial residential patterns, they suggest that racial/ethnic boundaries are malleable and can blur. In particular, the meaning of "white" has expanded to include the descendants of earlier Chinese and Japanese immigrants.[2] Alba and Nee's position reflects a trenchant American belief in fairness, in socioeconomic mobility for all irrespective of race, ethnicity, or nationality, and is closely linked to another enduring American myth, that of abundant opportunity (Wong 1999). Howard Winant observes that the progress made by Japanese and Chinese Americans has been in the arenas of structural assimilation and adoption of Japanese and Chinese cuisine only, underscoring the ease with which race and ethnicity are conflated in such discussions. He argues that the experience of these two ethnic groups has not altered the fundamental identity of mainstream America: "The system has a capacity to incorporate and hegemonize new immigrant groups without altering the dominant center."[3]

In other contemporary studies of immigrants and their children, assimilation is still the "master concept" (Portes and Rumbaut 2001:45), but scholars argue that assimilation is not inevitable or linear for immigrants and subsequent generations. Many elements point to the inadequacies of the classical assimilation paradigm: the changing racial and ethnic characteristics of new immigrants, the altered structure of opportunities, the recognition that a core culture does not exist but that "American culture" varies by locale and social class, the presence of ethnic resilience, and continuous reconstruction of ethnic social relations, institutions, and cultural practices rather than forced Americanization campaigns. New theories describing the experiences of adaptation among the second generation have stressed the changing contexts of reception and emphasize the multiple and uneven (Gans 1992) and segmented nature of this process (Portes and Zhou 1993). The influential "segmented assimilation" model, which has been further elaborated by Portes and Rumbaut (1996, 2001), Zhou (1997b), Rumbaut (1995, 1997), and Rumbaut and Portes (2001), focuses on the interaction of systems of race and class that shape adaptation outcomes and identifies two sets of factors, contexts of exit and contexts of reception, that can affect multiple acculturative and economic adaptation paths.

Given the socioeconomic statistics of Laotians in the United States, the segmented assimilation model predicts that second-generation Laotians will assimilate into the black underclass. However, as other case studies underscore (Kibria

1993; Wolf 1997; Espiritu and Wolf 2001; Fernandez-Kelly and Curran 2001; Stepick et al. 2001; Lopez 2003), the complexity of contemporary American society ensures that there will be multiple permutations in the adaptation outcomes for the new second generation. As Espiritu and Wolf contend, socioeconomic indicators and ethnic identity shifts can predict structural assimilation and direction of acculturation, but they do not reveal the *"process and meaning* of assimilation for those who live and experience it" (Espiritu and Wolf 2001:182–183; emphasis in original).[4] One promising approach to the study of adaptation experiences among the descendants of immigrants is to avoid seeing the second generation only in terms of the end point of assimilation. I suggest that we envision a two-way microscopic gaze. Rather than assess the assimilative and adaptation potential of the second generation in terms of a set of givens, we can understand "race," "ethnicity," "nation," "gender," and "class" as socially constructed, revealing the ideological underpinnings and power hierarchies girding these social locations. By shifting the analytical lens from product to process, we can bring both majority groups and immigrant communities into focus as actively involved in the construction and reconstruction of social identities (Brah, Hickman, and Mac an Ghaill 1999:4).

Race Matters: Citizenship, Racial Formation, and Immigration

Asking questions about educational attainment and ethnic identity shifts among the new second generation, while important, still leaves unaddressed the potential for symbolic belonging in the nation (Park 2005). Will new immigrants be accepted into the nation and on what terms? Where is "home" located for the new second generation? Is "home" membership in a distinctive imagined community and/or the emotional attachments to a place, located in the nation or the ethnic community? In other words, race matters.[5] Waldinger (2001:12) asserts that scholarly literature on assimilation has yet to conceptualize the mechanisms whereby dominant groups might exclude immigrants and perpetuate the disadvantages they experience. Recent sociological theorizing on immigration perceives the American nation as a neutral or benign context (Hsu 1996:54). It ignores the power relations between majority and minority groups and does not theorize the construction of difference within racialized social collectivities. As Lisa Lowe argues:

> Citizens inhabit the political space of the nation; a space that is, at once, juridically legislated, territorially situated, and culturally embodied. Although the law is perhaps the discourse that most literally governs citizenship, U.S. national culture—the collectively forged images, histories, and narratives that place, displace, and replace individuals in relation to the national polity—powerfully shapes who the citizenry is, where they dwell, what they remember, and what they forget. (Lowe 1996:2)

American citizenship and American nationality are not synonymous; citizenship carries with it the promise of equality in legal and political terms while nationality defines who "real Americans" are at any given historical moment (Lee 1999:6). The ostensibly *abstract* discourses of U.S. citizenship and individual rights are in fact structured in terms of racial, ethnic, class, sexual, and gender hierarchies (Kim 2008; Park 2005; Glenn 2004; Collins 2001; King 2000; Perea 1998; Lowe 1996; Mohanty 1991a; Pateman 1988). Rather than conceptualize the United States as a monolithic nation-state, I understand what is called "America" as a nationalist discourse that produces diverse—racialized, gendered, and classed—subjects. Nationality, then, "contains and manages the contradictions of the hierarchies and inequalities" of America as a social formation (Lee 1999:6).

Scholars have noted the ways in which "race" in particular has been a constitutive element in the formation of American national identity (Collins 2001; King 2000; Ngai 1999; Higham 1974, cited in Sanchez 1997). I find it useful to draw on Omi and Winant's (1994) notion of "racial formation" to understand the racialization processes experienced by Asian Americans and Asian immigrants. As a racial formation, America is a constantly shifting and contested terrain, in which citizenship laws and rights are the outcome of negotiations, contestations, and struggles over racial discourses and structures between the state and civil society. Contemporary racial formations bear the footprints of the historical debates and decisions taken by the racial state, which have come to project "American" identity as centered on white race and class interests and ordered the nation around the biracial black-white axis. However, changes in racial dynamics in the United States suggest that this white versus nonwhite structure is evolving into a triracial order, comprising white people, honorary white people, and a diverse collective black group (Bonilla-Silva 2004). Using objective indicators of standing such as income and occupational status, subjective indicators of "consciousness" such as self-reports on race and racial attitudes, and data on social interaction such as interracial marriage and residential segregation among members of the three racial strata, Eduardo Bonilla-Silva (2004:932–933) hypothesizes that the white group will include "traditional" whites, new "white" immigrants, and totally assimilated white Latinos; the intermediate group of honorary whites will comprise most light-skinned Latinos, Japanese Americans, Korean Americans, Asian Indians, Chinese Americans, Filipinos, and most Middle Eastern Americans; and the collective black group will include blacks, dark-skinned Latinos, Vietnamese, Cambodians, and Laotians. Aihwa Ong (2003) elucidates the processes of "whitening" and "blackening" that lead to distinctions within racial groups and differentially position Asian immigrant groups within the U.S. racial formation. In the contemporary era a neoliberal discourse "increasingly defines citizenship in economic terms, by insisting that citizenship is the civic duty of individuals to reduce their burden on society and to build up their human capital" (Ong 2003:14). Such human capital calculations and discourses on welfare, affirmative action, and immigration/immigrants, which define worthy citizens as white, structure the racial classificatory process so that some Asian immigrant groups and refugees, such as Laotians and Cambodians, are placed at the black pole (Ong 2003:14) and compared with African Americans in terms of low-wage employment, high rates of teenage pregnancy, and welfare-dependent families.

This triracial model sheds light on the racial positioning of Laotians, one of the newest immigrant groups to arrive in the United States. But as this model indicates, there is no overarching homogeneity of experiences among the broad ethnic and racial groups in each of these strata. Asian Pacific American (APA) communities have become extremely differentiated along lines of class, culture, language, histories of immigration, and patterns of settlement and adaptation (Espiritu and Ong 1994). The second-generation Laotians in this book belong to a recent immigrant community and represent a group that is distinct from other Asian and Pacific Islander groups in the United States in terms of ethnic and class composition. The struggle to improve their social and economic status suggests the potential for solidarity across "race" rather than within racial boundaries. Indeed, Bonilla-Silva (2004:942) anticipates "higher levels of collective action and consciousness among the poles of the racial order (i.e. among whites and the collective black strata)."

For Asian immigrants and Asian Americans, however, discourses of new scientific racism and eugenics have intersected with an orientalist discourse[6] that defined Asians as culturally and racially "other," as a "yellow peril," and as the "foreigner within," even when born in the United States and the descendants of generations born here (Lowe 1996:4–6; Lee 1999). Historically, these discourses have ideologically underpinned the series of legal exclusions, disenfranchisements, and restricted enfranchisements of Asian immigrants, who have been positioned as either "near-blacks" (as in aliens ineligible for citizenship but seen as cheap exploitable labor) or "near-whites" (as in model minority) (Espiritu 1997:109–110). Even so, many Asian American scholars (e.g., Gotanda 1999; Ancheta 1998) contend that anti-Asian subordination is qualitatively different from subordination of African Americans. Rather than based on notions of racial superiority and inferiority, anti-Asian subordination is centered on citizenship, which divides racially between American and foreigner.[7] If Asian Americans are "forever foreign" (Tuan 1998) and still considered outside America's national imaginary, then Claire Jean Kim's (2004:999) conceptualization of "racial positionality," which locates racialized groups on a plane defined by at least two axes—superior/inferior and American/foreigner—appears more apt. It would allow us to "recognize that Asian Americans and Latinos have been seen historically as *both* between black and white on the former scale and quite foreign on the latter scale" (Kim 2004:999). An understanding of the racial positioning of groups can reveal differences in socioeconomic status, power, and privilege, as well as provide clues to the nature and dynamics of interminority relations emerging in the changing U.S. racial landscape.

As Lisa Sun-Hee Park (2005) deftly demonstrates, the children of Korean and Chinese immigrants feel compelled to prove their "Americanness" and display their belonging in the nation through consumption. These two groups of the new second-generation Asian Americans have absorbed the neoliberal discourse on citizenship (Ong 2003) that delineates a "good" immigrant as one who pursues upward mobility and contributes rather than burdens the United States. Possession of material goods and pursuit of higher education—in other words, consumption—becomes a mark of social citizenship. However, given the reality of race, class, and gender barriers to full citizenship, pursuit of the American Dream becomes a disciplinary mechanism "that keeps in place normative, unequal social structures by enticing marginalized groups with the possibility of full participation" (Park 2005:8). The parents of second-generation Laotians, who also aspire to social mobility, as I discuss in Chapter 5, arrived with little human capital and few resources to put to the service of the pursuit of socioeconomic mobility. Thus, for them, the possibilities of full citizenship are even more remote within contemporary neoliberal discourses. Moreover, as Nadia Kim (2008) has recently shown, even those Asian Americans who arrive with human capital and achieve hard-won social mobility continue to be denied membership in the nation. For second-generation Laotians, participation in AYA provides an opportunity to gain an understanding of contemporary racial politics in the United States, to negotiate interminority relations, and to acquire the resources to participate in the polity in order to critique and contest the normative ideology of citizenship within collective contexts. In this book I investigate how opportunities for shifting cross-racial and/or cross-ethnic alliances based on political commitments and shared interests may challenge unequal social structures and exclusionary discourses. I am interested in understanding the possibility of challenging and altering the meanings and boundaries of racial categories, and constructing alternative notions of belonging and citizenship.

Conceptualizing the Social and Political Identities of Second-Generation Laotian Girls

It is crucial to conceptualize the adaptation and incorporation processes for the children of immigrants as mediated by intersecting systems of race, ethnicity, and class as well as gender and generation in order to capture their complexity and multiple permutations. But how are we to concretely understand the linkages and inscriptions of these intersecting structures of power? As discussed above, discourses and structures of race and citizenship at the local, national, and global levels position Laotians as a group on multiple planes of racial hierarchy and form the broader social and political contexts in which identities take shape. At the level of the individual, how second-generation Laotians experience these discourses and structures and how they become and are made into subjects is constrained by their social locations and the particular grids of power they experience. Thus it is important to link the macrolevel within which racial and ethnic group identities are formed to microlevel processes of identity formation.

In the United States second-generation Laotians are simultaneously positioned as refugees, immigrants, and poor, racialized minorities as well as subjected to discourses on young people and women of color. The popular conception of young people in the United States has a Jekyll and Hyde duality to it. On the one hand, ambivalent and contradictory discourses construct young people as the symbols of the future, representing hope and optimism; at the same time, young people are perceived in negative terms, as threats to the existing social order (Giroux 1998:25). Wyn and White (1997) identify three approaches that remain central to academic research on young people: youth development, youth subcultures, and youth transitions. The concept of youth development draws from psychological theories of human development, which constructs normative expectations of young people. Young people who do not conform to these norms are identified as "at risk," requiring specific programs and practices to help them meet these expectations (Wyn and White 1997:51–52). Peter Kelly (2000) also observes that in a time of profound social, economic, and cultural change, popular and theoretical discourses primarily construct young people as "at risk." This trend was particularly prevalent in the United States in the 1990s. Moreover, once youth behaviors, dispositions, and interactions are so identified, various programs can be implemented by schools, police, health services, the juvenile justice system, and funding bodies to increase surveillance, regulation, and intervention in the lives of young people.[8]

The youth transitions approach has drawn greater attention in Europe as a "response to the failure of traditional pathways towards achieving adulthood" (Wyn and White 1997:94). This approach focuses on the education system and the labor market, and how these institutions are failing to offer all young people real pathways to adulthood and becoming productive citizens. My aim here is not to evaluate these approaches except to highlight that both perspectives view young people as passive, their lives determined by individual psychological development and/or social institutions. Young people in general, and the children of immigrants in particular, are rarely portrayed as actively constructing their own life patterns and experiences, albeit within specific material and cultural contexts and relations of power (for exceptions, see Lee 2005; Alexander 2000).

In contrast, the wealth of studies on youth subcultures demonstrates young people's active role in the production and consumption of culture and processes of identity formation. In the 1970s the British Birmingham Centre for Contemporary Cultural Studies (CCCS) had a strong influence on the cultural analysis of young people. Detailed ethnographic studies of young, working-class, heterosexual males adopted a Marxist conception of cultural production and redefined young people as cultural producers and consumers rather than as delinquents and deviant. The concept of resistance offered in these earlier ethnographic studies viewed working-class young men as agents rather than as recipients of a dominant culture and highlighted the practices, fashion, and styles of expression in their everyday lives, such as mods, Teds, skinheads, and punks, that subverted aspects of the dominant culture (Wyn and White 1997:24).

In the United States, youth subcultures research had its antecedents in studies that emerged from the Chicago School in the postwar period (Zhou and Lee

2004:3–7). Much of this research has tended to focus on hip-hop artists and rappers, hippies, skinheads, punks, graffiti writers, low riders, ravers, or suburban "mall rats." Zhou and Lee (2004:1) argue that these popular images seem to exclude Asian American young people. Educators widely portray young Asian Americans as the "model minority" while peers often derogatively stereotype them as "nerds" or "geeks" rather than as consumers or producers of youth subcultures in the way "normal" teenage Americans are perceived to be. At the same time, studies on youth subcultures have tended to equate "resistance" and "struggle" with boys, according to Gelder (1997:86).[9] Women in general have been situated as passive victims of those with political and economic resources in vertical power relations, and as some feminists have argued (Mohanty 1991b; Puar 1996; Brah 1992a), studies of "Third World" women and women of color have cast this group as victims of particular socioeconomic systems and patriarchy (for exceptions, see Espiritu 2003; Lopez 2003). An edited volume by Lee and Zhou (2004) goes some way toward redressing the marginalization of Asian American young people and women in research on American youth cultures. *Laotian Daughters* also contributes to filling this gap but goes beyond Lee and Zhou's focus on Asian American young people creating and consuming or inhabiting distinctive cultures and identities to address community activism among young Asian Americans. While an emphasis on "resistance" and an attribution to subcultures of a creative agency, in which resistance is worked out in the realm of leisure rather than in a way that addresses structural change (Gelder 1997:86), has certainly been captured in many of the ethnographic studies emerging from the tradition of the Birmingham School, these scholars have been critiqued for promoting a simplistic view of "resistance." More recent youth culture studies have highlighted the nuances and contradictory political meanings of subcultures and "oppositionality" (Maira and Soep 2005:xxxi). Maira and Soep (2005:xxxi) further contend that that we need to retain the focus on "resistance" and that popular culture can provide a space and vehicle for contesting identity, community, and belonging. I agree with Maira and Soep on the potential role of popular culture, but I argue that we need to extend studies on youth resistance to include formal organized activism aimed at structural change.

While the media and politicians often blame racial/ethnic minority young people for a range of social problems, scholars such as George Lipsitz (1998) argue that youth research should be located within the racialization of social crises such as unemployment, poverty, ghettoization, school failure, alcohol, and drug and gang violence. Stacey Lee's (2005) in-depth study of first- and second-generation Hmong American high school students explains their experiences of school, identities, and responses to life in the United States in terms of the processes of racialization that confer power, privilege, and status to whiteness and associate poverty, failure, and reliance on public support to blackness. Lee argues that while the adoption of particular youth cultural practices and oppositional identities among Americanized Hmong students represents resistance to race and class exclusion, they are unable to link their personal experiences to processes of racialization or directly challenge racism. Racialization processes in the United States also explain the individual experiences and identities of second-generation Laotian women, as I argue in this book. But I also demonstrate how, through participation in a social justice organization, these young women acquire the language, the understanding, and the political skills to confront race- and class-based inequalities in the United States as well as gender and generational hierarchies within Laotian families and communities. However, I do not advocate swinging the pendulum in the other direction and seeing all action and inaction as resistance. By presenting and analyzing second-generation Laotian girls' oppositional and nonoppositional positions and complex subjectivities within intersecting relations of power, I hope to convey a nuanced understanding of the possibilities for these girls to actively shape their world.

Acknowledging the possibility of occupying oppositional and nonoppositional subject positions in different contexts suggests a conception of identity that is fluid, unstable, and situational. To view acculturation in terms of shifts in ethnic identity is to view the "original" and "American" cultures as static, fixed, hermetically sealed, impermeable, and always in opposition. Much scholarship on the new second generation understands ethnicity in terms of one's ethnic origins and heritage, bounded and rooted in place, and the distinctive cultural practices associated with such origins (see Portes and Zhou 1993; Zhou and Bankston 1998). Such a position implies that those ethnic attachments and cultural understandings and practices are either retained or, in the case of assimilation, lost. And becoming American is synonymous with the principles of freedom, progress, and individualism (Ong 1996:739).[10] Reconstruction is a more accurate description of ethnic institutions (Hein 1995), ethnic social relations, and cultural practices under the rubric of enduring but distinct ethnic categories. In this book I conceptualize culture as a process, in which there is no separation between culture and structure. Such a perspective does not invoke a fixed array of customs, values, and traditions, leaving scholars to simply describe the effects of culture on assimilation outcomes; rather, culture is processual and constantly reconstructed within shifting structural contexts.

The process of cultural construction also serves to build community when groups define the boundaries of collective identity, establish membership criteria, generate a shared symbolic vocabulary, and define a common purpose (Nagel 1994:163). Within the context of migration to the United States, such community building is important for ethnic groups that have been historically antagonistic but need to form pan-ethnic organizations in which common interests and common histories necessitate the construction of a shared culture (Nagel 1994; Espiritu 1992). For example, in the context of the United States, the sub-ethnic groups Lao, Iu Mien, Hmong, Khmu, Lahu, and Thaidam constitute the category Laotian, despite their cultural differences and past adversarial relations (Chan 1994:3). Debates over the label "Laotian" among Lao-Americans (see Anderson

2005:218) notwithstanding, U.S. institutions such as the California Youth Authority and the U.S. Census Bureau, scholars such as Portes and Rumbaut (2001), and social justice organizations such as APEN apply the umbrella category "Laotian" to the sub-ethnic groups that have migrated from Laos. Here I also use the term "Laotian" to understand the ways in which the context of an ethnic-specific community organization provides the space to build collective self-understandings (Brubaker and Cooper 2000:7) of social practices as well as of larger political issues that are important to this new immigrant community.

However, I view "Laotian" not as a singular, fixed identity for second-generation Laotian women but as one that is constructed and unstable. If we limit the inquiry into ethnic identity to self-labeling, then the struggles embodied in identity formation, or the meanings of particular ethnic self-identification, are not revealed in quantitative research, as recent ethnographies indicate (Stepick et al. 2001; Espiritu and Wolf 2001; Fernandez-Kelly and Curran 2001).[11] I am concerned with understanding the forces that shape and influence the contents of ethnicity. Critical scholarship (Moraga 1994; Alarcon 1990; Mohanty 1991a; hooks 1984; Smith 1990; Collins 1990; Crenshaw 1995; Anthias 2002) points to the intersection of gender, race, ethnicity, sexuality, class, and other axes of difference that structure people's images of themselves and their material lives. I draw from feminists of color and postcolonial feminists who have moved toward using the term "subjectivity" rather than "identity" to avoid a free-fall into relativity or the trap of essential categories and an authentic being (Moya 1997; Alarcon 1990; Sandoval 1991; Alexander and Mohanty 1997). They view subjectivity as multiple, dynamic, and continuously produced in the course of social relations that are themselves changing and at times contradictory. Additionally, they insist that subjects are constituted only in their situatedness in multiple and intersecting axes of domination (Alarcon 1990; Sandoval 1991). Thus at each moment any given identity may take a range of meanings and encompass a range of experiences. Acknowledging the interacting webs of ethnic, race, gender, class, and other systems of stratification allows us to move away from essential notions of identity and to understand the dynamic and contradictory ways in which multiple relations of power construct the subjectivity of second-generation Laotian girls. I analyze their cultural practices and actions, which are governed by particularistic self-understandings (Brubaker and Cooper 2000:6) and the multiple subjectivities produced through generation, gender, class, ethnicity, and race. Thus we can begin to understand how it is possible to challenge a particular cultural practice from a feminist perspective, for example, without maligning a whole cultural group (Brah 1996:92). Or how teenage Laotian girls can challenge dominant representations of them and potentially transform relations of power without rejecting all of dominant "American" culture. Second-generation immigrants can occupy oppositional or nonoppositional subject positions as they negotiate, contest, and collude with cultural forms and practices in different contexts and situations.

Negotiating Power, Exercising Agency

Recent academic scholarship has documented the emergence of Asian American community organizations from the 1970s onward as vehicles for political action and, increasingly, for resistance to dominant narratives of assimilation, incorporation, and becoming "American" (Chung 2007; Das Gupta 2006; Võ 2004). These writings undermine both ideological constructions of Asian Americans as the "model minority" and the liberal ideology of universal citizenship. In so doing, they go beyond recognition of heterogeneity in the racial category "Asian American" and cleave open ethnic categories to reveal differences in interests and experiences along lines of class, gender, sexuality, and generation within particular Asian American ethnic groups. I place my study of the process of sociopolitical incorporation among second-generation Laotian women within this body of critical literature. But rather than ask questions about what induces Asian Americans to mobilize (Võ 2004), or what role ethnic bridging organizations play in new immigrant communities (Chung 2007), or how Asian American community organizations construct a set of rights that are not confined within a nation-state but are mobile within a transnational field (Das Gupta 2006), I focus on the strategies and vision of an ethnic organization with a broad environmental and community justice agenda to investigate the nature of sociopolitical incorporation experienced by second-generation Laotian women. Through APEN young Laotians learn that instead of focusing on individual triumphs within existing hierarchies, they can secure gains for the whole community by challenging unequal structures in the wider society and ethnic community. In addition, my concern with citizenship as social practice and my emphasis on an agency-oriented perspective (Smith 2001:6) leads me to analyze how such critical discourses and community organizing influence the political subjectivities and the political and social practices and identities of the young Laotian women in this book.

Communities of color and immigrant communities in the United States have been organizing since the 1980s around a range of environmental justice concerns, such as issues of toxic waste siting and public health (Bryant and Mohai 1992; Cole and Foster 2001; Timmons Roberts and Toffolon-Weiss 2001), land and water rights and industrial workplace safety (Pellow and Park 2002), pesticide use and working conditions on farms (Pulido 1996), disposal of solid waste in urban areas (Pellow 2002), and urban planning and environmental health concerns in the context of privatization and deregulation (Sze 2007). In documenting efforts to challenge unequal toxic burdens, the environmental justice movement and environmental justice scholarship have adopted a civil rights framework linking environmental and social exclusion and inequities. Environmental justice advocates have been concerned with the unfair distribution of environmental risks and problems and with processes that produce social inequality. As Dorceta Taylor (2000:535) argues, environmental racism as a concept is important because it "bridges past social justice activism that focused on racial injustice and civil rights with past and present environmental experiences." These linkages are represented in the six ecological and social justice components enshrined in the Principles of Environmental Justice adopted at the First National People of Color Environmental Leadership Summit held in October 1991: ecocentric principles; environmental and human rights; autonomy and self-determination; corporate-community relations; policy, politics, and economic processes; and social movement building (Taylor 2000:538–539).

This investigation of mobilizations against the environmental and social injustices faced by Laotians further extends environmental justice scholarship. I document how one of the newest Asian immigrant groups and their children relate to and engage with environmental and social injustices in the San Francisco Bay Area. The book demonstrates that when working with new immigrant communities, which have few formalized structures for achieving social change and are linguistically isolated, environmental justice advocates must focus on political socialization: generating new social capital and a sense of political efficacy to facilitate mobilizations against environmental and social injustices. In this goal the bilingual second generation play a vital role. However, as this book also demonstrates, environmental justice advocates must address issues specific to the children of immigrants living in urban multicultural environments if this group is to actively participate in achieving social change. This case study on Asian Youth Advocates provides a unique and in-depth analysis of APEN's work with the Laotian community in Richmond, California,[12] and mobilization of young women in the pursuit of environmental and social justice. The specific political values that shape APEN's work in the Laotian community include (1) the belief that whatever the citizenship status of new immigrants and their children, they have social and political rights; (2) the importance of participating in the democratic political process; (3) the political value of direct collective action; and (4) common struggle with other communities of color. These values and ideologies influence APEN's political practices in ways that depart from both those in mainstream U.S. society and those in the Laotian community. Asian Youth Advocates thus provides a unique opportunity for investigating environmental justice activism as well as the politics of incorporation and mode of incorporation into the American polity for second-generation immigrants.

Scholars and activists working with immigrant women assume that disempowered communities need forms of knowledge to negotiate and change the inequities that keep them disadvantaged (see Benmayor et al. 1992). These efforts have combined critical literacy, leadership development, and skills building to create individual and collective capacities for change, enabling immigrant women to exercise full citizenship. Such efforts acknowledge the possibilities of challenging what Ong (1996) identifies as complex relations of power linked to the state, institutions, and social groups that define the criteria for belonging. The agency-oriented perspective adopted in this book recognizes the micropolitics of power where power is relational, multiple, and mobile (Dreyfus and Rabinow 1982:208–

226). A relational notion of power challenges simplistic binaries such as oppressor/oppressed (Mohanty 1991a:13) and public/private dualities that keep Asian immigrant women powerless (Lowe 1996:162), and shifts the terrain of politics from a focus on abstract political identities, or a singular narrative of emancipation (Lowe 1996:58), to negotiation, resistance, and accommodation in everyday relations within institutions and spaces such as the law, workplaces, schools, community organizations, family, sexual life, churches, and popular culture. This induction into American society is not an uncritical emphasis on adaptation but a conscious and deliberate attempt to foster what I call *critical incorporation*. Contemporary social justice organizations such as APEN engage in cultural politics because they believe that groups suffer injustices and inequalities on the basis of unequal and unfair distribution of not only economic capital but also symbolic, social, and cultural capital. Thus critical incorporation involves a set of practices in the cultural political realm that contest, transform, or accommodate power relations within the nation and civil society as well as within the family. In the following chapters I analyze both the creative potential and the sometimes uncertain effects of this radical political orientation.

4

The Politics of Race

Political Identity and the Struggle for Social Rights

My idea of a perfect school is a school that has money, has all available school materials, can afford to go to field trips where students can learn with a "hands-on" experience, a school that has very good, intelligent, fun and humorous faculty, a school that has counselors who guide students to their goals and to the right direction; a school with clean bathrooms, no graffiti; and a school with students who do not discriminate, no bad attitude, and students who are just there to learn and have fun.

—Cuo, Group 2 (Journal entry, 2 July 1999)

At various times and in a range of contexts, second-generation Laotian women in the United States are portrayed as the model minority, as "problems" and at risk of becoming single mothers, and as refugees and perpetual foreigners. In this chapter I demonstrate how teenage Laotian girls challenge these discursive delineations through political action. Specifically, I discuss their involvement in three organizing efforts: the demand for a multilingual emergency warning system in Contra Costa County; a campaign to improve school counseling services; and electoral work to oppose Proposition 227, which sought to dismantle bilingual education. These issues were only some of the major concerns facing the Laotian community, given its members' history as recent refugees, their class position, the neighborhood demographics, and their socioeconomic milieu.[1] In addition to anti-immigrant and anti-Asian racism, Laotians experience racialization through the structural "neighborhood race effects" (Espiritu et al. 2000:136; Lopez 2003) of underfunded and resource-deprived schools, environmental pollution, and low-wage jobs that Laotians share with their African American, Latino, and even poor white neighbors. Such structural race effects not only undermine successful socioeconomic adaptation but also deny new immigrants and their children substantive citizenship, or a sense of belonging, participation, and equal access to rights and opportunities.

In September 1998, with four cohorts of teenage girls in the program, APEN staff decided to harness the knowledge, confidence, and leadership skills the girls had developed during their involvement in AYA and engage them in direct organizing activities. This shift in strategy came about from the realization among the staff that no other group in the Laotian community was in a position to build the

Laotian Organizing Project. As Miya Yoshitani, who was of Japanese Anglo heritage and worked as lead organizer for LOP at the time of my research, explained:

> We will have to do this with the people we work with the most, which is the youth, the young women and teenage girls who we have been working with and ... have really been directing most of our resources into. And that waiting for another group to step up or something is not going to happen as a first step. (Interview, 22 September 1998)

The shift also acknowledges that young people already play an important role as the link between their parents and grandparents on one hand and the wider American society on the other hand. As the first English-speaking generation in the community, they have a powerful position, and "so we're just sort of recognizing that and trying to build on that, to take advantage of that," noted Miya (interview, 22 September 1998). In this chapter I discuss the roles the second-generation Laotians undertook and their reactions to APEN's efforts to link personal experiences of neighborhood race effects to structural analyses of social inequalities in the United States. I analyze the contents of APEN's political strategies to understand the kind of political subjects and ethnic and racial identities that are created through participation in AYA. In addition, I discuss APEN's creativity, as well as the tensions and limitations of their organizing strategies. The chapter underscores the importance of understanding youth political identities and how they develop within the context of a community organization that foregrounds race at a time when the dominant discourse attempts to erase it. At the same time, APEN has attempted to avoid the pitfalls of essentialism by linking concerns about environmental protection to issues of linguistic and social equality and community empowerment. As the environmental justice refrain underscores, the environment is "where we live, where we work, where we play, where we learn" (Cole and Foster 2001:16). Contemporary social justice organizations like APEN acknowledge the intersectionality and simultaneity of processes of racialization, class exploitation, and exclusion based on language, age, and other axes that shape individual and collective experiences. Conceiving of identity in terms of multiple subjectivities, whether consciously or not, allowed APEN to mobilize the Laotian community around its multiple needs in their specific location in west Contra Costa County, as well as to emphasize connections with other communities of color within common contexts of struggle along class lines. Such organizations provide space for second-generation young people to learn to be "Americans": they gain a critical understanding of the links between personal experiences of inequalities and wider structural race and class inequalities, as well as acquire resources and a sense of efficacy to participate in the polity.

While the media and politicians often blame racial/ethnic minority young people for a range of social problems, in this chapter I advocate for viewing young people as active agents working to address the racialization of social crises such as poverty, school failure, alcohol, drug and gang violence, and unfair burdens from environmental degradation. In so doing, I draw attention to young people as citizens in their own right rather than as "incomplete" adults whose rights can be ignored (Wyn and White 1997). Citizenship is predominantly viewed as an adult experience and ignores efforts by young people to achieve social change (France 1998:99–100). As the studies on youth subcultures demonstrate, when we do hear youth voices in the contemporary era, they appear in subcultural sites such as underground magazines, alternative music and style, and computer hacker clubs (Giroux 1998:24). Rarely do we hear of young people engaged in politics in its widest sense or involved in alliances with other subordinated groups to achieve social transformation. The daughters of one of our newest immigrant communities, a group that has been invisible or ignored to date, demonstrate that they too have a right to equal citizenship and belonging in the nation.

Race and New Immigrants:
The Environmental Justice Angle

A vivid and immediate example of what environmental justice means to the Laotian community in west Contra Costa County occurred in the early afternoon of 25 March 1999, when a fireball erupted at the Chevron refinery. This incident highlighted issues of environmental justice, race, and citizenship in a new immigrant community.

The accident occurred when Chevron's hydrocracking unit, used to remove impurities from crude oil when it is refined into gasoline and jet fuel (Squatriglia 1999), developed a leak and released hydrogen sulfide and sulfur dioxide into the air.[2] The explosion shook nearby homes and sent a fireball and thick clouds of smoke hundreds of feet into the air. It took sixty-eight firefighters from Chevron and Richmond three hours to control the blaze, which engulfed an area of seventy-five square feet. Sulfurous smoke rose two thousand feet, causing respiratory difficulties and sore eyes for hundreds of local residents (Squatriglia 1999; Ferris 1999). This incident exposed major inadequacies in the county's warning system, which is supposed to inform residents of "shelter-in-place" procedures.[3] The severity of the accident demanded that each household receive a warning by an automatic phone-alert system operated by the Contra Costa County Health Services Department. Yet many households never received a call. Other households received the message several hours after the explosion, when residents had already been exposed to the toxic gases. Seventeen-year-old Gabriela, a committed and vocal member of Group 1, recounted that Chevron called their home at midnight, several hours after the incident, to inform them about the accident and asking them to stay in place. And then five minutes later the Health Department called them (field notes, 30 March 1999). Of those Laotian households that received timely calls, many of the residents did not understand them because the message was in English. Elder Laotians, especially, have limited English proficiency (Kong 2001:18). Moreover, unlike the Spanish-speaking residents, who are able to receive emergency information and warning alerts from local media channels, the Laotian community in west Contra Costa County has no full-time television or radio station that could have served as a source of information.[4]

At a subsequent youth meeting, on 30 March 1999, discussion on the Chevron explosion revealed some of the side effects of exposure to sulfuric gases that the residents had suffered, as well as the confusion that surrounded the incident. Grace Kong, of Korean heritage and the Youth Program Coordinator for AYA, asked the eighteen girls present what information they had about the incident and their experiences of it:

> "I want to do this check-in about Chevron. Who knows what happened?" asks Grace. Various people shout out that it was sulfur and it could be smelled in the Oakland hills, but that it was no risk to people. After allowing the girls to share what they know, Grace goes through what actually happened. She tells them that the hydrocracking unit had a fire but there was a twenty-minute lapse before the sirens went off. She states that "in many ways the emergency systems failed." She also tells the girls that while the public line that Chevron is holding to is that there was no risk, LOP is hearing from the community that people had difficulty breathing and had burning eyes, and that long-term effects such as cancer, respiratory problems, and asthma are exacerbated.
>
> Grace then inquires, "What happened at school?" Someone reports that the bell rang and teachers allowed students to leave Richmond High School. Leah says that at Middle College, classes were canceled and students were allowed to go home. She adds, "Police officers walked around telling people to stay in." At Richmond High School an announcement was made over the loudspeaker that there was an accident at Chevron. Gabriela reports that the school was not notified until one hour later. She also mentions that parents were calling to get students, but school staff asked students to stay in.
>
> Grace asks people to pair up and interview each other about how they felt and what happened during the accident. [There is a lot of energy today, and everyone is lively.] She gives them ten minutes and then asks people to shout out a few of the answers. The girls report that they were scared, confused, worried about their health, and some people had suffered minor ailments. (Field notes, 30 March 1999)[5]

This discussion indicates that although the official position from Chevron suggested that the smoke was nontoxic, many area residents suffered minor ailments, including nausea, skin rashes, headaches, and respiratory problems (Kong 2001:18).[6] More significantly, the girls were not sure how to respond when the emergency sirens sounded. Rather than arrange for "shelter-in-place" procedures, school authorities at Middle College permitted students to go home, in the process exposing them to the toxins in the air. Large numbers of elderly Laotians were unaware that an industrial explosion had occurred and thought that the black smoke came from a burning house. In the southwest section of San Pablo an elderly Laotian said that he had climbed the bunker behind his apartment, beyond which was the Chevron refinery, to see where the smoke was coming from (field notes, 19 April 1999). Others could not understand the English-language news announcements on television and radio asking residents to "shelter in place" (Kong 2001:17). These elders, and the grandchildren they typically take care of at home during the day, were particularly at risk to exposure from toxic chemicals.

At a small community meeting soon after the accident, APEN staff heard adult and senior Laotian members of LOP express anger over the inadequacies of the emergency warning system. They knew that the explosion on March 25 was one of many that had occurred in Richmond. They expressed frustration at the frequent and ongoing exposure to toxins (Kong 2001:18). In these emotions APEN staff saw an opportunity to galvanize the diverse ethnic groups in the Laotian community to fight for an environmental justice issue that directly affected them. Over the ensuing months a team of APEN staff and elderly Laotian men and women devised a campaign to press for alternatives to the monolingual emergency warning system that was in place at the time. They decided to target Contra Costa County's Health Services and the Internal Operations Committee of Contra Costa County's Board of Supervisors to implement this change (Kong 2001:8).

Previously, APEN and LOP had joined efforts with the West County Toxics Coalition to demand corporate accountability from large corporations such as Chevron, which have a history of environmental accidents, as detailed in Chapter 2. But in this campaign APEN staff decided that LOP did not have the capacity or the power to confront a large corporation that plays a significant role in the economy of Contra Costa County and the larger Bay Area (Kong 2001:19–20). Instead, they insisted that the government has the responsibility to ensure the community's well-being and protect residents' health. In making this strategic decision, APEN linked environmental justice to race and citizenship for new immigrants.

Second-generation Laotians played multiple roles in the campaign. Several of my respondents in AYA took an active part at meetings and events. A few weeks after the incident APEN organized a "small, controlled" community meeting with Mr. Walker, the director of the County's Health Department and the person with the authority to make decisions about the current warning system (conversation with Grace Kong, 12 April 1999). In addition to Bryanna of Group 4, Tsiet of Group 3, and Gain of Group 2, two other girls from Group 4, elderly Laotian men and women, and APEN/LOP staff members were present at this meeting. This was the first meeting of its kind for LOP, and the staff was unsure how it was going to unfold. The atmosphere was quite tense, and Vicki, an APEN staff person, remained in charge of facilitating the meeting (APEN 1999).

Mr. Walker heard testimonies from the Laotian seniors as well as fifteen-year-old Tsiet about their experiences on 25 March 1999. Tsiet described what happened at Richmond High School: "The school broadcast said that there was an explosion at the oil refinery, but we were let out of school at the usual time, making us walk home as usual." Tsiet stated that later that night she felt dizzy after coming home. She was extremely angry because "the school should have made us stay within the classrooms and not let us out to breathe the poisoned air" (APEN 1999). Tsiet's anger appeared genuine, and her involvement in this campaign reflected her desire to fight for linguistic equity for Laotians. In informal conversations she had often mentioned that she wanted to become a lawyer or work in the field of criminal justice on behalf of her community, and giving testimony was the beginning of achieving that aspiration.

After the testimonies, Vivian, of Chinese heritage and working as APEN organizer, presented Mr. Walker with four demands: that the County Health Services Department should reach out to diverse populations in the county; conduct a language equity analysis of its capacity to serve non-English-speaking populations, particularly Laotians, in the event of an emergency; develop a plan that addresses language access for limited-English-speaking populations, particularly Laotians; and conduct community-based education activities on emergency warning procedures for Laotian residents. To the surprise of everyone present at the meeting, Mr. Walker categorically accepted each of the demands presented to him (APEN 1999). This was a powerful moment for everyone at the meeting, but especially the girls. Grace recalled:

> It was new for them to see seniors speak in Mien at a public meeting to a decision maker, and it was great to present our demands to Mr. Walker and have him say yes to all of them. This was a positive and exciting experience for the youth. It was also the first LOP meeting for them. (Conversation with Grace Kong, 12 April 1999)

A few weeks later, when Grace asked the girls involved in the LOP campaign to share their thoughts at a youth meeting, fourteen-year-old Bryanna reported that the campaign work for the multilingual warning system has "been great! We put in a lot of work and they've [director of the County Health Department] supported us." Sixteen-year-old Gain enjoyed being interviewed by a local television channel about the campaign (field notes, 3 May 1999).

Ten days after the meeting with Mr. Walker, APEN staff organized a press conference in front of two apartment buildings in southwest San Pablo to publicize their mini-victory. They selected this location to highlight the proximity of Laotians, mostly from Khmu and Thaidam ethnic groups, to the refinery. An excerpt from my field notes describes the scene:

> The two apartment buildings are at a T-angle to each other, separated by a driveway. A large tree provides shade for the two cars parked in the driveway. A chain-link fence separates the apartments from a huge bunker with a railway track sitting atop. No trains passed by while we were there, but when a train does go by I am sure it is deafening and shakes every home. Beyond the bunker I can see the rooftops of a couple of factories. The Chevron refinery that had the explosion is in that vicinity.
>
> A few of the Laotian residents are at home on this Monday afternoon. An elderly man, who is holding a baby in a sling, is standing in the doorway to his apartment; a middle-aged man and a couple of teenage boys are standing

on the sidewalk; and a teenage girl is observing from her apartment. Some of the African American neighborhood kids come to watch too. (Field notes, 19 April 1999)

Ten elderly Laotian women stood in a line in front of the bunker, holding a banner that read "The Laotian Organizing Project" in Lao script. Eight of the youth from AYA, including many of the youngest from Group 4, were standing behind the women holding signs that said "Safe systems for all people," "We deserve health & safety," and "Everyone deserves to be safe." The press conference was organized and supported by five of the APEN/LOP staff members, who were either talking to reporters or standing with the Laotian teens and elders. As the press conference began, one of the elderly Laotian women spoke in Mien, and Tsiet translated for her: "On that day I heard the alerts and saw the dense smoke from afar but didn't know what happened, and didn't understand the news reports. I thought that was a fire from someone's home and was extremely afraid." Gain, a confident and vocal member of Group 2 who aspired to be a pediatrician, ended the press conference by stating in English, "Our community's health and safety should not be put on hold when these accidents happen so often." Before and after the press conference, reporters from two local television channels and two newspapers (including one from the Asian press) interviewed Vivian, the elderly Laotian woman, and LOP's Laotian organizer (field notes, 19 April 1999).

At these two public events second-generation Laotians acted as translators and communicators for the non-English-speaking elderly Laotians, as so often happens in immigrant communities. They also made visible the Laotian community in west Contra Costa County and asserted that they too have a right to a safe and healthy living environment. Moreover, they observed elders speak in Mien at a public event. These actions signaled a growing self-esteem and sense of efficacy among both generations of Laotians. Susan James argues that to speak in one's voice and put forward one's own views in the polity requires self-esteem, or "a confidence that one is worthy to participate in political life" (1992:60, quoted in Lister 2003:39). Through such political acts Laotian immigrants and their children were forging substantive citizenship in the United States.

Small-scale political action is often frustrating, however, and has many twists and turns. After their initial success APEN and LOP made little progress with the County Health Department to have their demands implemented and instead faced "entrenched resistance" (Kong 2001:19). Thus they decided to take the initiative to develop concrete proposals for improving the emergency warning system and to present them to the County Health Department. Through language-specific house meetings in the Laotian community, APEN/LOP staff began to prioritize the development of a multilingual phone-alert system rather than a multilingual radio station or simply community outreach and education. Mr. Walker was invited to another meeting to discuss these proposals, but this time APEN and LOP staff found that he was quite inaccessible. In order to have its proposal heard, the campaign team agreed to a meeting with a county health ombudsman and a press officer from the Health Department.

Two elder Laotians, Bryanna, and Tsiet took turns to present each proposal. The two County Health Department representatives were polite and expressed great interest and commitment to working with LOP. They acknowledged the time and work that had gone into putting these proposals together but held their ground, referring to the established budget process and the County Board of Supervisors as the decision-making body for the allocation of funds for these proposals. They also asked that LOP remain open to other ideas besides the ones being proposed, such as installing radio frequency devices in each Laotian home. Grace stated that they were very open but insisted that they saw these proposals as a baseline of what the community needed. Vivian expressed disappointment that the two representatives could not make any decisions and tried to impress on them the urgency of this matter.

Tsiet, Bryanna, and the two elder Laotians listened attentively during the meeting. As the meeting was coming to an end, Bryanna raised her hand and asked Teri, the ombudsman, how much the radio frequency devices would cost. Teri told her that they would cost about sixty dollars apiece. "At that price we can buy them too," asserted Bryanna.

The first meeting, with Mr. Walker, was a powerful and positive experience, but this meeting gave Laotian elders and second-generation teens a real insight into local government bureaucracy and the power structures they were challenging. The multilingual warning system campaign became a protracted struggle with the county's elected leadership and public workers. Reflecting the general political climate and trend of privatization of key government responsibilities to voluntary organizations and individuals, some members of the County Board of Supervisors believed that community organizations such as LOP should do the work of educating the Laotian population (Kong 2001:21).

During this time the APEN/LOP staff sought to maintain momentum on the campaign by extending contacts in the Laotian community, increasing membership, and deepening the involvement of interested Laotian adults and elders who had been difficult to organize previously. For APEN, this was an opportunity to do base-building work and strengthen LOP, thereby furthering the goal of creating an Asian Pacific American face in the environmental justice community. LOP's Laotian staff, with the help of its Organizing Committee, which consisted of elder men and women from the Iu Mien, Khmu, and Lao ethnic groups, organized language-specific house and neighborhood meetings, made personal visits to those who showed a keen interest in the campaign, and conducted presentations at churches, adult education classes, and Laotian ethnic associations (Kong 2001:23). Members of the Organizing Committee asked family and friends to sign postcards demanding that Mr. Walker and the Department of Health Services take steps to protect the health of the community. Toward the end of the campaign there were one hundred Laotians actively involved in campaign pressure activities (Kong 2001:21). Several delegations, which included APEN/LOP staff, Laotian elders, and/or Bryanna and Tsiet, met with various members of the County Board of Supervisors.

After six months of organizing and sustained pressure, on 27 September 1999, the County Board of Supervisors agreed to a new multilingual phone alert system in Contra Costa County.[7] For APEN and the Laotian community, this campaign demanded that all county residents—immigrants and non-immigrants alike—have a basic right to a safe environment, regardless of their race or class, English-language ability, or citizenship status.

APEN/LOP sought to execute the campaign for a multilingual emergency alert system through the leadership of monolingual elders (both men and women), as well as other adult women and teens. These sections of the community challenged the authority of a few established leaders. Early on in the campaign, these leaders had disparaged the ability, and viability, of a grassroots membership to represent the needs and concerns of the Laotian community to the county.[8] Perhaps these established leaders were also questioning the legitimacy of individuals exogenous to the Laotian community to convey the needs of the community to state officials.[9] As my discussion of the various campaign-related meetings suggests, Bryanna, Tsiet, and Gain, along with some elders, provided testimony and presented previously defined solutions to the problem the campaign was addressing. The participation of Laotians in this campaign was circumscribed within these specific roles, and it was Vivian, the lead organizer for the campaign (and a third-generation Chinese American), and sometimes Grace (a second-generation Korean American) who controlled the meetings and took responsibility for the delicate political negotiations with state representatives. This distribution of roles highlights the fact that the U.S. political system rewards those with language skills and political sophistication, both of which most Laotians do not have (Espiritu and Ong 1994).

Nevertheless, the campaign for a multilingual emergency warning system made the needs of Laotians in west Contra Costa County, as a new immigrant community, more visible and built a sense of political efficacy among some young, adult, and elder Laotians. Miya described LOP's roles as

> building desire or building, like, the vision, that is, building the possibility in people's minds that you have the right to do this. And you have the right to demand a better life for the community and for your children . . . that there are possibilities of participating and having a voice and demanding your rights. (Interview, 22 September 1998)

APEN/LOP staff found that many grassroots campaign participants had little experience in expressing their views in a formal setting, let alone an understanding of community organizing and civic participation (Kong 2001:33). In part, this may be due to what Jeremy Hein (1995:100–101) calls a "deferential view of authority figures" among Laotian refugees. In contrast to participatory democracy in the United States, political decision making in Laos was the province of elites rather than ordinary citizens. Moreover, many Laotians have memories of the way politics were conducted in Laos under authoritarian and then Communist governments. Hein (1995) argues that experiences under these governments, as well as the negative connotations associated with the very term "politics," act as further disincentives to political participation.[10] And in the United States, where assaults on existing social support systems have increased, immigrants are wary of questioning and challenging public officials. For example, one Iu Mien grandmother was reluctant to speak with local government representatives about her experiences and concerns for her family's health because she was afraid she would lose her welfare benefits. This elderly woman was eventually featured on television voicing her view that the government was responsible for protecting the health of her community (Chiang and Chiang 1999:9), but other Iu Mien members ended their participation early in the campaign due to this fear (Kong 2001:33). Nevertheless, in a community with little community-organizing experience and still fearful of government authority, many members were empowered to speak in front of government officials.

The campaign for a multilingual emergency warning system also highlights the tension between identity politics and coalitional politics. Clearly, the inadequacy of the emergency warning system affects the lives of other limited-English-speaking communities in Contra Costa County. Previously, APEN had joined efforts with West County Toxics Coalition, a multiracial organization, to address the impact of toxic threats in west Contra Costa County, but on this occasion APEN/LOP staff made a strategic decision to emphasize the vertical relationship between the Laotian community and the established decision makers in Contra Costa County. In this decision APEN activists displayed an awareness of the American sociopolitical environment and the ways in which interest-group politics on the racial model shapes access to resources and political influence (Gamson 1995:400-401). APEN thus also defined social rights in terms of the group, in the process challenging liberal definitions of citizenship that construct all citizens as equal in terms of status, rights, and duties. At the same time, the organizing strategy in this campaign called attention to the need for an increased role for the state, not a diminished one, to ensure social rights so that all citizens can be full and active members of the nation.

Lack of staff capacity may have been one practical reason for the decision to focus on mobilizing the Laotian community through this campaign rather than nurturing coalition politics. Certainly, the protracted struggle with the county's leadership and public workers had severely stretched APEN and LOP resources. But perhaps more importantly, following the environmental justice principle of people speaking for themselves, APEN/LOP staff sought to use this incident to develop capacity in the Laotian community for first- and second-generation Laotians of various ethnic groups to "speak for themselves." During the campaign APEN/LOP staff made an effort to extend contacts in the Laotian community, increase membership, and deepen the involvement of interested Laotian adults and elders who had been difficult to organize previously. By focusing on the

Laotian community, APEN prioritized base-building work in a community that lacks resources, experiences extreme poverty and invisibility, and whose older members are linguistically and culturally isolated.[11]

The ramifications of this campaign may eventually spread to all non-English-speaking residents in the county, including the large Spanish-speaking population. However, given the state's practice of allocating scarce economic resources along racial lines, there is no certainty that an adequate multilingual emergency warning system will emerge without a sustained multiracial campaign. In this campaign APEN and LOP built a strategic Laotian identity to bring together three of the ethnic Laotian groups in west Contra Costa County for which the staff had the language capacity to communicate with and organize. In pursuing this political strategy, APEN downplayed historically present internal divisions of ethnic affiliation and nurtured a new collective political identity.[12] Laotian political identity, constructed out of different languages, cultural traditions, classes, genders, and generations, is shaped by the shared experiences of racialization and its consequences. In the next section I discuss how APEN sought to maintain the Laotian political identity as fluid, dynamic, and open to making connections with other limited-English-speaking communities.

Race, Language, and Belonging: The Fight against Proposition 227

On 2 June 1998, Californians decisively rejected bilingual education by approving Proposition 227, the so-called English for the Children initiative. Proposition 227 represented a continuation of an extreme antipathy toward non-English languages embodied in previous "English Only" legislation that has swept the nation (Sanchez 1997:1020). Such legislation, together with attacks on multiculturalism and affirmative action prevalent during the 1990s, as discussed in Chapter 2, asserts what George Sanchez (1997:1019) has called a racialized nativism at the end of the twentieth century.

In the 1990s, issues of immigration, race, ethnicity, and language preoccupied and often divided Californians (Crawford 1999). The passage of Proposition 227 represented a fear among sections of the population in California that linguistic difference would undermine the American nation (Sanchez 1997:1020). Upholding English as the language of the nation is thus seen as protecting a way of life.[13] However, Proposition 227 raised not only questions of race, language, and belonging for immigrant and refugee communities but also the issue of language minorities having access to a good and adequate education.[14]

Over a period of six months in 1997 and 1998 the Organizing Committee of LOP, consisting of LOP staff, adult Laotians from the community, and four girls from the youth project—Sarah of Group 1, Gain of Group 2, and Pham and Tsiet of Group 3—had met to identify and discuss the barriers facing the Laotian community in their local schools. Parents did not have access to their children's schools because many did not speak English but also because they were not familiar with the most basic practices of American schools. This meant that parents could not participate in matters dealing with the education of their children. In addition, during the 1997–1998 school year over 50 percent of the Asian students categorized as limited-English-proficient in the West Contra Costa Unified School District (WCCUSD) were Laotian (California Department of Education 2002a). If voters approved Proposition 227, these students would be directly affected.[15] Thus, for APEN, organizing a campaign against Proposition 227 was an opportunity to mobilize Laotian parents against a ballot initiative that would be detrimental to the needs of their children and those of other immigrant families in the community. Peggy Saika, APEN's executive director, emphasized that APEN/LOP's "ability to be involved in working against 227 was really predicated by the growing understanding of what the barriers were for the [Laotian] community in their local school and they couldn't have access" (interview, 21 October 1998).

APEN decided to join forces with Californians for Justice (CFJ), a grassroots multiracial social justice organization, to work in key precincts in west Contra Costa County. CFJ was organizing a campaign against the initiative and conducting a voter registration drive. For APEN/LOP staff, this electoral campaign represented an organizing effort that would be completed in a short time frame, would not require a lot of staff resources since CFJ was leading the organizing effort, and would give the AYA girls experience in electoral organizing against a statewide initiative that directly affected the community (Miya Yoshitani, interview, 22 September 1998). At the same time, bilingual education was an issue that was also important in the Latino community. Thus, for APEN, involvement in the "No on 227" campaign provided an opportunity to draw connections among all the immigrant communities in Contra Costa County.

Staff members introduced Proposition 227 and the issues surrounding it to the AYA girls at a Whole Group Meeting in March 1998:

> It is a gray and rainy afternoon, but this store-front office is buzzing with the sound of teenagers excited to see each other and rock music blaring from the radio. Nineteen of the youth are here today from Groups 1, 2, and 3. Only three of the girls are not present. Almost everyone is dressed in blue jeans, black T-shirts, rain gear, and black lace-up platform boots or Fila running shoes. [The first 90 minutes of this meeting were filled with an ice-breaker, announcements of upcoming events that AYA staff wanted some of the girls to attend, updates on the retreat in April, and a short ceremony honoring Peggy, APEN's executive director, for winning the Woman Warrior Award.]
>
> After a ten-minute break, Gain of Group 2 and Pham and Tsiet of Group 3, with the aid of staff, present a short skit on bilingual education and Proposition 227.
>
> **SCENE 1:** A non-English-speaking parent comes to school to meet with one of the school administrators. Someone goes to pull her daughter out of class to translate for the parent, but the daughter is extremely reluctant to go

because she will miss part of the class. Later that day there is a LOP meeting during which time the upcoming Proposition 227 is discussed.

SCENE 2: A subsequent day in a classroom with a bilingual teacher and students. The teacher explains something in English, but the students do not understand her. So the teacher repeats it in the students' native language, Mien. Then two people, holding placards with Proposition 227 and "English Only," stomp through the classroom.

SCENE 3: AYA youth are trying to persuade people to vote "No" for Proposition 227 and asking them to sign a petition against it. (Field notes, 23 March 1998)

After the presentation and a short debriefing about what happens in each scene, Grace Kong, the Youth Program coordinator, asked the girls to suggest some other ways to get people involved in such a campaign. Someone shouted "phone-banking." Another girl offered, "Door-to-door." This prompted Seng to mention a difficult experience that she and Gain had had when working precincts during the campaign against Proposition 209.[16] Grace affirmed their experience and explained that one can meet unsympathetic people who are difficult to persuade, "but you also meet some cool people" (field notes, 23 March 1998). Grace went on to summarize the discussions of school issues that had occurred in LOP's Organizing Committee (OC) and stated, "If Prop. 227 passes, OC has no grounds to ask for bilingual education and bilingual services in schools." When she asked the girls if there had been any other, similar propositions in the last few years, no one seemed to remember. She prompted them by mentioning Proposition 187 and Proposition 209 and again asked if anyone remembered them. Seng and Gain chimed together, "Cutting affirmative action," with respect to Proposition 209.

Most of the girls remained attentive during this discussion, and when Grace asked for volunteers to work on the "No on 227" campaign, Tsiet, Paeng, Tracy, Pham, Lai, Gain, and Leah immediately signed up. While Tsiet and Pham of Group 3 and Gain and Leah of Group 2 had been actively involved in both AYA and LOP activities, I was surprised when Paeng, Tracy, and Lai, all of Group 3, volunteered to become involved in electoral organizing. Paeng and Lai were particularly shy and studious, but both were also involved in their church youth groups. As I argue below, for these teenagers the ways in which Proposition 227 would directly affect their limited-English-speaking peers struck a chord.

Tsiet, Pham, Cuo, Leah, and Rachel got their first experience of informing others in the Laotian community about Proposition 227 and persuading them to sign a petition against it at the annual Lao New Year celebration at the Richmond Auditorium in early April.[17] With a clipboard and petition in my hand, I accompanied Pham and Tsiet as they walked around the reception area outside the auditorium. Several organizations, including LOP, had set up information booths by the front entrances. Adjacent to the side entrances there was a mini-market where vendors sold Laotian textiles, readymade clothing, and food cooked on the premises. Several hundred guests were inside the auditorium watching a beauty pageant, but the reception area was quiet.

Pham and Tsiet decided to approach people as they were standing around chatting to friends and family. I observed Tsiet confidently introduce herself as a member of LOP and inform them about Proposition 227 and why they should oppose it. Pham found it difficult to approach individuals at the event. When I tried to encourage her and suggested that she use the words Tsiet was using, she said, "I am too embarrassed." AYA staff had coached the girls earlier in the day to tell people that in addition to cutting bilingual education and services if it passed, Proposition 227 represented an attack on Laotian cultures and languages. This was a powerful argument for some Laotians, who already feared that their children would be monolingual in English. They signed the petition without questions or discussions, and Grace reported that she heard many people say, "They can't take away our language" (field notes, 6 April 1998). Others refused to sign the petition, stating that they were not citizens. Still others were fearful of signing because it might mean they would have to give money to someone or to an organization. They were also afraid of being included in some kind of list. Despite reassurances, these Laotian community members were not persuaded by three unknown individuals—Tsiet, Pham, and me—representing a little-known organization, LOP (field notes, 4 April 1998). Nevertheless, the youth volunteers, staff members, and I were able to gather eighty signatures that afternoon.

In response to media polls showing that Proposition 227 had strong voter support, all my respondents were urged to work precincts, carry out phone banking, distribute flyers, get petitions signed at school, and hang information on doors in local precincts. During a meeting for all the teens in early April, AYA, APEN, and CFJ staff showed them how to work precincts and carry out phone banking through role plays. The CFJ staff person emphasized to the twenty young people attending that they should always ask for three things when working a precinct: "to vote, volunteer, and donate money for the production of campaign materials" (field notes, 6 April 1998). At the end of this training Grace reiterated to the girls that their involvement in the campaign against Proposition 227 and working with CFJ was "a learning experience" and "ties in with LOP's school issues campaign." In other words, it was an important part of their work as members of AYA/LOP. However, she did not elaborate on LOP's school issues campaign even though only four of the girls had been involved in those discussions with LOP's Organizing Committee. While there were no questions or signs of resistance from the girls, AYA staff did not create a space at this meeting for a conversation with them about the importance of their role, whether they wanted to be involved in electoral organizing, or their reactions to the proposition (field notes, 6 April 1998).

How did involvement in the campaign against Proposition 227 shape my respondents' political subjectivities? When asked how they felt about Proposition 227, many of the girls expressed confusion about the supporting and contrary arguments. They were categorical about needing to learn English if one wants to live in the United States, but at the same time they objected to the proposition's provisions for learning English (a one-year intensive program) and what this meant for getting a good education. For example, sixteen-year-old Lon, of Group 1, who had participated in phone banking and had talked to family members about the initiative, believed that bilingual classes were necessary because non-English-speaking students would not understand or learn anything in English-only classes:

> **BINDI:** So, do you think classes should be held in Spanish for chemistry or algebra so they learn enough in it or should they just go to an English-speaking class?
>
> **LON:** Well, I think certain subjects—say, chemistry—could be; it doesn't have to necessarily have to be taught in all Spanish. It could occasionally, like, have English, you know. It could be on and off or something. But then I don't think it should be all English and I don't think it should be all Spanish. Because, if it's either, then they'll never learn. If it's all Spanish, how are they gonna learn English? If it's all English, they'll never learn English. So, it should be, like, mixed.

Lon, who was born in the United States and aspired to attend college, believed that it was necessary for the children of immigrants to learn English. Perhaps this view was reinforced by her father's experience of working at Lao Family Community Development, Inc.[18] But Lon recognized the necessity for flexibility in teaching methods based on the needs of the students, something that was threatened by Proposition 227. Other respondents drew on their experiences of learning Spanish to argue that it was impossible to learn adequate English in one year. Seng, who had taken Spanish as a second language for three years, noted that it takes "that long to learn some words." She believed that "people will get frustrated" if they are pressured to learn English in one year (field notes, 6 April 1998).[19]

Two other respondents, fifteen-year-old Maya, from the third cohort, and Leah, from the second cohort, both of whom had worked precincts, asked friends to sign petitions, and participated in phone-banking, made a direct connection between schools not meeting the educational needs of some students and those students dropping out or engaging in criminal activity:

> **MAYA:** Leaving them in all-English classes, of course they, like, learn to adapt and mix in and learn, like, what they're saying in English or doing whatever. But then when they have, like, help from a translator and stuff, they understand that. They are more eager, you know, to learn about more stuff instead of, like, because they can be pulled down, right, like, if they don't understand any of it. "What's the point of me coming to class if I don't understand what they are saying?" Or like, you know, "I'm having such a hard time and stressing over this," you know. They just, like, they give up.
>
> **LEAH:** What I was thinking about 227 is if we were to say No, and then you cancel all the things like they say . . . I think that it's going to cause crime,

> crime rates. People tend to cut when they don't understand school. . . .
> Then if they cut, then they doing something out there, not good for their
> health and not good for their community. So that's why I supported it
> [the APEN campaign against Proposition 227].

Maya and Leah, both of whom were born in the United States, attended a selective high school in Richmond, and were keen to take advantage of the educational opportunities available to achieve social mobility, delineated a connection between bilingual education and academic performance.[20] Maya and Leah's comments echo the alienation experienced by some Laotian teens that Laotian social workers have observed in west Contra Costa County. All my respondents knew of Laotian peers who were involved in gangs or who had become teen mothers. And Maya had recounted in her interview that her male friends had often told her there was no point in working hard and going to school because the teachers did not care about them. Here Maya's friends were reacting to the racial stigmatization young Laotians and other young people of color experience in schools.[21]

In their comments my respondents focus on the pedagogical issues involved in bilingual education rather than the proposition's nativist implications, which motivated APEN staff to join forces with CFJ in challenging it. However, I argue that this does not necessarily represent a rejection of APEN's interpretation of the proposition. Rather, it appears to be a response to the dominant framing of the proposition as a children's "right" to learn English in the media and the purported failure of bilingual education programs (Crawford 1999).[22] But some respondents were concerned about the unfairness of not allowing immigrants to maintain their language while taking advantage of the opportunities in this country. Fourteen-year-old Bryanna said:

> It's not fair. I mean, what's wrong with people from another country not being able to speak English. I think we should give them opportunities 'cause this is a land of opportunities. But that's like kinda, that's kinda unconstitutional for them to do that stuff.

Bryanna, who was also born in the United States, recognized, along with some of the other girls, the anti-immigrant elements of Proposition 227. Three days after California voters approved the elimination of bilingual education, Maya reported that "earlier today a Spanish lady was speaking in Spanish and someone else came and said to her, 'Have you guys heard about 227?'" (field notes, 5 June 1998). Seventeen-year-old Seng also viewed the proposition as a direct attack on language and cultural minorities. While training AYA girls how to work precincts, the CFJ staff person asked, "Why is it [Proposition 227] bad?" Seng responded passionately, "Most people in here can't even talk in their own language. They are so caught up in learning English and doing school work that when they go home they forget to speak their language" (field notes, 6 April 1998). For Seng, the strategy of intensive English for one year that Proposition

227 proposed would put even more pressure on the children of immigrants to speak English at all times and abandon their home languages. Bryanna had been involved in the campaign even before she became an official youth member of AYA; she and Seng and Maya had all been very active in the electoral organizing activities because the proposition directly affected the Laotian community. But once they were engaged in the campaign, they began to understand the implications of the proposition for other communities, as well as its ideological underpinnings.

For other respondents, the campaign against Proposition 227 presented an opportunity to inform their immigrant parents and get them involved in fighting for their rights:

> **SARAH:** In that it was, like, a good issue for us to try and help them, you know... 'cause some people didn't know what it was about, so we, so APEN explained it to them.
> **TRACY:** Yeah, it also gives me a chance to let the people be aware, like the Proposition 227, like most of us Asians, like our parents, everyone, they didn't, like, know what's going on.
> **PHAM:** And they think, they either think it's good or bad. They don't know the real reason, you know, so they'll just pick one or the other.
> **TRACY:** Yeah.
> **PHAM:** And then we try to, like, let them know that it's a very bad thing.

Here sixteen-year-old Sarah, of Group 1, who was born in the United States, and Tracy and Pham, of Group 3, both of whom arrived before the age of six months, recognize the critical role they play as cultural brokers and bridge builders in a community that is linguistically isolated. Working with APEN/LOP on the campaign against Proposition 227 provided AYA teens both information and a perspective on the bill, and created an opportunity to educate family and friends about the consequences for bilingual education if the proposition was approved.

In this campaign to defeat Proposition 227, APEN provided the language and created the conditions for my respondents to get involved in mobilizing the Laotian community. Although the initiative passed in California,[23] it was defeated in every precinct that APEN and CFJ worked. When I asked my respondents what they were most proud of being involved in at APEN, fifteen-year-old Fiey, from the third cohort, who came across as quite shy and reticent, mentioned her role in this victory (interview, 7 January 1999). Gabriela, from the first cohort, was also ecstatic that their efforts had paid off:

> Another thing about it is that it passed within all the other cities but it didn't pass in Richmond. That really like, that really like, you know, that's like one of the biggest moments in this thing—it didn't pass. Yehhh!

For these Laotian teenagers, who could not vote at the time, getting involved in this electoral campaign showed them that they could still influence voter opinion. And it illustrated the importance of exercising one's right to vote and to participate in building a democratic society. Almost all the girls participated in one or more of the campaign-related activities, whether it was asking friends to sign petitions, passing out information, or actually working precincts with other young people of color from CFJ. Many of these activities, such as walking in unfamiliar neighborhoods and talking to strangers in person, required some level of courage. Some respondents participated because of the strong expectations from AYA staff that they become involved even though they did not care about the issue. Other respondents got involved "because of, like, their obligation and loyalty [to APEN]," according to Grace Kong (interview, 9 October 1998). But for a core group of my respondents, Proposition 227 struck a chord. Even though none of them needed bilingual classes, they all knew of Laotian peers in school who did. And most of the teens had had the experience of being pulled out of class to translate for their parents when they came to meet with a school official. Among this core group there was a collective self-understanding of the implications of Proposition 227 and a realization that no one else was mobilizing the Laotian community against a ballot measure that would affect them directly.

In the campaign to defeat Proposition 227, APEN made a link between immigration, culture, and citizenship. The staff viewed the appearance of such an initiative as part of the rise in nativism and attacks on people of color in the 1990s. As the CFJ representative categorically stated to the twenty AYA girls during a training session, "This is an attack on some people, on immigrants and African Americans" (field notes, 6 April 1998). Thus, besides the practical aims of getting the community involved and educating members about their rights, the campaign sought to make connections between immigrant communities and communities of color. However, as I stated above, there was no explicit discussion during the campaign about the connections and commonalities between different communities of color in Contra Costa County. Consequently, my respondents understood Proposition 227 as an attack on "difference," and were aware of the practical implications of banning bilingual education in schools for Laotians and other limited-English-speaking students, but failed to reach a "complex antiracist consciousness" (Angela Davis in Lowe 1997:320), the possible reasons for which I discuss in Chapter 5. The campaign against Proposition 227 highlights the need for clear, intentional strategies to create a politics based on commonalities.

In the next section I discuss a campaign that sought to build the Laotian Organizing Project and to make explicit connections with other communities in west Contra Costa County.

Race and Education: The School Counselor Campaign

My respondents attended inner-city public schools, where they experienced surveillance and intervention and were constrained from reaching their full potential because of a lack of resources and textbooks, inadequate numbers of teachers with credentials, nonchallenging curricula, and the prevalence of violence.[24] At a brainstorming session early in the 1998–1999 school year, I remember being aghast at the litany of problems the girls in AYA identified at Richmond High School, the school most of them attend: not enough counselors to give adequate advice, favoritism exercised by security guards, inadequate numbers of textbooks, crowded classrooms with fifty students per class, dirty and unusable bathrooms, violence among students and weapons brought to school by students, lack of respect from some teachers, and drugs (field notes, 23 November 1998). On the occasions that I had visited the school it had felt like a low-security prison with security guards everywhere, locked gates, crowded classrooms without windows, and absolutely no greenery to soften the gritty concrete environment. I could not imagine learning anything in what appeared to me to be a very alienating school environment. But the girls did not express anger; the tone in which they stated the problems was very matter-of-fact. Perhaps this was because they had to build a protective barrier around themselves and get on with school.

Some of my respondents' school experiences had origins in past tax policies in California and changing funding priorities at the local, state, and federal levels. In addition, the rapid demographic changes in California since the early 1990s have led to severe competition for resources. Other reasons for these experiences stem from dominant constructions of urban youth as "at risk" in the 1990s, with proclivities for teenage pregnancy, gang involvement, violence, drug addiction, and reliance on public assistance. Despite a steady decline in youth crime and violence over the last few decades, the categorization of youth as "at risk" provides a rationale for increased surveillance of and intervention into young people's lives by schools, police, health services, and the juvenile justice system (Kelly 2000; Collins and Kearns 2001).[25]

Yet other experiences were particular to schools in the West Contra Costa Unified School District. In the late 1980s the then Richmond Unified School District was unable to fund a continuance of instructional services and was faced with bankruptcy. The district accepted a multimillion-dollar loan from the state of California. By 2000 the district had repaid approximately $22 million of the loan but remained burdened with the outstanding $19.9 million of debt (Superintendent of Schools 2001:16). The district's near-bankruptcy and resultant state oversight meant that it was prohibited from participating in the State School Facilities Program from 1993 to 1998. Consequently, existing facilities had deteriorated and custodial and other maintenance staff were reduced by 50 percent, all of which created "teaching environments [that] are depressing to both students and staff" (Superintendent of Schools 2001:17). More significantly, the district's budgetary problems led to a focus on financial survival rather than supporting and facilitating student achievement (Superintendent of Schools 2001).

Based on discussions with adults in LOP's Organizing Committee and the youth members of AYA, who had identified multiple problems at Richmond High School, AYA staff decided to organize a campaign around a school-related issue.

At an AYA meeting on 23 November 1998, with twelve girls from Groups 1, 2, 3, and 4 in attendance, Grace Kong presented four problems in schools that Groups 1 and 2 had identified in previous meetings: insufficient attention from counselors and too few counselors to give adequate advice, teachers unfamiliar with Laotian cultures and cultural norms,[26] racism among security guards, and inadequate resources and textbooks. In the ensuing discussion Sarah stated that she did not think the second issue was appropriate, as no school teaches Laotian history and culture. Leah responded that while that may be true, she would like to learn about other Asian groups, not just about Chinese history and culture. Pham and Rachel pointed out that friendships rather than race governed favoritism and discrimination by security guards (field notes, 23 November 1998). In order to select the best issue to organize around in a more systematic way, Grace asked the girls to evaluate each issue in terms of the following criteria:

- Is serious enough to get specifically Lao youth involved.
- Is not just one person's issue but affects a lot of people.
- Will motivate people to get involved.
- Builds alliances with people of other races. It doesn't isolate us.
- Makes a real and specific change happen at school.

Grace further elaborated on each criterion. On building alliances with other races, she reminded the young women present, "We would never want to work against other races, especially other people of color, because that divides us. That often happens [that others try to divide people of color]" (field notes, 23 November 1998). Thus Grace emphasized another of APEN's political values: that any campaign APEN/LOP conducts must meet the goals of building the organization but also promote bridges with other communities of color.

At subsequent meetings in early 1999 the teens voted to work on the issue of the lack of sufficient support and guidance for students at Richmond High, thus deciding to take a proactive stance on a long-term problem and one that directly related to educational performance. Most of my respondents were performing well at school and were highly motivated. They had learned the cultural codes required for high academic achievement and navigating school life. Thus they did not encounter cultural dissonance or problems from security guards. The lack of adequate academic counseling was also an issue that affected all the communities in west Contra Costa County because 95 percent of students at this school are students of color.

The first step in this campaign was to find out how other students at Richmond High felt about the issue. The core group of teens working with the staff to devise campaign activities—sixteen-year-old Blia of Group 1, who was also active in a multiracial student group at Richmond High; sixteen-year-old Cuo of Group 2; Maya and Fiey of Group 3; and Bryanna, Lisa, and Yen of Group 4—led the design of a survey questionnaire. At a meeting in April 1999 the staff trained them on how to introduce the surveys to their friends and peers and reminded them to be careful to avoid alerting the teachers and the principal that a campaign was under way:

> "What's the rap?" asks Chit [one of the AYA counselors]. Grace requests suggestions from the girls. Bryanna rattles off "try to get more counselors," "doing survey for student opinion." Blia offers another version, "I am part of AYA, a student here, and concerned that students are not getting enough academic counseling." Grace nods in approval but is concerned about not alerting the teachers and principal about a campaign. She asks the girls to emphasize the information-gathering aspect only when introducing the survey in class, but if they are talking to their friends, she encourages her to talk about the campaign stuff to excite them. (Field notes, 20 April 1999)

The young women then used this script to role-play and to practice implementing the survey at school. During the month of May my respondents administered over five hundred surveys to students at Richmond High (field notes, 3 June 1999). Other teens, accompanied by staff but still taking the lead, interviewed academic counselors and deans at four high schools in the school district. At the final AYA school-year meeting in June, the mood was celebratory and buoyant. Grace congratulated the thirteen girls present on their hard work and told them that the valuable information they had gathered was an achievement in itself because "students don't normally go out and interview 500 students and counselors." She announced that they were going to use the data to "influence state policy!" (field notes, 3 June 1999).

In the wake of recent high-school shootings, such as that at Columbine High School in Littleton, Colorado, in 1999, much public attention has focused on the role of counselors at high schools. With more than fifteen hundred students in 1999, Richmond High had only two-full time counselors. They were responsible for supporting students' academic and social development in a variety of ways, including scheduling classes, providing college and career guidance, meeting with parents, giving referrals, and handling crisis situations. In other words, students expected them to be accessible caring adults in the school, trained to provide guidance and support to students.

The survey conducted by the AYA teens found, among other things, that (1) there were not enough counseling resources to meet all students' needs at Richmond High; (2) a large number of students surveyed had never seen a counselor; (3) students felt an inequity in service due to their age, with seniors getting priority; and (4) students desired and would use more counseling resources if they were available (field notes, 23 June 1999). These findings also reflected the AYA teens' own experiences with school counselors (field notes, 23 June 1999) and reinforced the overall lack of resources available in WCCUSD to support student achievement. For the seventeen girls from Groups 2, 3, and 4 who were participating in this summer session, the need for an adequate number of academic counselors was transparent. When staff asked them to think about the consequences of insufficient support, the teens listed "gangs," "welfare," "pregnancy" (field notes, 23 June 1999), and "no good jobs" (29 June 1999). The survey found that students often feel lost and detached from school, resulting in poor attendance and weak academic performance.

Emboldened by these findings, during the summer of 1999 the APEN staff developed a curriculum for the second, third, and fourth cohorts of girls that addressed a broader understanding of the problem in the school district and the state. The AYA teens spent the early part of the summer program in intense sessions of analysis and learning about the state of education at Richmond High and WCCUSD, the counseling-related needs of the students, and the dominant perception of young people. The staff used a range of interactive techniques to help the teens construct this collective knowledge. One afternoon early on in the summer program, Grace reviewed the findings of the survey in detail. Subsequently, she split the girls into four groups and asked them to create a three-minute skit to "to bring to life what these numbers mean" (field notes, 23 June 1999). I observed Pham, Bryanna, Lisa, and Ruby create the following scenario quite effortlessly:

> A tenth grader goes to see the counselor about SATs and college. The counselor tells her to come back next year, at which the tenth grader is upset and stomps her foot as she walks out. Then a ninth grader goes to see the counselor, wanting to know more about the school. This student is told to look in the school planner. Next a senior walks in and tells the counselor that she needs credits to graduate and asks what she can do. The counselor tells her that she needs to fulfill some more requirements before she can graduate and that she should have come to seek advice much earlier. (Field notes, 23 June 1999)

Once all four groups had created and performed their skits, Grace drew out two key themes: (1) counselors want to help but are too busy; (2) counselors should help all students, not just the seniors. She concluded that in all the skits, counselors were providing "Band-Aid" solutions rather than addressing the problems early on. After a short break Grace announced that the next session was going to consist of a game-show format based on the popular television shows "Jeopardy!" and "The Price Is Right." She asked for nine volunteers to be the contestants and informed them that they would receive candy for each correct answer. Such competitive games and rewards generated a lot of excitement, and several girls volunteered immediately. Grace called on them one by one. Each contestant chose a category behind which there was a question related to students at Richmond High School or students and schools in west Contra Costa County or California. While the game show was going on, Tsiet was plucking Lisa's eyebrows but still paying attention. Fiey asked several follow-up questions to some of the game-show questions: "How did Richmond High School become bankrupt?" "How much more is left to pay off the debt?" At the end of the session Grace wanted to make sure that the girls understood the implications about the facts that were presented and asked, "What was striking about what we learned today?" Maya stated, "The dropout rate and the number of people who graduate." Fiey was struck by "how much money we owe," and Pham remarked on "the ratio of counselors." Grace smiled and nodded, pleased that the teens had understood the key messages about the needs of students from this session (field notes, 23 June 1999).

Other tools included eye-catching charts and the dissection of relevant news articles. During one afternoon session the girls were reminded of how young people are portrayed in the media and the key actors involved in disseminating such views. They reviewed two news stories, one that reported on how the police were maintaining safety in schools and the second on funding for more counselors. Grace asked the girls to consider how each story portrayed young people, which voices were predominant, and whether a student voice was included. After they had had time to read the stories, the girls shouted out what they had found in each story. In the first, they thought the key point was that young people were bad and that police were present in schools to stop fights and vandalism and to train teachers to disarm students. The predominant voices quoted in this story were from the police and school staff. There was a minor student voice that suggested that money should be spent on a nurse and centers for young people rather than on policing. In the second news story, the girls identified the key message as one of moral decline among young people and the need for early guidance. The only voices heard in this story were adult voices—then California governor Gray Davis, school board members, and the school principal. Grace used this discussion of the news stories to emphasize that the report the girls were going to produce on their survey findings not only would counter dominant representations of young people and provide a student voice, but also would identify solutions to address the lack of adequate academic guidance for students in WCCUSD (field notes, 24 June 1999).

The next step was to brainstorm feasible solutions and demands that would not divide different communities and groups. During a subsequent afternoon Grace separated the participants into three groups and asked them to brainstorm solutions to the following problems: lack of student access to counselors, access based on race, and access based on age. The list of solutions they generated involved teachers having a greater role in academic counseling, a reorganization of the existing counselors' time, better promotion of the roles and responsibilities of counselors, and hiring more counselors of color. Several youth opposed the last solution: "I don't like that," stated Tsiet, referring to hiring someone based on race. "No, I don't either," added Lai. "It's complicated. We need to talk about it more," responded Grace and left it at that (field notes, 29 June 1999). The young women suggested that inadequate resources of all kinds, not racial bias, prevented all the students at Richmond High from getting quality and timely counseling. This exchange illustrates different understandings of the politics of race in the United States among the children of recent immigrants and among second- and third-generation East Asian American activists. It also reflects the everyday experiences of Laotian young people growing up in inner-city multiracial neighborhoods, where their friendship groups are racially mixed, though generally do not include white teens.

APEN had two key goals in conducting any campaign: to build LOP and to develop links with other communities of color. The young women participating in the AYA summer program identified potential allies, both Laotian and non-Laotian, at Richmond High School and in the wider community. At a brainstorming session at the end of June, the staff divided the girls into three groups and asked each to develop two lists identifying other groups in school and in the community that might be interested in getting involved in the campaign. I observed the group led by Martha:

> Martha asks the girls to think about groups that would help build LOP. Gain shouts "ACTION" [All Colors Together in One Nation, a multiracial student club founded by Seng]. She thinks ACTION is a good candidate because it's mixed (racially) and the problem affects them. Martha tries to clarify the immediate task at hand by saying that "this isn't about exclusion but would they be ongoing members of LOP?" Then she asks them to think about groups to help build LOP. Consequently, Gain suggests that ACTION should be on the allies' list.
>
> The girls identify the youth group of Lao Family, Laotian students in CSF [California Scholarship Federation], and various ethnic cliques and social cliques. Molli suggests the Khmu Association and then asks about RYP [Richmond Youth Program]. "It's mixed," says Gain. Martha moves it to the "allies" list, which already has a number of entries under it. The girls identify additional groups such as Alma Latina, the International group, popular social cliques, and smart cliques.
>
> Martha asks the girls to pick two or three groups they would start with since they cannot work with all of them right away. Gain suggests Lao Family because they have a lot of groups. Everyone agrees with this, and they also prioritize the Khmu Association and the freshman group. Gain states that the recently immigrated will not be of help "because they are too shy." On the allies list they prioritize RYP, Leadership [a group of students elected each year to serve on the Leadership Committee to represent the whole student body and to organize events for students], and Alma Latina at Richmond High. (Field notes, 30 June 1999)

The girls identified social organizations and service agencies in the Laotian community as potential sources for recruiting members for the Laotian Organizing Project. But what was significant about the potential allies list is that except for Alma Latina they were all multiracial groups that were either academically oriented or already involved in improving their school and community. The identification of these groups as potential allies suggests that a "racial caste system" based on myths about racialized intelligence (Robles 2006) did not exist at Richmond High; the girls believed that students of all races would be interested in this campaign to improve access to academic counseling services. Though the majority of students on the California Scholarship Federation roll were Laotian and a greater proportion of students categorized as Asian completed all courses required for entrance to the University of California and California State Universities at the time of the study, there were also large numbers of Laotian and Asian students who were not high achievers.[27]

Over the course of the summer Grace reiterated to the girls that the campaign to improve counseling services at Richmond High, and potentially at other schools in the district, was not just for girls, or for Laotian teens, but "we are trying to improve the whole community for everyone" (field notes, 3 July 1999). The young women in AYA conveyed this message as they developed, with the help of staff, interactive presentations on the campaign issue. They made five presentations to students in summer school classes and to other youth groups, gaining some experience in persuading others to get involved. These presentations, which included information from the survey, a short humorous skit that illustrated the problem and the possible consequences for students of a lack of high-quality and timely counseling, and a discussion of possible solutions, ended with a call to sign action cards and the following statement:

> We believe that all youth deserve a good education, even us, who live here in Richmond. We deserve to have lots of people in the schools who will help us with our classes, help us graduate, help us go to college, or whatever we need. In our survey, 91 percent of students said they would use more counseling services if they were available. We're going to try to improve our school by looking more at this problem. We need people who want to do something to make our schools better for us. No one is going to do it for us. We have to act now—*our* future is at stake. (Presentation at Kennedy High School, field notes, 15 July 1999)

This statement conveys that the goal of the campaign was to improve counseling services at Richmond High and perhaps at other schools in the district, while underscoring that all young people, regardless of race or class, have a right to a high-quality education. Furthermore, by urging other young people to join them and take immediate action, the Laotian teenagers were showing how young people could be active citizens who shape their own futures.

Toward the end of the summer session, the AYA staff identified key decision makers and targets for the campaign, as well as sources of potential funding for any solutions they devised. The AYA staff also facilitated discussions on campaign strategies and tactics, conducted training through role-plays to implement some of these tactics, and created opportunities to put them in practice. For example, one afternoon in July, the girls, staff members, and I divided into four teams, and each team traveled to a designated site in Richmond or the neighboring cities of San Pablo and El Cerrito where young people might be located. Our objective was to talk to as many high school students as possible, inform them about how the problem affects young people, and have them sign a postcard in show of support. Seventeen-year-old Rachel and sixteen-year-old Blia, both of Group 1, who were working with AYA as youth counselors for the summer, accompanied sixteen-year-old Cuo of Group 2, as well as Bryanna and Maya, to the El Cerrito train station in search of potential supporters. I joined them too, anticipating staying in the background and simply observing them. But as the following excerpt from my field notes indicates, this sort of community organizing work was difficult for even the oldest teens in AYA. I felt compelled to shift my role and support them actively:

> We don't see any high school students at first. Two guys are walking into the BART [Bay Area Rapid Transit] station, but nobody wants to approach them. Everyone in the group, except Maya, is too shy to talk to people they don't know. So I break the ice by asking two Asian girls if they are high school students. They say "yes," and so I turn to Rachel and Cuo and ask them to take over. That seems to have got the ball rolling for Rachel.
>   Cuo and Bryanna are still nervous about stopping strangers, so I decide to do the initial approaching. If the young people say they are high school students, then I ask Cuo to take over and do the rap, and get them to sign a postcard. Bryanna still doesn't want to talk to anyone. I try to encourage her. "It's embarrassing," she responds. Maya is the only one who is not shy about approaching people and talks to them with confidence. Cuo doesn't exude confidence, but she is overcoming her shyness. (Field notes, 20 July 1999)

The 1999 summer session was eye-opening, intense, at times difficult, and often tedious for the girls, who were on their summer break. At the beginning of the six-week program, most of the girls claimed to be moderately excited when Grace asked them about the campaign. However, fifteen-year-old Maya was very excited because she believed that mostly Asians were dropping out and she wanted to work on the campaign for that reason. Tsiet, Maya's peer in Group 3, wanted to help her community, and Pham stated that "we want to build a future for ourselves." As the summer progressed, Grace tried to maintain morale and motivation by acknowledging their feelings of discomfort, nervousness, or disappointment and noted that "this kind of work is hard." She reminded all the young women that most teens do not engage in this kind of activism and that they should feel good about such work (field notes, 21 July 1999). A core group that included Maya, Tsiet, and Pham of Group 3 remained engaged and made astute comments and evaluations of the various demands, tactics, and solutions they discussed. Although other young women appeared to be bored, they nevertheless continued to attend the program, perhaps because they were earning a stipend or had the chance to spend time with friends. On many afternoons I watched them while away the time by braiding each other's hair, sharing photo albums, or napping.

The AYA staff frequently reminded the girls about the reasons behind organizing and doing campaign work. At one session Grace asked them about the merits of being involved in organizing versus getting a lawyer to advocate on their behalf. Fiey, of Group 3, responded, "Because we don't want it that way." "Why not?" Grace fired back. Fourteen-year-old Bryanna, of Group 4, answered, "Because you don't know what our problems are." Grace affirmed both of them and reminded the young women that "we are trying to build a voice for the Laotian community" (field notes, 30 June 1999). In this and other ways the AYA staff attempted to keep all the teens motivated, build a sense of power among them, and develop the skills they needed to use that power more effectively in the pursuit of change. Also significant was the greater leadership taken by the Laotian teens in meetings and presentations with other young people while the APEN staff provided more supportive roles. The young women's language skills, knowledge of the school environment, and growing collective self-understandings of the issues affecting young people of color in Richmond facilitated this increased participation.

Based on analysis of other programs that addressed the issue of inadequate academic counselors, as well as potential monies available to fund any kind of program, the AYA girls and staff decided that an advisory program would be the most valuable and feasible solution to the lack of counseling guidance for students at Richmond High.[28] Decisions concerning such a program could be made at the School Site Council, which the staff perceived to be an easier target to approach than the WCCUSD or higher levels of authority. In the fall of 1999, after I had left the field, the girls and the staff built on all the preparation they had done during the summer. Despite competing commitments of school, jobs, and responsibilities in the home, the young women talked to hundreds of students at Richmond High, collected over five hundred postcards in support, and identified other potential allies at school, such as Healthy Start, Leadership, and Youth Together. The AYA staff believed that the campaign's success required alliances with diverse school groups that shared an interest in improving the quality of education. Thus the staff and the teens organized a coordinated effort to win a program to improve guidance for students at Richmond High (Toommaly 2000).

On 25 May 2000, more than forty Laotian, Latino, and African American students, teachers, and parents packed the School Site Council (SSC) meeting at Richmond High to speak out and urge council members to approve a pilot teacher advisory program. The council did so for the following school year (Toommaly 2000:15), adding an advisory period to the regular school day as well as mentoring time for students and teachers. The advisory program placed a small number of students with a teacher-adviser to guide them through school. After this victory the AYA teens involved in the campaign highlighted the value of collective action and the role of young people in organizing for structural change. One said:

> The more important thing I learned working on this campaign is how to work together. It was hard working together because everyone has their own personal lives. The only time we had together was when we met with APEN and some of the girls didn't show up. It was hard to work on something as a group, but I learned that together, youth can achieve anything! (Quoted in Toommaly 2000:16)

Another young woman noted, "Not a lot of students speak out, they are afraid no one will care, but trying is worth it because we can change things if we want to. Youth's voice can be heard" (quoted in Toommaly 2000:17). APEN and AYA staff constructed a politicized youth identity on the common structural location of young people attending inner-city, severely resource-deprived schools. Since some 95 percent of students attending Richmond High School are people of color, this politicized youth identity draws on Laotian, other Asian and Pacific Islander, Latino, and African American students. Yet the campaign did not assert a rigid black/white difference, aiming instead to also reach white students, who constituted 4 percent of the student body and experienced a similar lack of high-quality and timely counseling services. This campaign sought to improve the quality of education for all students at Richmond High School and potentially in the whole school district.

The victory capping this campaign also challenges popular media constructions of young people of color as "at risk," as involved in gangs and drugs and prone to teenage pregnancies; it shows how students in inner-city schools and young people of color can positively influence decisions that affect their lives. Students of color did not accept blame for lagging achievement and failure; rather, they drew attention to and challenged the structural sources that lead to achievement deficits, dropping out, and a future in low-paying jobs. They created visibility for themselves and a positive voice for change, illustrating that schools can be sites of resistance and contestation even as they constrain young people from reaching their full potential.

Conclusion

Contemporary social justice organizations such as APEN adopt the position that whatever the citizenship status of new immigrants and their children, they have social and political rights, and political mobilization and active participation in the polity are necessary to secure these rights. In that regard, the Laotian Organizing Project plays a critical role as a vehicle for leadership training in a group that is marginalized in multiple ways, through race, class, gender, and generational hierarchies. Despite the tensions and limitations of the political strategies implemented and the prevalence of interethnic power differentials within the organization, I argue that through AYA and LOP, APEN cultivates resources, sparks community mobilization, and creates a basis for communication and negotiation among groups differentiated by race, ethnicity, and generation (Saito and Park 2000:441; Chung 2007). My respondents' community activism and involvement in APEN's youth program is significant for two reasons. It highlights the role of children of immigrants in the political socialization, or the process of developing attitudes, values, beliefs, and behaviors, of parents who may face linguistic, experiential, and structural barriers to political participation (Bloemraad and Trost 2008). It also represents the generation of new social capital for the Laotian community, the networks, trust, and information channels that encourage and facilitate greater community involvement in collectively solving the social problems this group faces. In this sense, LOP represents a "bridging" organization (Chung 2007) that enables Laotians to shift from immigrant and refugee politics to ethnic/race-based group politics.

Involvement in AYA and LOP generates a sense of personal and collective efficacy and creates opportunities and networks for second-generation Laotians to actively participate in efforts to improve the quality of their material lives. Fam Linh Saechao, one of the AYA members, explained why she remained committed and involved in APEN's work throughout her high school years:

> My family and the people I care about live here. As a young person I want to work with other youth to change the toxic web in Richmond into a place where we can breathe clean air, drink clean water and play on uncontaminated land. (Quoted in Dang 1998)

Nontraditional politics provides an avenue for politically marginalized groups to acquire substantive citizenship. Learning methods of organizing, analyzing power dynamics in the wider society, participating in voter registration, and making representations to politicians, the media, and other community groups enables second-generation Laotians to gain leadership skills as well as knowledge of American political norms, values, and political participation. This is a process of Americanization but with a difference: APEN is creating a critical political subjectivity that links everyday experiences of "neighborhood race effects" (Espiritu et al. 2000) to a structural analysis of race and class inequalities in the United States and empowers new immigrants to demand equal social, economic, and political rights through collective action. It represents a different claim to be an American than that constructed by the welfare system and social workers, schools, churches, and so on. It is not an uncritical emphasis on adaptation but a conscious and deliberate attempt to foster critical incorporation.

APEN's decision to shift to youth organizing reflected a desire to harness the energy of young people to help build LOP as an organization that can eventually form part of an Asian Pacific American face in the environmental justice movement. With this explicit strategic change, APEN directly challenged the gender and generational hierarchies within immigrant Laotian families, as I discuss in Chapter 6. But APEN was also signaling that young people as a group in U.S. society, and particularly young people of color and young women, are important and have a voice. Second-generation Laotian women's activism undermines dominant "model minority" stereotypes that portray *all* Asian Pacific American students as overachieving or math and science nerds (Zhou and Lee 2004) uninterested or unwilling to engage in political activism; such activism also disrupts dominant constructions of young people of color as "at risk" (Kelly 2000) for delinquency, gang involvement, and teenage pregnancy. APEN, in contextualizing youth issues within the broader economic, social, and cultural issues facing the Laotian community, showed that it viewed young people as agents and as having a key role in defining and constructing their future. France (1998) argues that for young people to participate actively and have a sense of responsibility for their community, they must believe that they have social rights and that certain adults will not exclude them from making change. APEN's shift in strategy made young people the core of the Laotian Organizing Project and positioned them as subjects with a stake in their community. In the next chapter I examine how political engagement shapes the racial identities of second-generation Laotians and the prospects for future cross-racial and pan-ethnic coalitions.

5

Negotiating Racial Hierarchies

Critical Incorporation, Immigrant Ideology, and Interminority Relations

> *Well, environmental justice is like, it's like your, it's sort of like your basic right in the constitution. . . . And I just, like, basically believe that environmental justice, like, like, the right for everyone to live in a healthy safe environment, you know.*
> —Lon (interview, 7 December 1998; emphasis in original)

The post-1965 demographic revolution has changed the racial landscape of many urban areas. Settlement patterns of new immigrants indicate that it is an urban phenomenon (Waldinger and Lee 2001) and one that is shaped by class status. Ethnic and racial minorities are beginning to form majorities in many cities (Camarillo 2004), and processes of acculturation are shaped more by interaction between nonwhite groups than by contact with white people or a core American culture (Kasinitz 2004:293). These demographic shifts demand that we examine the interminority relations emerging from the changing racial dynamics (Võ and Torres 2004), particularly the prospects for cross-racial/cross-ethnic coalitions to contest existing racial hierarchies and to dismantle related structures and processes of racial inequality in the United States.

In recent times the media and some academic analyses have portrayed African Americans, Asian Americans, and Latinos as competing for scarce resources and political inclusion rather than as potential allies and coalition partners (Lie 2004; Camarillo 2004). These encounters and interactions between racial and ethnic groups in the contemporary U.S. urban landscape are fashioned by larger economic and political structures, government policies, and racialized perceptions and misperceptions. Nevertheless, opportunities exist at the local level to create cooperative cross-racial relations through, for example, efforts to keep neighborhoods free of crime and drugs (Camarillo 2004) or coalitions to address environmental pollution or improve schools in the local community. Võ and Torres (2004:310) call such opportunities "border spaces" where racial groups interact, sometimes with overt or covert tension and other times quite amicably. APEN is one such border space; operating within an environmental justice framework, it advocates for common struggle with other communities of color and resists artificial racial boundaries in favor of fluid, multiple identities where race, class, gender, and generation intersect. In this chapter I analyze the macro-

and microlevel processes that create possibilities for and constraints to challenging structures of racial difference. Specifically, I examine the impact that involvement in AYA/LOP and community organizing has had on second-generation Laotians' political identities and collective self-understandings (Brubaker and Cooper 2000:7) around race. As I demonstrated in Chapter 2, Laotians in northern California share a common economic, social, and environmentally impacted context with their African American and Latino neighbors. While many analysts would assume that in this common material context lies the potential for shared class interests across race (see, for example, Murguia and Forman 2003: 72; Camarillo 2004), I argue that the possibilities for and limits to APEN's goal of engendering critical racial subjectivities and a sense of being "kindred people" (Okihiro 1994:34) are also influenced by an "immigrant ideology" (Cheng and Espiritu 1989) among Laotians and their children, as well as shaped by racialized perceptions and stereotypes. At the same time, this immigrant ideology, together with class position and the desire for ethnic distinctiveness, also shapes the possibilities for identification and solidarity with other Asian Americans.

I analyze second-generation Laotians' particularistic self-understandings, or one's sense of one's social location and the range of experiences related to it (Brubaker and Cooper 2000:17), around "race." Processes of racialization in the United States affect Laotians in contradictory ways. Though the migration of Laotians to the United States emerged because of the history of U.S. involvement in Southeast Asia and the deep entanglement of Laotians in the Vietnam War, Laotians arrived as refugees with high aspirations for rebuilding their lives and obtaining opportunities for their children. These aspirations and a sense of optimism are prevalent among their children, though as I demonstrate below, it is a gendered phenomenon. Moreover, as Asian Americans, they are perceived by the dominant society as the "model minority." Second-generation Laotians are acutely aware of the racialization processes that attribute racial power and prestige to white people and assign black people to the bottom of the racial hierarchy. At the same time, dominant representations of Laotians and other Southeast Asians as refugees, poor, and dependent on welfare also positions them at the black pole. Eduardo Bonilla-Silva (2004) argues that the positioning of multiple racial groups in the collective black strata suggests the potential for solidarity across "race" and higher levels of collective action. However, as a number of scholars have argued, Asian Americans are seen as perpetual foreigners (Ong 1996; Tuan 1998; Ancheta 1998; Gotanda 1999; Kibria 2000). Thus Kim's (2004:999) conceptualization of "racial positionality" highlights multiple dimensions of relationality among different racial and ethnic groups. Such a complex relationality allows for shifting cross-racial and/or cross-ethnic alliances based on political commitments and shared interests that are highly contingent and situationally specific.

The notion of "the social geography of race" (Frankenberg 1993:43) is useful for understanding the effects of contemporary racial politics on my respondents' racial and ethnic identities and the meanings these identities have for them. An understanding of racial social geography enables us to ground individual attitudes and beliefs in the material world. Racial politics in U.S. society and the informal meanings and stereotypes emanating from it, which structure everyday experiences of minority groups, construct these material worlds. Thus it becomes possible to examine how racialized perceptions influence intergroup relations between Laotians and African Americans, and between Laotians and other Asian Americans, and link these to the larger social, historical, and political forces that brought these environments into being.

Collective Self-Understandings around Race

APEN staff members presented an underlying analysis of race, class, and citizenship in all the discussions, activities, and campaigns that involved the girls. Moreover, a basic principle of APEN's organizing is that its work should not create a wedge between Laotians and other communities of color. Rather, the goal should be to identify linkages and produce alliances across race. This principle stems from both an ideological belief and a pragmatic position based on the situation of Laotians in Contra Costa County. Peggy Saika remarked that she was proud to have held onto and worked toward the "same vision of a multicultural democracy" in the United States for the last twenty-five or twenty-six years, one based on the belief "that people of color in this country have a particular history, a shared history and a shared struggle that needs to be, that's lifelong" (interview, 21 September 1998). In stating her ideological beliefs, Saika evokes Gary Okihiro's (1994:33) question "Is yellow black or white?" in his discussion of the bipolar race-relations model of American society. At the same time, APEN staff understands the practical necessity of working with other communities in order to achieve systemic change. LOP organizer Miya Yoshitani explained:

> You know, there's a substantial population of Laotians here, but we won't do enough for the community if we keep organizing just Laotians. So part of building their skills, like building their leadership skills, I think part of it is working with other groups. (Interview, 22 September 1998)

The low numbers of Laotians as well as the racial tension that Laotians experience with their Latino and African American neighbors necessitates coalition work with other communities. These conflicts breed "a wedge between groups" and create "another barrier to the community not coming together," as Miya noted (interview, 22 September 1998).

As we saw in the previous chapter, through the ongoing education on environmental justice issues and issue-oriented community campaigns, APEN has sought to foster not an abstract political identity among Laotians but one that arises out of the concrete material realities that the Laotian community faces. Even though APEN's goal is to create an Asian American face for the environmental justice movement, it does not impose an Asian American pan-ethnic identity on a community that thinks of itself as refugees, immigrants, poor, and low-wage workers. Rather, APEN acknowledges multiple relationality and seeks to mobilize a politicized Laotian identity, which has connections to other communities of color in Contra Costa County. In order to understand the impact of such political action on my respondents' collective self-understandings, I asked them what environmental justice means to them. The responses from the first and second cohort of girls, who had been in the youth project for four and three years, respectively, suggest that they have absorbed APEN's perspective and language on environmental justice. Leah, from the second cohort, wanted to educate other young people about what she learned in APEN because

> then, it's like, "Oh! Environmental justice, what's that?" And they think it's the grass, the trees, and the water and the air, that's it. But they don't really know what's really in between those things and what really makes the environment.

Leah stated that most young people understand environmental activism in terms of the traditional narrow focus of U.S. environmental movements on conserving land or cleaning air and water. For Leah, the environment also included hazardous homes, schools, and workplaces. Seng and Blia, from the first cohort, articulated a specific race and class analysis of environmental issues:

> **SENG:** [*no hesitation*] I think just having the things like as any, like, girls, like rich people have, you know, all that. Clean air and, like, no refinery or whatever behind your backyard and all that stuff. Like having the same right as they do and, like, I think that it's not fair that just because we are minorities and then we live in a, like, lower, like, you know, lower-income, you know, neighborhood and, like, we don't have as much as money as they do and all that stuff. That, you know, we get all this, you know, discrimination and get all that stuff.
>
> **BLIA:** [*long pause*] What it means to me is, like, having equality in the environment. . . . It's, like, every community, it's not perfect, but then they should all be treated equal regardless of color because the way Chevron is treating us, it's not right. 'Cause just, just because we're colored, it doesn't mean that we can't do anything about it. And to me, it also means to have a right to everything else that, like, the rich people up in the hills get.

Seng and Blia emphasize the language of rights, of the right to live in a clean and healthy environment regardless of one's race and class. Lon, another member of the first cohort, stated it much more emphatically in the epigraph to this chapter. For her, the right to live in a clean and healthy environment was a basic right enshrined in the Constitution. Blia's comments challenge another common assumption: that people of color, poor people, and immigrants do not care about the environment as much as they care about jobs and economic development (Bullard 1992). Blia and Lon were born in the United States, and Seng had arrived at the age of two and a half. As citizens, they expected equal rights and equal opportunities to everything the United States had to offer. However, after four years of exposure to political education and action through AYA, the girls from the first cohort had adopted a race and class analysis and understood the linkages between environmental issues and civil rights and social justice issues. Their words echo the efforts of poor communities of color in the United States that have been organizing around environmental justice concerns since the 1980s.

This was not the case for girls in the third and fourth cohorts, who had spent less time in the youth project and had not absorbed the language of rights or a clear analysis of race and class. The third cohort had spent the summer of 1998 learning about various aspects of environmental justice, giving "toxic tours," and meeting with a Latino group and a multiracial youth group in Oakland that were cleaning up a local park and pressuring owners of a medical incinerator to curb pollution levels, respectively. They articulated the meaning of environmental justice in terms of educating others in the community about environmental hazards and supporting the work of other groups. Moreover, as we saw in the previous chapter, APEN's environmental justice work with the Laotian community in Richmond encompassed a broad social, political, and environmental agenda. Thus for many of the girls, it was difficult to define environmental justice in specific terms. However, the ongoing political education by APEN staff on the environmental hazards in their community, homes, and schools means that the longer they participate in AYA, the greater the likelihood that they will adopt a race and class analysis. APEN gives them the information and the language to understand what they and their families experience viscerally, that of rising cancer rates and respiratory problems.

A discussion on drug dealing in the community provides a second example of the kind of collective self-understandings APEN was nurturing about the perception of young people, and particularly young people of color, in the dominant society. At a meeting in November 1998, when twelve of the young women from Groups 1, 2, 3, and 4 were present, Grace Kong asked them to consider how the current California governor, Republican Pete Wilson, would respond to the problem of drugs and drug dealing in the community. The girls offered several ideas:

> Maya says, "Put more police on the corner." Tsiet suggests, "Boot camp." Fiey suggests, "Build new prisons and longer sentencing." (Field notes, 23 November 1998)

A little later in the discussion, when Grace asked the girls to suggest the kinds of policy responses that LOP could propose, Tsiet suggested "workshops," while Maya believed that "recreation centers" that included "fun stuff with some learning" could address the problem. Cuo suggested working with parents to improve parent-child communication, and Leah thought that the girls could "be peer educators. Like go into schools and talk to the kids about drugs" (field notes, 23 November 1998). Then Grace highlighted the economic motivations of selling drugs and asked the girls if there was an alternative. Rachel emphasized the need for "an organization that helps kids find jobs," and Sarah believed that "training programs" would be useful. Grace had drawn a circle on her flip chart and listed the solutions the girls thought Pete Wilson would offer for the problem of drug dealing on the top half and the solutions that LOP would offer on the lower half. She pointed out that each half of the circle projected "different values" and emphasized that "when LOP is working on an issue, we need to be aware of what kind of values we want to project" (field notes, 23 November 1998).

During this meeting, of the twelve young women present, the most active and vocal participants were mainly from Groups 1, 2, and 3. These teens, who had been involved in AYA for one to three years, displayed an understanding of the consequences of punitive measures focused on the individual versus supportive solutions that placed the problem of drug dealing in the context of problems in the wider community. They did not believe that incarcerating youth and handing down tough sentences would address the structural causes of drug dealing in poor, inner-city neighborhoods. Rather, they suggested measures such as job training, supportive parent-child structures, meaningful education, and recreation centers that offered a safe place for young people. During the study the teens had frequently cited the lack of recreation centers for young people in Richmond and San Pablo as the reason why they congregated at the local mall. The public library had become another safe venue for teens to gather after school. In suggesting these solutions, they displayed solidarity with other young people in their multiracial and impoverished neighborhoods and community.

By framing the siting of toxic plants in communities of color, monolingual emergency warning systems, and inadequate school counseling services as evidence of deep-seated societal racism and classism, in this "border space" APEN aimed to build a critical racial solidarity with other communities of color in Richmond. Involvement in APEN's youth program exposed second-generation Laotians to both a civil rights framework and the power of collective organizing. However, the key question is whether such collective self-understandings transcend the context of APEN. Does political socialization through APEN lead second-generation Laotians to develop a common consciousness and coalesce with other members of the "collective black" stratum (Bonilla-Silva 2004) or to distance themselves from this stratum and instead, as Bonilla-Silva (2004:944) puts it, struggle to "position themselves higher in the new racial totem pole"?

Distancing from African American Young People: "I Ain't Ghetto"

What individuals think and believe about the members of other racial and ethnic groups—stereotypes—are commonly recognized as a critical factor in intergroup relations (Allport 1958). During my two years in the field I often heard my respondents use the term "ghetto." They would say, "Oh, that's ghetto," or "I ain't ghetto." I wondered what meaning the term "ghetto" had for them and how they related to it since they too lived in very poor multiracial neighborhoods, went to impoverished schools, and often spoke in Black English. Focus group discussions revealed that the term "ghetto" referred to language but also to a specific part of the city, housing conditions, dress styles, behavior, and "black people." My respondents enlightened me that not "talking properly," using a "lot of profanity," and using slang were part of ghetto culture. However, while they attempted to distance themselves from this culture, my respondents were "not secluded from the environment," as Ms. Collins, the ninth-grade English teacher at Richmond High, put it. She admitted to being surprised to hear her Iu Mien students "all speak Black English, Ebonics," and sometimes even "write Ebonics" (conversation with Ms. Collins, 1 June 1999). The familiarity with what the English teacher called "playground language" was most evident among the youngest girls in Group 4. For example, at the end of one afternoon during the summer of 1998, the APEN staff was facilitating an evaluation of some of the activities that Group 4 had participated in that afternoon. When staff members asked the girls what they had liked, Julia said, "Magazine thang." Angela immediately corrected her and emphasized "thing," and then asserted, ironically in improper English, that she "ain't no ghetto." In another conversation during a focus group with Group 4, Marn expressed her opinion about the way some of her peers dress: "I be hating people that be hella, I don't know, they be wearing some tight-ass pants even though you can't fit them, they still wear it. It's hella ugly. I don't like that."

Fourteen-year-old Julia and thirteen-year-old Angela were both born in the United States, and fourteen-year-old Marn had arrived at the age of two from Thailand. This familiarity with Black English reflects interactions among Laotian and African American young people and immersion in local cultures, highlighting the resettlement of Laotian refugees in poor, inner-city neighborhoods where the majority of the population is African American. While improper English peppered my respondents' everyday conversations at APEN, they rarely used slang and never uttered profanity. As fourteen-year-old Bryanna noted: "It's easy for us 'cause we can switch because we have APEN. Because we have APEN, we can switch really easily." The use of Ebonics was not as striking in the older girls, though they too would use the Ebonics "be" verb. For the most part, they were more self-conscious about how they talked and had had four years of high-school English as well as numerous opportunities for writing and public speaking in APEN. The college-educated staff at APEN created an environment in which the use of standard English was the norm. While they did not correct the young women when they spoke Black English, staff members helped my respondents write in standard English when they were drafting speeches and essays or creating published journals.

The term "ghetto" also referred to a particular culture, according to the girls. Pham stated, "It's all about the attitude when you're ghetto . . . like, I don't know, just the way that you present yourself." Tsiet explained what Pham meant by the attitude:

The way you talk, it's the way you dress. Like when you're outside and then, like, there's elder people and stuff, you, like, have no respect, you just always yelling and [*a loud chorus of laughter from everyone*]. Yeah.

All the girls agreed that ghetto culture was signified by doing "whatever looks bad to other people," including wearing baggy clothes or clothes that don't match. For Cuo, ghetto culture referred to "where you do stuff that's not really proper, like when you wear your pants backward or something, like, inside-out." Gain gave another example: "they use cardboard to pick up your dust, [use it] as a dustpan." Gain's use of "they" suggests that she does not participate in this ghetto culture. Indeed, in over two years of fieldwork, I observed that none of my respondents wore baggy clothes or clothes inside-out. In fact, many of the girls expressed a 1970s retro dress style, with black, blue, or white flared jeans, short T-shirts that hugged their figures, and black platform shoes or sandals. In contrast to the 1970s, the colors were muted and the clothes often bore the logos of Tommy Hilfiger, Nautica, The Gap, Old Navy, and Bebe.

In their attitudes and behaviors the young women also displayed a culture different from the ghetto culture they described, though I acknowledge that I observed them only in the context of AYA meetings, activities, and retreats, and not when they were around their peers outside AYA. But within the context of AYA and APEN, the staff fostered a respectful and supportive environment, and each young woman was regarded as a valued member. During meetings and other activities, the staff immediately addressed disrespectful and negative statements. They attempted to create a culture in which everyone was recognized as having a particular skill, experience, or perspective to bring to the group, all of which were to be valued. Older teens in the program acted as role models for the younger members and monitored their behavior. Thus I rarely heard my respondents being disrespectful to each other or to the staff.

A few of the girls specifically associated the term "ghetto" with African Americans, indicating that they have adopted the wider society's negative portrayal of poor blacks.[1] For fifteen-year-old Fiey, of Group 3, the word "ghetto" usually referred to black people:

That's how I see them. They be, like, tough, like, and they speak in slang; they don't speak in, like, clear English, you know. And they usually wear, like, a lot of baggy clothes; they don't have any respect.

Though Fiey was born in the United States and went to Middle College High School, an "early college" high school that offered underserved students with academic potential the opportunity for dual enrollment in high school and college courses, where her friends were other Laotian and Vietnamese students, she clearly indicated that she was not immersed in local youth cultures. Sixteen-year-old Sarah, of Group 1, made the same association even as she admitted that she called herself ghetto: "And, like, I talk ghetto. I talk like black peoples . . . that's like the majority of black people 'cause majority of black people talk that way. So that's what I consider ghetto." The desire to distance themselves from other communities of color was powerfully evident when I asked my respondents how they would like a reporter to portray Laotian women. As Sarah went on to say:

> Yeah, the thing is that mostly that we work hard for what we want. I mean we build our own goals, you know, and we work hard for it. We don't get it like other people; we don't, like, ask for it; we work for it, you know. That's what they need to understand.

Sarah was born in the United States, had participated in AYA for three years at the time of the study, and attended the same selective high school as Fiey. Sarah's uncle had founded the Lao Mutual Assistance Association, which was active in organizing the annual Lao New Year Festival in Richmond as well as helping members of the Lao sub-ethnic group during the resettlement process. As her comments illustrate, while she identified as being ghetto, and many of my younger respondents spoke in Black English and listened to rap music, she and others did not embrace the African American peer culture. Even though Sarah was not explicit, she contrasted Laotian culture and values to those of poor African Americans. Her comments suggested that she attributed African Americans' lower economic status to individual values, such as lacking a work ethic, being lazy, and having few aspirations for social mobility, rather than to inequalities in society and their lack of power.[2] Sarah wanted reporters to recognize that Laotians reject the ghetto culture of their African American peers. In the process, she positioned Laotians as a "model minority" that did not accept handouts from the state but instead worked hard to achieve the American Dream, like other immigrant groups in the United States. These young women's considerable efforts to distance themselves from ghetto culture suggests resistance to the process of "blackening" (Ong 2003) that Laotians and other Southeast Asian refugees experience. However, as we see in the next section, many of my respondents reacted to the "model minority" label with a great deal of ambivalence.

Other girls were much more explicit in disassociating themselves from ghetto culture. Maya, a self-assured and articulate Group 3 member, exemplified the extent to which some of them went to distance themselves:

> Well, I have, I guess, like, I can call myself ghetto, right, 'cause I guess I was born and raised in, like, worst part there is in Richmond, you know. That's why everybody's like, "Oh, that's the ghetto!" you know, north Richmond, right . . . but most people don't say that to me, right. 'Cause I'm, like, I could come from the ghetto and, you know, I could be ghetto, I could talk ghetto, but that's not the way I present myself, you know. It's like I could present myself as, like, I feel, like, corporate . . . if you didn't know me, I would be, like, from the street, you know, the rich hills, you know.

She was right. She was always dressed smartly, her clothes and nail polish were color coordinated, she wore a lot of gold jewelry, and she spoke standard English. Based on her appearance and the way she carried herself, I had made an assumption about the class status of her family. So when I went to pick her up for our interview date, I was quite astounded to see that she shared a small dilapidated house with her parents, three siblings, and a cousin on the edge of north Richmond, the area that other respondents had described as decidedly ghetto. Earlier in the interview she had recounted her parents' migration stories and had indicated that she had absorbed her parents' belief that hard work, determination, and the adoption of middle-class U.S. norms would lead to success and social mobility.

The labels my respondents used to describe where they lived revealed another strategy for distancing themselves from ghetto culture. Leah noted that other people described where she lived as the projects "just 'cause they have a lot of houses around it." But she believed "it look like no projects," and called it "the manors." Others expressed a sense of denial that where they lived was ghetto when compared with other parts of Richmond. Fourteen-year-old Yen, of Group 4, noted that she "used to live down there [north Richmond], but it wasn't that bad." North Richmond and central Richmond were considered the worst parts of the city in terms of gangs, garbage on the streets, broken windows and peeling paint on houses, few working streetlights, no trees, and close proximity to industrial sites. The young women saw north Richmond as an especially dangerous part of town. Lisa, of Group 4, remarked: "You never mess with north Richmond," because, as Yen explained, "they do have ghetto people down there. When you go there, people be throwing rocks at you." While a few Laotian families live in north Richmond, African Americans predominate. In fact, Yen noted that "everybody leaves the ghetto," reflecting her own experience of having been born in north Richmond but living in San Pablo at the time of the study.

The identification of only specific parts of Richmond as ghetto implied that my respondents did not perceive the neighborhoods where the majority of them lived as ghetto. While two of my respondents lived in north Richmond, the rest lived in the "flats" (as opposed to the hills), which are still generally considered the poorer parts of the cities of Richmond and San Pablo. Moreover, these neighborhoods were racially mixed, with Asian, Latino, and African American residents rather than predominantly African American, as in north Richmond. My respondents' attempts to differentiate parts of Richmond in this way represented an effort to avoid the stigma of living in Richmond, since most people living in the San Francisco Bay area associated Richmond as a whole with high levels of poverty, poorly performing schools, and a prevalence of crime and gang activity. It also represented an attempt to rehabilitate specific locations in Richmond as pleasant places to live in, since, as focus group discussions revealed, the young women had no desire to move to the affluent suburbs, which they characterized as "white" and, therefore, where they would be more likely to experience overt racism.

Even though some of my respondents spoke Ebonics, listened to R&B and rap music that was mainly associated with black artists, had frequent social interactions and sexual relations with African Americans, and were exposed to APEN's radical political ideology, these preferences, desires, and ideologies did not necessarily lead to a critical understanding of political and economic disenfranchisement or to racial solidarity outside the context of APEN. Laotians, like other recent immigrants and their children (see Waters 1999; Prashad 2000; Dhingra 2003), as well as earlier immigrants (see Kasinitz 2004), have adopted a negative portrayal of African Americans in the United States. Though my respondents came from poor families and lived in impoverished urban cities, they represented a self-selected group of young women who had middle-class aspirations and had adopted their parents' belief that hard work, perseverance, and the right values and attitudes will lead to social mobility.[3] Their attitudes reveal what Cheng and Espiritu (1989:528–531) have called the "immigrant ideology," or a "frame of reference different from that held by native born Americans." Those immigrants who are impelled to leave their home countries because of economic or political turmoil often view America as the land of opportunity. They are willing to work hard because they have a sense of optimism that their aspirations and dreams will be realized, as was the case with earlier European immigrants to the United States. This is in contrast to African American experiences, which are rooted in the historical legacy of slavery and the associated legal and institutional discrimination and inequality. African Americans often perceive America as a country where opportunities to achieve the American Dream have been denied to them (Cheng and Espiritu 1989).

In addition to displaying an immigrant ideology, second-generation Laotians' attempts at distancing themselves from ghetto culture reveal an awareness of the racialization processes operating in the United States, which attributes racial power and status to white people and links urban poverty to the pathological values of black inner-city residents rather than to structural inequalities and barriers to opportunities for success. Such processes privilege assimilation into middle-class white America as a route to gaining social prestige and full citizenship. An awareness of differentials in power and opportunity among racial groups leads new immigrant groups, as well as longer-term citizens, to maximize distance between themselves and African Americans and to attempt to minimize distance between themselves and majority whites (Bobo and Johnson 2000; Murguia and Forman 2003).

However, not all second-generation Laotians practice distancing strategies; rather, gender and generation intersect with race and class to shape racial stereotypes held by young Laotians. Some of the young women reported that their male peers perceived them as having adopted white norms because they spoke standard English, did not wear baggy clothes, and had not adopted black ways of acting. If ghetto culture is associated with "black people" and a "black attitude," then not being ghetto is the exact opposite and associated with being white. Cuo's uncle called her a "white girl":

CUO: He's like, "'Cause, the way you talk, the way you act." I'm like, "You know, how do I act and stuff like a white girl?" I'm like, "Why, because I don't slang and stuff, 'cause I don't act in all, you know, ghetto whatever, slanging, using Ebonics whatever?" I mean, that don't make me a white girl whatever.

BINDI: But that wouldn't make you Laotian either, to speak Ebonics; that would be more like some African American girls. [*Some of the others laugh.*]

CUO: Yeah. But then, like, you know, my uncle, he uses slang, he's all trendy. He's with the Honda Civics and, you know, the hooboo and the clothing and stuff.

BINDI: The hip-hop stuff?

CUO: And I'm not doing, like, wearing that kind of clothes or whatever, and he calls me a "white girl" and stuff. But then I don't see myself as a "white girl."

Sixteen-year-old Cuo, born in the United States, was one of the more introverted young women in AYA. She attended Richmond High School, where she had both Laotian and Latino friends and enjoyed her writing class, which prompted her to write poetry. She was studious and had a grade point average that put her in the California Scholarship Federation roll. As far as Cuo's uncle was concerned, her educational success and dress preferences indicated that she had adopted white norms, and this phenomenon of "acting white" was not "cool."[4] For Cuo's uncle, adopting black styles perhaps mirrored the embodied masculinities dominant among his peers. Boys are more likely to suffer social stigma if they speak standard English among their friends, while girls have more leeway to code-switch in speaking when the situation calls for it. It may also represent his alienation from school and wider society and reflect an understanding of how racism and poverty operate in American society.[5] On the other hand, the second-generation young women in my study believed that America offered freedom, more power for women, and opportunities for education and work regardless of social status, unlike in Laos. The majority of girls who became involved in AYA had positive attitudes toward school, were performing well, and had high aspirations for college and careers, as we see in the next section.

In the future the second-generation Laotian girls in this book may follow the Asian American staff at APEN and adopt a progressive ideology of alliance and a sense of being "kindred people" (Okihiro 1994:34) as they continue to be exposed to the history of racisms in the United States. However, at this stage of their life, as teenage girls, they perceive the United States to be an open, fair, and meritocratic society; if they talk "proper," act "right," dress stylishly, and work hard, they will set themselves apart from blacks and not experience racism. In short, they are convinced that if they become middle class (read "white"), they will have the possibility of upward mobility and acceptance into U.S. society by the dominant culture. In expressing an "immigrant ideology" and optimism about their future social mobility, these young Laotian women appear to fit into the dominant mold of Asian Americans as the "model minority," to which I turn next.

On Being a Model Minority

From interviews I knew that the majority of the young Laotian women in AYA were performing well at school and were committed to attending college and having careers. These attitudes were emphasized and reinforced in AYA; the staff created a culture and a set of expectations in which attending school regularly, maintaining grades, going to college, and acquiring skills while at APEN were seen as important aspects of becoming responsible and productive adults. My respondents' educational performance and attitudes were in marked contrast to general statistics on Laotian youth in Contra Costa County, cited in Chapter 2. They also deviated from patterns of achievement and aspirations among Southeast Asian young people found by earlier studies[6] and contrasted with dominant representations of Laotian girls as teenage mothers. I was curious about how teachers perceived these young women and other high-performing Laotian students at Richmond High, where Laotians made up 10 percent of the 1,587 students in the school year 1998–99, according to Dean Saechao of Richmond High (conversation with Dean Saechao, 29 April 1999).[7] Did my respondents complicate the dominant perception of Laotian teens in Contra Costa County? Did teachers and fellow students label them a "model minority"? If so, did the young women understand the ideological underpinnings of the stereotype? And how did they react to being called a "model minority?"

In the spring of 1999 I informally interviewed several teachers at Richmond High, all of whom painted a very mixed picture of the educational performance of Laotian students. Dean Saechao, who had been teaching at Richmond High for seven years, who was previously a student there, and who claimed to be the first Mien teacher in the country, noted that up to the mid-1980s Laotian students viewed education as an opportunity. However, from the mid-eighties to the late eighties Laotian "youth adapted," and they "accepted the negative values similar to the population around them," according to Saechao, suggesting that they were mirroring an adaptation trajectory predicted by the segmented assimilation model (Portes and Zhou 1993). Academic achievement was "no longer the goal" for Laotian young people, and they viewed school as a place for "social gathering." As found among Iu Mien boys in other parts of the San Francisco Bay Area (Jeung 2002; Kwon 2008), gang activities in Richmond had been on the rise since the mid-eighties, and incarceration and suspension of Iu Mien/Lao students had "increased dramatically" since 1992, according to Saechao.[8]

However, when I asked Dean Saechao about academic achievement levels among Laotian students at Richmond High at the time of the research in the late 1990s, he proudly reported that "today, Mien students are the highest achievement group," and they have the highest grade point average (GPA). He recalled that in the past many Laotian students were in English as a Second Language (ESL) or remedial classes and few were in college prep classes. Other teachers also described Laotian students as spanning the spectrum of educational performance. Ms. Behrens, who taught ESL 4 and was the resource teacher for the

Bilingual Program, informed me that Laotian students fall into two groups: one group that is "extremely diligent, hardworking, studious, and with high-level skills" and another group that has "low-level skills, is truant, into drugs and into gangs" (conversation with Ms. Behrens, 19 May 1999). Mr. Richards, a veteran teacher of eighteen years at Richmond High School who taught Economics and ESL 4, attributed the very low level of performance among some Laotian students to not wanting to appear "geeky" or "nerdy," not wanting to stand out (conversation with Mr. Richards, 19 April 1999). Having said this, however, Mr. Richards pointed to the California Scholarship Federation (CSF) roll for 1999 that was pinned on a wall in his classroom and highlighted the fact that while only about 30 students out of 1,587 were on the list, the majority of them were Mien, judging by their last names. A student needs a 3.00 GPA to be on the CSF roll.

Other teachers who taught college preparatory classes and therefore saw only college-bound students confirmed the high performance levels among some Laotian students. Ms. Murray, a teacher of English 1 and college preparation classes, described Laotian students as "good students" who "do their homework pretty well" (conversation with Ms. Murray, 12 May 99). In fact, Ms. Collins, who taught both college preparation and nonpreparation English to ninth graders, told me that most Laotian students speak English well and "some of them are more advanced than some of the American kids without ESL" (conversation with Ms. Collins, 1 June 1999).[9] She also mentioned that she had a lot of Mien students in her college preparation class, but few white, black, or Latino students.

I also inquired about the gender breakdown in the school performance of Laotian students since several of my respondents acknowledged that their brothers were in gangs or faced peer pressure to join a gang. Some teachers affirmed that Laotian boys experienced a great deal of pressure to join gangs, and Ms. Behrens observed that "boys are more into the gang culture." At the same time, Mr. Sweeney, who taught ESL 4 and English 3 to juniors, reported that while girls take school seriously, "a whole slew of students," mostly girls, disappear, and more of the Laotians than girls from other groups are teen mothers (conversation with Mr. Sweeney, 25 May 1999). However, in Ms. Behrens's experience, Laotian girls did better in school though they did not significantly outnumber boys, and they exhibited high career aspirations, wanting to be doctors, lawyers, or fashion designers.

Thus, in the late 1990s at Richmond High School, patterns of academic performance and aspirations among Laotian students were not clearly demarcated. Teachers positioned Laotian students both within and outside the discourse of academic achievement, though none labeled highly achieving Laotian students a "model minority."[10] Nevertheless, I was curious whether the young women in AYA, the majority of whom were performing well at school and aspired to attend college, were singled out as being "smart" and perceived as a "model minority" by their peers. In focus group discussions I asked them if their educational performance and aspirations had earned them the label "model minority" and how they would feel about being called that. Their initial response was that they would react positively and take the label as a compliment. Pham's response typified how most of the girls felt:

PHAM: I'll take that as a compliment.
BINDI: You would take that as a compliment.
PHAM: Not just, just because you're a model minority or whatever, but for myself, you know. Just, just, just the fact that I'm doing good.

These Laotian teens, who attended a severely resource-deprived inner-city high school, felt proud to be called a model minority or smart because it implied a recognition of their individual performance. They embraced the stereotype because this stereotype appeared flattering, especially when compared with the stigmatized stereotypes of other racial minorities (Lee 1996). Maya said she would be proud to be called a model minority because it affirmed her parents' hopes and desires for their children:

> I feel proud to hear that 'cause it's like, 'cause that's what my, most our families came for, right. Like, you know, they always tell us, "We came to America to get education, for you guys to do better." Like when we, you grow up, you know, like Asian people do better. We're like, "Yeah, we're really determined, you know." Like we're not just here just to be here, you know. So that's why I would be happy to hear that kids these days are, you know, really striving for something, you know, better and all that.

Leah's response struck a nationalistic tone:

> It's like sometimes, I mean sometimes I feel proud to be Asian 'cause of that stereotype. It's like, "Yeah, us Asians this and this and Asian that" [*raises her voice*].

Maya's and Leah's comments convey an opposition to the ghetto culture of their neighborhoods and schools, discussed earlier. They had adopted their immigrant parents' values and beliefs that hard work, determination, and a willingness to delay immediate gratification for future gains will lead to success and social mobility. Leah's comment in particular is pregnant with the divisive implications of the model minority myth. The media, politicians, and some educators regard Asian Pacific Americans as more socially and culturally integrated into mainstream America than are other racial and ethnic groups, and ideologically construct them as model minorities. These commentators perceive Asian Pacific Americans as embodying the Protestant work ethic necessary to achieve the American Dream (Ho 2003). In viewing the stereotype as positive and laudatory, Leah appeared to have bought into the culturalist argument that attributes her achievements to her "Asianness."

However, as my respondents considered how the model minority label affects them in their daily interactions with fellow students, there was an overwhelming sense that certain expectations were being imposed on them just because they are Asian.[11] My respondents expressed annoyance and anger because the stereotype brought expectations with it that they did not fulfill or did not wish to fulfill. Fiey was annoyed when an African American student in her science class told her, "All Asian girls are smart, you know," because she herself doesn't "get" science and she doesn't like it. When I asked if she would consider it a compliment in some situations, she said:

> **FIEY:** It varies, like, like let's say, like, I aced something, you know, and they say, "See, I know you're smart." I know I'm smart; you can call me that [*laughter from everyone*]. But, like, if I wasn't doing well and then they just say it, then, you know, I feel offended.
> **BINDI:** So it's like putting you down almost, like "Why aren't you smart?"
> **FIEY:** Yeah.

While Fiey believed that she was intelligent, she did not want to lose face with peers on the occasions when she was not able to conform to these expectations. What the girls objected to strongly was the assumption that smartness is a genetic trait among Asians. As Fiey went on to remark: "They all think we're naturally smart. It just depends on how hard you work." What irked my respondents most was that when peers attributed their educational achievements to their Asianness or natural ability, they failed to recognize the planning and effort that contributed to that achievement. And if at times Laotians failed to do well, then fellow students chastised them for not measuring up to high expectations, as Alison commented in focus group discussions:

> I mean, like, okay, my algebra class, right, it's like, it's not a lot of Asian people, it's only a couple, and then me and her cousin, right. Like whenever we go to class and stuff and when we do our work and stuff and we get good grades. And then there be, like, African American kids, right, and they sit right in back of us and they always ask us for help and stuff. And then when we don't get it, they be like, "What, you don't get it!" They're like, "You supposed to know, you're smart," you know, "You're Asian." We're like, "No, we don't get it," you know, but they think that we just, we're just lying to them. We just don't want to help them. [*Several people say "yeah" and "uh-huh."*]

Similarly, Maya was exasperated with her peers who failed to recognize that she "tried her best" and simply assumed that she is " smart anyways" in order to explain away why she did better than they in school work. She emphasized that "we worked hard to deserve the A, not just teacher come in and then, you know, "Oh, I could get an A," you know what I'm saying. Uh-uh." Tsiet remarked that she would "be mad" when someone says to her, "Oh, you're smart 'cause you got an A on this test," because

> I know that everybody tried, so that, I mean, you can't just say that "Oh, you're smart." I mean, everybody's smart. It's just that they didn't do well or

something, like get a B grade and stuff. That's why I wouldn't feel bad; I would feel proud if somebody said, "Oh, you are a model minority." But in a way I would feel bad and stuff with that compliment.

For Tsiet, everybody is capable of getting good grades if they make an effort and work hard. So while she would be proud to be called "smart," she also did not want to be stereotyped by culturalist or biologistic assumptions. These responses from the young women do not represent a sophisticated racial and class analysis of the operation of the model minority myth but focus on how the stereotype shapes their daily interactions with fellow students. In most of their comments I hear a desire not to be set apart, not to be seen as belonging to a distinctive group, but to be recognized for the diverse individuals they are, for their humanity, as well as for their effort. While they oppose the "ghetto culture" of some young people in Richmond, within the context of school they do not employ culturalist explanations to denigrate those who do not perform well. Perhaps this so because at least half of my respondents stated that they had a mixed group of friends at school that included African Americans, Latinos, and Asians, and four had African American boyfriends. In the minds of my respondents, Richmond High did not have a racial caste system (Robles 2006) that relegated African American and Latino students to the bottom of the educational achievement hierarchy, with Laotians, as Asian American students, hovering somewhere between them and white students. Nevertheless, they seemed unaware of the ways in which Laotian, Latino, and African American students are racialized in wider social and political contexts. They had accepted the ideology of meritocracy and the possibility of educational success through individual achievement and hard work.

One teen, who was actively involved in campaigns against welfare reform and Proposition 209 through APEN, offered a more sophisticated response to why she objected to being labeled a "model minority." Gabriela recognized that this image not only pitted Laotians against other communities of color but also served to obliterate the specific situation of Laotians in this country:

GABRIELA: I don't fall under none of those categories. Another thing is that I think that it's *such* a stereotype about Asian Americans because, like, um, it might help one Asian American group but then at the same time it might hurt another group.
BINDI: Uh-huh. How?
GABRIELA: For example, like the welfare reform, like when they said that, um, you know, Asians are supposed to be the perfect, you know, Asian role models or whatever. And then, like, they are talking more about, like, um, Chinese American, how somebody can't be like that, you know . . . or Japanese American or Korean American or whatever. How come, like, none of these other ethnic groups can be like that, right. And it's just because we are Asians they assume that we are like that, you know,

quote-unquote, you know, that, um, model minority. And we [Laotians] are not even like that, you know, 'cause we have only established our roots in America for, like, the last fifteen years and nowhere near the fact of running a university or starting our own corporation within America, you know, unlike the Chinese.
BINDI: Except perhaps the Vietnamese.
GABRIELA: Yeah. So we are nowhere near that, and at the same time they are putting us under the same group and it hurts because it hurts us socially in terms of climbing up the social ladder of America.

Seventeen-year-old Gabriela, who was born in Thailand and migrated to the United States at age six, had acquired her political analysis by passionately embracing all the opportunities offered to her through AYA. She was also a senior editor and writer for *Youth Outlook,* a monthly news magazine written by young people and published by Pacific News Services, an alternative media source. Gabriela understood that the stereotype of Asian Americans as a model minority masked the struggle of Laotians with poverty and racism. It led to the needs of non-affluent Asian groups such as Laotians being unrecognized and, therefore, unmet. She also recognized that politicians and the media employed cultural explanations of economic success and integration into the mainstream U.S. economy among Asians to negatively judge the lack of economic success among groups such as African Americans, Native Americans, and Latinos, without regard to structural inequalities that create barriers to achievement. Gabriela's comments contain the seeds of the critical racial solidarity that APEN is attempting to foster across class and ethnicity but also reveal the possibility of uncertain outcomes.

Ethnic and Class Constraints on Pan-Asian American Racial Solidarity

The second- and third-generation Japanese, Chinese, and Korean American permanent staff at APEN and AYA, who all identified with Asian American activism, APEN's expressed political goal of promoting the specific concerns of Asians and Pacific Islanders within the broader environmental justice and social justice movements, and learning about Asian American history during the summer program all directly and indirectly exposed the young women in AYA to Asian American frameworks. Like other Asian American forums, APEN provides a critical arena for second-generation Laotians to develop an Asian American identity based on the understanding that Asians share a racial status and history in the United States (Espiritu and Ong 1994).

The political category "Asian American" arose in the 1960s to express the similarity of experiences, and treatment from state institutions, of specific Asian ethnic groups, such as the Japanese, Chinese, Koreans, and Filipinos (Omi and Winant 1994:109–110). However, in the post–civil rights era, Asian American communities have become extremely differentiated along lines of class, culture, language, histories of migration, and patterns of settlement and adaptation. Even though state and nonstate institutions continue to identify different Asian ethnic groups along racial lines, and therefore the Asian American racial category remains institutionally relevant in the political and legal system, it is likely that class and ethnic cleavages will mitigate racial solidarity (Espiritu and Ong 1994; Omi and Winant 1994). Indeed, in the late 1990s ethnic identities had more meaning than membership in "Asian America" for second-generation Chinese and Korean Americans (Kibria 1997).

In this section I examine how teenage Laotians interpret the label "Asian American" and the prospects for pan-Asian racial solidarity among the children of one of America's most recent refugee communities. As I discuss in detail in the following chapter, almost all my respondents self-identified as Lao, Mien, Khmu, or Laotian, and in the process affirmed ethnic identities that emphasize ethnic distinctiveness and national boundaries. However, ethnic identifications were used selectively by individuals and shifted with context. On occasion my respondents would identify as Asian. For example, Cuo, who said she would identify herself as Mien or Laotian, later qualified this assertion by noting that she might label herself Asian, depending on the social context and the race of the other person:

> I think who asks me too, but if it's, like, a white person, then I'll tell them that I'm Asian. If it's someone, like, from San Francisco or whatever, I'll probably say Asian, but if it's, like, around Richmond or something, then I'll probably say, like, Mien or Laotian because, you know, they know more.

Here Cuo revealed that her interactions in Richmond, where she lived and went to school, were confined to nonwhite people—to other Laotians, Southeast Asians, African Americans, and Latinos.[12] And as several respondents noted, many of their peers, teachers, and others in west Contra Costa County were familiar with the label Laotian.

Other second-generation Laotians identified as Asian, even in west Contra Costa County, in order to avoid lengthy explanations of the ethnic group they belong to. When I asked my respondents in Group 4 if they would always identify as Mien or Lao, or if they would choose to label themselves Asian Americans, they said:

> YEN: Mien.
> BRYANNA: I just say Asian.
> BINDI: How about you, Karouna?
> KAROUNA: I say Lao.
> BINDI: How about you, Marn?
> MARN: I say Asian.
> YEN: I say Mien. They say, "What's that?" "Don't trip, it's Asian." *[Everyone laughs]*

BINDI: Is it easier to say you are Asian?
BRYANNA: Yeah.
MARN: 'Cause I don't wanna explain.

Even though Laotians are the dominant Asian group in Richmond and San Pablo, my respondents were categorized by their peers as Chinese, Vietnamese, or Filipino. Thus they often found it easier just to call themselves Asian. For Leah, the identification she chose depended on how much she wanted to reveal of herself: "It depends [on] how much I wanna tell them about myself. So if I don't wanna tell them that much about myself, then I'll say Asian, you know." Rather than express a sense of commonality, identifying in pan-Asian terms was a strategic move, as Maya noted, to avoid having "to explain the whole process" and a refusal to help peers and others unravel assumptions of racial sameness. Thus second-generation Laotians saw no contradiction in identifying in terms of ethnic or pan-Asian categories; the girls assessed different settings and audiences and selected from a range of pan-ethnic and nationality-based identity categories based on their strategic utility and symbolic appropriateness.

However, in the late 1990s identifying as Asian was not synonymous with the category "Asian American" for this group of second-generation Laotians. They did not resort to the pan-ethnic label "Asian American" to avoid lengthy explanations of Laotian migration history. Maya conveyed the complicated dance my respondents went through in selecting ethnic identifications:

> But then when I think Asian American, sometimes I think, like, American-born Asian or, like, being here for so long we can name ourselves as Asian American, right. But, like, when other people ask us "What are you?" or "What's your nationality?" you know, and then we don't want to say Asian American because they gonna think our ethnicity or whatever is Asian, you know. They won't understand which one, so . . .

For Maya, the label "Asian American" not only referred to someone who was born in the United States or who had lived here for a long time; it was also a label that denied ethnic specificity. Yet twenty-three out of thirty-one of my respondents, including Maya, were born in the United States. Their understanding of the label "Asian American" became clearer to me when I asked if they could be Laotian, Mien, Lao, or Khmu and also identify as Asian American. For them, identifying as Asian American represented a dissolving of ethnic boundaries and a blending into dominant American norms. For Pham, it meant a loss of traditions and lifestyles:

> Hmm, I think that when you talk about being Asian American, like, you change, like you go from being, like, Laotian or whatever and then just changing your whole lifestyle and becoming American, you know. And, like, your whole religion or tradition or whatever, it's all gone. It's just American tradition, you know.

As Pham suggests, identifying as Asian American represented an erasure of what made Laotians different and unique, even though she admitted to not practicing many of the Laotian traditions. Sarah distinguished Laotians and Asian Americans in terms of education, English-language facility, and community organizing:

> They [Asian American staff at APEN] talk more English, they seem way smarter than us, like they have more education than we have, and they just come across as more Americanized. . . . And like in Laos, people, we don't do stuff like this. Or now they do, you know, because they are in America but. . . . Like we don't have officers, we don't sit here in meetings, you know, just go in the house and talk. They are different people, so Americanized.

Here Sarah contrasted the political and cultural capital and class characteristics of the predominantly Asian American staff at APEN with that of the Laotian community. Though all the APEN staff had a long history of community organizing, they also all had college degrees, and several had attended elite universities such as the University of California–Berkeley, Stanford University, and Oberlin College. By identifying them as "so Americanized," Sarah also highlighted the fact that the APEN and AYA staff are not part of the recent Asian immigrant and refugee communities that she encounters in Richmond and San Pablo.[13] At the same time, she equated the category "American" with the conduct of politics, a sense of individual and collective efficacy, and particularly the tradition of civic participation in the United States.

On the occasions when my respondents opted to label themselves "Asian American," it was an imposed identity, when others classified them in terms of a pan-ethnic label rather than an ethno-national label. Maya noted the times when she, as a second-generation Laotian, had no choice but to check the "Asian American" box:

> It's like the surveys we have to take at school, like you would never have a category like Laotian, it's like Asian for everyone, right. It's just like African American, Asian American, Latino, or just white. We have no other choice but put Asian American, so they don't really know.

The preceding narratives indicate that second-generation Laotians understood the category "Asian American" in both cultural and political terms. Within an ethnic-specific community organization connected to a larger Asian American political framework, APEN staff was cognizant of shifting contexts and encouraged multiple and fluid identities, one of which became salient in a given context. Indeed, like other pan-Asian activists in California (Võ 2004:225), they believed that strengthening the Laotian community furthered the goal of creating an Asian Pacific American face for the environmental justice movement. In contrast, the young Laotian women in this book appeared to resist this fluidity; instead, they juxtaposed the boundary of "Laotian" with that of "Asian

American" in terms of a series of rigid oppositional dichotomies—immigrant versus American, traditional versus modern—that helped define their second-generation experience (Kibria 1997). However, as I demonstrate in the following chapter, even though Laotian teenage girls selected ethno-national categories that differentiated them and connected them to their parents' homeland, the content and meaning of these categories were reconstructed within the specific context of the United States. By resisting the imposition of an Asian American category by state and nonstate institutions, second-generation Laotians underscored their specific immigrant experience and ethnic distinctiveness, thus challenging the tendency in dominant discourses to lump all Asian ethnic groups into the racialized category "Asian"[14] and asserting their emotional attachments to a single ethnic community.

Moreover, identifying with a political label such as "Asian American," which arose in the 1960s, also implied identifying with a certain political perspective on the position of racial minorities in the United States, one that included an emphasis on shared histories of immigration and common experiences of discrimination. As Deborah Misir observed of South Asian activism against the racial violence of the Dotbusters and other anti-Indian sentiments,[15] the "progressive ideology of alliance and identification with other people of color espoused by student activists is in many ways itself an *elite* ideology" (Misir 1996:72; emphasis in original). Like the South Asian student activists, the third- and second-generation Asian American staff at APEN and AYA viewed the issues that affect Laotians in Contra Costa County within the prism of larger sociopolitical and economic structures and a historical continuum of racism in the United States. However, second-generation Laotians in this book belong to a recent immigrant community that was not involved in the struggles of the 1960s. Laotians also represent a group that is distinct from other Asian ethnic groups in the United States in terms of ethnic and class composition. Even though the older cohorts of girls were exposed to Asian American history and organizing, they appeared not to understand the legacies of the civil rights movement. Moreover, identifying with pan-ethnic labels such as "Asian American" is also more common in college.[16] For working-class Laotians, the immediate and primary concern was to improve their social and economic status rather than to challenge their ongoing racialization as "foreign" and "alien." This suggests the potential for solidarity across race and within class (Bonilla-Silva 2004; see also Lee 2004) rather than within race and across class, confirming Espiritu and Ong's (1994) prediction that class divisions will constitute the greater barrier to racial solidarity.

Conclusion

Interminority relations are a complex web of cooperation and conflict, intermingling and distancing, and assertions of ethnic distinctiveness influenced by geography, immigration histories, race, class, gender, and generation. The ways in which new immigrants and their children make sense of racializing processes reveal the complexities of racial politics in the United States and the difficulties of nurturing long-term prospects for cross-race and pan-ethnic coalitions. As indicated by socioeconomic status, residential patterns, low rates of interracial marriage to white people, and friendship groups that include African Americans, the Laotians in this book fall into the "collective black" stratum. This common social location on the racial hierarchy in the United States, together with shared experiences of marginal social and economic conditions and environmental degradation, suggests the potential for cross-racial coalitions. Indeed, within "border spaces" such as APEN we see the emergence of collective self-understandings around race and ethnicity and cooperation with other members of the collective black stratum, exemplified in the campaigns against toxic emissions by corporations, monolingual English-only emergency warning systems in communities where at least 40 percent of the residents are new immigrants, and inadequate counseling services in a school that is 95 percent students of color.

However, collective self-understandings around race are also constrained by contemporary racial politics in the United States. These racializing processes and the informal meanings and stereotypes emanating from them structure everyday experiences of minority groups, shaping the material worlds in which new immigrants live. The social geography of race reveals how these material worlds influence second-generation Laotians' daily environments and interactions. Second-generation Laotians' desire to distance themselves from blacks indicates an awareness of racialization processes in the United States which attribute the positioning of African Americans at the bottom of the racial hierarchy to moral deficiencies and negative values rather than to racial discrimination and structural inequalities.

The variable positioning of Asian immigrants and Asian Pacific Americans along the biracial hierarchy suggests that ethnic and racial hierarchies are not given or stable. The shifting and contradictory constructions of racial meanings can provide second-generation Laotians with resources that are interpreted and mobilized in new contexts (Sewell 1992). The young women's attitudes and self-identification in ethno-national terms suggest an "immigrant ideology" (Cheng and Espiritu 1989). Unlike many of their male peers, the majority of Laotian girls in this book were educationally oriented, had high aspirations, and were strongly connected to their families' immigrant communities and values. They perceived American society to be open and meritocratic, and one that offered many opportunities. Through the adoption of appropriate values and attitudes as well as individual effort, they believed they would fulfill their aspirations and achieve individual social mobility and acceptance in U.S. society. This optimism was bolstered by the positive images that teachers and peers had of Laotians performing well in school, which in turn provided second-generation Laotians with additional resources, albeit divisive resources, to challenge the positioning of Laotians at the bottom of the racial hierarchy. While not used consciously to denigrate the underachievement of many of their African American and Latino peers in school, the "model minority" label together with an "immigrant ideology" provided young Laotian women with resources to resist their positioning as racialized minorities who experience mobility barriers and levels of discrimination similar to those experienced by African Americans. This suggests that growing up in poor inner-city neighborhoods populated by native-born minorities does not necessarily lead to an "adversarial stance" (Portes and Zhou 1993) toward the dominant society among all the children of immigrants. Rather, these adaptation outcomes are shaped by gender intersecting with class, race, and ethnicity.

Second-generation Laotians' attitudes and aspirations reflect the power of racialization processes in the United States which attribute racial power to white people and which privilege assimilation into middle-class society as a route to gaining social prestige and full citizenship. The ideology of assimilation into middle-class white America limits the effectiveness of "border spaces" such as APEN and its goal of nurturing collective self-understandings and critical racial solidarity among Laotians and other communities of color in Contra Costa County. At the same time, young Laotian women resist the continuing imposition of racial boundaries and classification on Asian groups by state and nonstate institutions and the American public. They affirm ethno-national identities that emphasize ethnic distinctiveness and national boundaries. My respondents' attitudes and ethnic identifications suggest that they do not see themselves as racialized minorities who experience structural barriers to mobility or exclusionary national discourses that represent them as foreigners or alien; rather, these young women reflect the optimism of new immigrant groups that expect to achieve mobility and incorporation into America through individual hard work. The contradictory and multiple effects of contemporary racial politics on second-generation Laotians' racial subjectivities appear to undermine the potential for racial solidarity across race or a collective pan–Asian American identity across class within "border spaces" such as APEN. But I would argue that such uneven effects may actually serve to maintain collective identities as contingent and open up the space for cross-race and pan-ethnic alliances to counter inequalities related to specific issues and in specific contexts.

6

Family, Culture, Gender

Narratives of Ethnic Reconstruction

It's a cold, crisp but sunny Tuesday afternoon in February. As I walk in, almost everyone looks and smiles or says "hi." The front room of this small house in Richmond, which serves as LOP's offices, is packed today. Twenty-one of the youth members are here, waiting for the Whole Group Training on campaign options to start. Bryanna and Huk are sitting close to the radio, tapping their feet to Eminem rapping "My Name Is . . . ." Once the song ends, Bryanna turns the dial to a station that plays alternative and R&B music. Two girls are sitting on the floor in the middle of the room, sharing thumsom, *a green papaya salad. Others are sitting on the chairs placed in a circle, munching on nachos, burgers, and burritos and sipping on soda.*

A lot of the girls are dressed in black today—black flared trousers, black tops, and black jackets. Others sport blue or white flared jeans, short T-shirts or shirts that hug the body, and platform shoes or sneakers. This '70s retro style transports me back to my own dress preferences as a teenager. Bryanna wears an oversized orange rain jacket, nylon pants that bunch up around her ankles, and sneakers. Others resemble the style of the majority of their peers in the city, wearing blue jeans, long T-shirts, and sneakers or high-tops.

Their conversations revolve around boys, school, and clothes. My by-now-trained ear picks up both Black English and standard English, with a smattering of Mien and Lao words that I don't understand.

—Field notes, 23 February 1999

Gabriela: *Most of us who grew up here, we have both ways of thinking, you know. Both techniques of doing that, you know. It's a choice whether we should approach this way or that. That's what I'm trying to say. So it's kinda hard to really identify as a Laotian or, you know.*

—Focus group, 12 August 1999

Most media stories characterize second-generation Laotians as experiencing turmoil and as being involved in fervent battles over dual identities, loyalties, and feelings of belonging. A *San Francisco Examiner* article on Mien girls was titled "Mien girls straddle two worlds," with a subtitle of "New journal charts teen life for Laotian immigrants caught between streets and tradition" (Chao 1999). In a review of the documentary film *Kelly Loves Tony*, about a young Mien couple, the *San Francisco Chronicle*'s John Carman (1998) described Kelly as "gripping American culture with a desperate hold, while the Iu Mien tribal culture of Laos pulls at her ankles." A series in the *Sacramento Bee* on the Hmong ended with a feature on a sixteen-year-old girl titled "Hmong teen builds future in two conflicting worlds" (Magagnini 2000b). This theme of conflict and two separate cultures is a recurring one, especially in reference to Asian women.[1] In contrast, the chapter epigraphs suggest that as second-generation Laotian girls navigate different cultures and "socio-ideological points of view" (Ong 1995:357), they experience both conflict and solidarity with their parents and with the Laotian community. These second-generation Laotian girls defy easy ethnic labels and categorization. The stories of my respondents express muddled, contradictory, and ongoing negotiations around identity and culture that cannot be contained in the essentialized term "Laotian women." Constructing second-generation women's identities in terms of cultural conflict and in either/or frameworks renders the children of immigrants without voice, space, or autonomy. Rarely are second-generation women portrayed as active agents or as negotiators of their cultural values within specific social contexts and relations of power (Puar 1996).

In this chapter I examine the social practices of second-generation Laotian girls, practices that are governed by particularistic self-understandings (Brubaker and Cooper 2000:17) and shaped by multiple subjectivities produced through their particular location in social relations of generation, gender, class, ethnicity, and race. I am concerned with the meanings of ethnic identity for young Laotian women as individuals, and the forces that shape and influence the contents of that ethnicity. As my respondents' narratives demonstrate, the children of immigrants are active in constructing and reconstructing Laotian cultural practices. I also examine how these particularistic understandings are transformed within collective contexts. While Asian Youth Advocates provides a social space for the young women to navigate these differing socio-ideological points of view, the youth program also plays a role in influencing cultural norms and practices within the Laotian community.

Patterns of Ethnic Identification

When asked how they would self-identify if I met them at a party, the young Laotian women in this book chose without hesitation to label themselves Lao, Mien, Khmu, or Laotian. The ethnic categories that my respondents selected for themselves reveal a desire to challenge the tendency in dominant discourses to lump all Asian ethnic groups into the racialized category "Asian." But they also reflect struggles to articulate an identity that is ethnic without being perceived as foreign and un-American. In the context of U.S. racial discourse and the dynamics of racial labeling, all Asian ethnic groups are automatically categorized as "Oriental" or "Asian" (Kibria 1997:531). Concurrently, certain Asian immigrant groups such as the Chinese, Filipinos, and Vietnamese are more visible in popular discourse and are included in aspects of American history taught in California schools. With little knowledge about the specific history of Laotians, peers at school and the media often mistake them for members of one of these groups, something that many of my respondents experienced. For Sarah, it was important that the media make an effort to distinguish Laotians from other Asian ethnic groups and learn how Laotian culture is different:

> **SARAH:** I think he [a newspaper reporter] should write about, like, our culture and that there are different Laotians. It's not one culture, and then they need to start labeling, label, like, Laotian people instead of thinking that we are . . .
> **GABRIELA:** Chinese.
> **SARAH:** Chinese, whatever, right. And that there's different culture, and we speak different and that, I don't know. You need to realize that there's different Asian people.

Gain also expressed frustration when her peers did not distinguish Laotians from other Asian groups. She rebuked her African American peers at school and in the community for adopting dominant assumptions of racial sameness:

> I mean I be, like, "Oh, if you guys don't like us calling you Kenyans or whatever, then don't call us no Chinese or Filipino whatever. 'Cause it's a lot of us from Asia but it's like different things." . . . And after that, like, "You want me to call you all Somalians, do you?" I know Africa is heck of big . . . I was, like, it's just like Asia is made up of a lot of different countries.

In the face of being mistaken for being Chinese or Filipino or Vietnamese, my respondents affirmed ethnic identities that emphasized ethnic distinctiveness and national boundaries. They drew on ethno-national identities to challenge assumption of sameness, of the racialized assumption of "homogenized Asianness" (Kibria 2000:84–85). During focus group discussions my respondents also conveyed a strong desire to maintain ethnic distinctiveness through the preservation of particular aspects of Laotian culture. When asked what they liked about being Laotian, the teenagers in my study, twenty-three of whom were born in the United States and all of whom had grown up here, mentioned being unique, different, having pride, and having two cultures and languages. This is how Maya expressed it:

> I think it feels good to, like, have your own culture. But when you think of, like, well, not say, like other cultures, you know, like they just, like, speak English or whatever, and it seems like they just do the basic stuff. But you usually have your own language, and, like, do your own, like, traditional stuff and it's really, like, different.

When I asked them what they specifically liked about Laotian culture, these second-generation Laotians pointed to its symbolic markers, such as food, ceremonies and celebrations, family, clothes, dances, and language. Yet they did not necessarily engage with these outward manifestations regularly or with deep understanding. In fact, most girls had worn the traditional clothing for women within their sub-ethnic group only once in their lives, though those who identified as ethnic Lao had worn the traditional Lao dress for women to temple, wedding parties, and the annual Lao New Year celebrations. Many expressed dislike for traditional ceremonies that required animal sacrifice, and Pham stated, "We don't even pay attention, like, don't even do all that stuff. Sometimes I don't even be home." On the other hand, most of my respondents cooked and ate Laotian food at home, though a few of the younger girls noted that parents sometimes cooked "American" food for them such as spaghetti. In addition, despite the desire to maintain the Lao, Mien, Hmong, or Khmu languages, the young women admitted that while they understood (one of) these languages, they spoke it only with grandparents and parents and at church or temple. Daily interactions with siblings, Laotian peers, and sometimes even parents were conducted in English. Nevertheless, I argue that their ethnicity is concrete, tangible, and part of their everyday lives. Even though they may not have engaged in traditional ceremonies, celebrations, and dances with deep understanding or frequency and they disliked wearing traditional clothes, often accompanied with heavy silver jewelry among those with a Mien heritage, they were enmeshed in social ties and surrounded by ethnic networks that reinforced the "original" culture and its values on a daily basis. In particular, the family and family gatherings, as I discuss below, and annual celebrations such as Lao or Mien New Year served to strengthen the young women's ethnic identity.

These cultural markers enabled my respondents to demarcate the boundaries of ethnic membership and ethnic authenticity; they allowed the young women to locate themselves away from dominant culture in the United States and be "unique in our own ways," as Yen of Group 4 remarked, or in "how we speak a different language," as Gain of Group 2 noted. In highlighting what she liked about Laotian culture, Paeng of Group 3 also stated:

> I like the fact that, I don't know, we're different. I don't know, that's like a good thing to me because you get to do, like, different stuff, you know. It's like we do feel Americanish, like, one time and the Laotian [*laughs*] the other; it's, like, Laotianish. It's fun.

An emphasis on ethnic distinctiveness pointed to a positive attitude toward the Laotian culture of their parents and grandparents. While this is in contrast to previous studies (MacDonald 1997) in which young Mien believed that their parents' language and culture were old-fashioned and backward, this desire to maintain ethnic distinctiveness extended to the coming third generation. Some respondents were resolute in wanting to pass down the languages, cultural values, and history of Laotian people to their children because, as Maya said, "if they [their children] don't spend time with their culture or whatever, and their kids come out, it will be, like, straight." When second-generation Laotians identify symbolic markers as elements of Laotian culture, such as food, languages, ceremonies, dances, music, and history, they inadvertently contribute to the perception that "ethnic" culture represents the "original" culture that is imported rather than that which has been created in their encounter with U.S. society. Yet their actions and narratives in other contexts indicated that these young women were active in transforming and reconstructing Laotian culture in specific ways.

Intergenerational Family Relationships

One of the main themes that surfaced repeatedly in focus group discussions and interviewees' discussion of family relationships was alienation from parents. Conflicts stem from communication problems, parental expectations, and strict parental control, especially of young women. Although a few respondents had good and open communication with some family members, overwhelmingly they talked about alienation as a result of not being able to communicate with their parents, parents comparing the lives of their children with their own adolescent lives in Laos, and parents not being able to grasp the pressures and demands of living and going to school in urban, multicultural, poor neighborhoods. Lon, a seventeen-year-old, complained that her parents thought that going to school was much easier than the life they had had in Laos, but she contended that Laotian teenagers in the United States had to deal with other pressures:

> They [parents] always talk about, like, in "back in Thailand I used to do this, I used to do that, you don't have to do that stuff," you know, and all that stuff. And then I think they kind of resent us that we don't have to go through all that kind of stuff. But then, like, you know, going to school is just as hard as, you know, like, working in the field, 'cause there's so many pressures, you know, out there and stuff like that. They don't realize it.

Gain, a confident sixteen-year-old, as we saw in Chapter 4, appeared exasperated as she talked about her parents wanting her to work hard and do well at school and then come home and cook, clean, and take care of her siblings. Many girls reported that they could not relate when parents tried to motivate them by describing how they would get up at dawn to go and work in the fields all day. Thirteen-year-old Lisa recounted that "they [parents] are always bringing up the past. Like, 'oh, up in Laos, up in Thailand, we did this, we did that.'" And Yen interjected, "You guys should do it too," noting that she heard similar things from her parents. Lisa continued, "It's, like, the nineties. You can't do that. We don't farm, we don't go out, we don't wake up, we have school." From the perspective of the young women, these stories reflected a lack of understanding among parents about "what we are going through," as Pham complained.

In one sense this generational strain is familiar and an inevitable part of adolescent life. However, within immigrant families it acquires a particular resonance.[2] Laotian parents, who experienced poverty and marginality along the axes of race, class, and gender in relation to the larger society, also feared losing their children. Although most Laotian parents believed that academic advancement would lead to economic success, according to my respondents, many also felt that U.S. institutions such as schools and media, along with various informal settings, exposed their children to dominant American ideals of individualism, freedom, independence, and the fulfillment of personal desires. The desire for autonomy and individuality may well lead to educational achievement and economic success for the second generation, but like other Southeast Asian immigrant parents (Smith-Hefner 1999; Lee 2005), Laotian parents feared that this path would distance their children from their families and communities.

Dominant American ideals of individualism, freedom, and choice run counter to the collective nature of Laotian family life and parental expectations of filial respect and authority, as discussed in Chapter 2. In the United States, Laotian parents found it increasingly difficult to control and discipline their children. In this new context, corporal punishment is not tolerated, and parents' opinions and decisions become irrelevant if a teacher, Child Protective Services, or a judge decides that a child's rights have been violated (Tayanin and Vang 1992; Smith and Tarallo 1993:111). By recounting specific stories from their youth, the young women's parents were attempting to preserve their severely weakened parental authority and to shame their children for their perceived unwillingness to work hard. Through these stories parents hoped to obligate their children and ensure the young women's continued loyalty, interdependence, and cooperation with their families while submerging their individual desires. Laotian parents also had expectations of their sons, but these expectations did not revolve around learning household responsibilities or exercising appropriate dress, behavior, attitude norms, and in-group marriage practices, as I discuss below. According to my respondents, parents' conflicts with their sons centered on involvement in gang activities, school performance, and learning traditional ceremonies related to rites of passage such as funerals, namings, and weddings. As in other immigrant communities (Espiritu 2003), among Laotians in the United States the stakes for keeping cultural boundaries impermeable are much higher for girls than for boys. Women are the bearers and conveyors of culture, and the norms that regulate their behaviors become a means of determining and defining group status and boundaries (Anthias and Yuval-Davis 1989).

Reproductive Work: "I Have More Responsibilities Than My Older Brother Just Because I Am a Girl"

In order to understand Laotian cultural practices that embody gender relations, I asked the young women about gender socialization and expectations in Laotian families. Sixteen-year-old Blia immediately moaned, "Don't get me started." Fourteen-year-old Bryanna complained:

> I kinda hate it 'cause I'm the only girl there, and my brothers, they get to go play outside until, like, late. And I'm, like, the one who has to clean, like,

"Because you're a girl, you have to cook, you have to clean! Go do the laundry!" ... On Sundays they [her parents] take me to the Laundromat and I have to do the laundry alone. So it's, like, [laundry for] eight people.

As Gabriela and other respondents stated, by the time Laotian girls are eight or ten years old, parents expect them to cook, clean, take care of younger siblings, and sew in preparation for "a life of family," according to Pham, or their adult roles as wives and mothers. And Gain's comment above indicates that her parents expect her to work hard and do well at school, then come home and assume all her responsibilities for the care and sustenance of her siblings. My respondents particularly resented what they perceived as gender inequity within the family: the fact that their brothers had far more freedom, flexibility, and favored status than they did. Sixteen-year-old Sarah noted that when her brother is ill, her parents expect her to miss school and stay at home to look after him. But when she is sick, they simply tell her to take medicine and go to school. Lisa spoke about her brother, who was two years younger than her: "'Cause he's, like, the first boy and, like, he's bad and all, but no matter how bad he gets, they still favor him." All the girls, from the youngest to the oldest, complained about how their parents favored their brothers, that brothers were lazy, and that parents appeared indifferent toward them as girls. Moreover, in Asian families "girls have to bow down to the guys ... and the guys are the head of the house," according to Sarah. Parents and extended family members often reminded the young women that they should treat their brothers well "'cause one day you gonna have to run to" them, as Bryanna recounted.

These gender expectations within Laotian families are linked to the preservation of ethnic identity. Gabriela told me quite bluntly that she is "not up to the Mien standard, like being the perfect, ideal Mien girl," because she doesn't cook and clean every night, nor does she listen to her mom all the time but does what she wants if it's important to her. Cooking and cleaning and listening to one's parents are part of a "good" Laotian daughter code. When Sarah's mother tried to teach her to cook and clean, she told Sarah, "This is how you gonna get a husband. This is for your husband." When my respondents resisted parental expectations and gave preference to fulfilling personal desires, parents often reprimanded them and reminded them that they will not find a husband because they have not learned the skills to be a good wife and daughter-in-law. Pham stated that when she refuses her mother's exhortations to cook and help with household chores, her mother warns her, "Oh, watch, when you get older, no one will marry you because you can't cook, like, traditional stuff." Parents viewed their daughters' actions as misguided, and the derogations were meant to obligate second-generation Laotian women to fulfill their responsibilities as well as to ensure that they will be acceptable as potential daughters-in-law within the Laotian community.

Characterizing young Laotian women's choices as "untraditional" or "nonethnic," parents were attempting to regulate their daughter's choices and resistance "by linking them to cultural ignorance or betrayal" (Espiritu 2003:173).

Laotian women were expected to dedicate themselves to the family and community through their labor and transmission of cultural traditions (Anthias and Yuval-Davis 1989). When I asked my respondents how they felt when parents scolded them that no one (meaning no Laotian) would marry them, they asserted their independence and individualism. Pham retorted, "I don't care." Maya stated, "[I] can live by myself for the rest of my life," and Alison added, "I don't need no man." Seng insisted that Laotian parents should "accept their girls for who they are and not push them into something else." Yet the young women are unable to translate this bravado and rebellious streak into day-to-day negotiations with their parents, as I discuss below.

Dress, Behaviors, Attitude Norms: "I'm Not Hoochie"

Second-generation Laotian girls were also expected to maintain cultural boundaries through appropriate dress codes and behavior norms, as I learned during a skit about "good" girls and "bad" girls performed by some of young women at the 1998 AYA summer retreat. In the first scene two mothers are chatting about their daughters and expressing satisfaction that their daughters are "good." They take pride in the fact that their daughters listen to them, work hard, can cook, and are doing well at school. In the next scene one of the daughters walks past the two mothers and goes out. As she leaves home, she is wearing baggy pants and a jacket, but as soon as she is out of her mother's sight, she peels these clothes off to show off the tight shorts and tank top she is wearing underneath. When she comes back home, again "properly" attired, her mother tells her to ask her older sister to start cooking. As the daughter goes up to the sister's room, she smells cigarette smoke coming from inside. She frantically waves her arms to waft the smoke away in case her mother gets a whiff of it. In this skit Laotian girls are shown to navigate two sets of cultural norms, that of their parents and families and that of their peers. They fulfill their parents' expectations by living dual lives, or "code-switching" (Ballard 1994:31).

During a break, after the culture session was over, some of the girls were discussing this skit. I overheard fifteen-year-old Tracy, who performed the role of the daughter wearing seductive clothing underneath baggy pants and a jacket, telling another girl, "I'm not hoochie [that is, sexually promiscuous]." Tracy, who had dropped out of school, was engaged, and lived with her future in-laws at the time of the study, was attempting to distance herself from the role she had just played, that of a "bad" Laotian girl who flaunts her sexuality, and was asserting her identity as a "good" Laotian girl. These strategies of "code-switching" suggest that even when Laotian parents are unable to monitor and control the behaviors of their daughters, their disapproval acts as a powerful sanction and shapes the social practices of second-generation Laotian young women (Espiritu 2003; Wolf 1997).

My respondents often complained that parents enforce these cultural expectations much more vigorously for girls than for boys, resulting in additional responsibility for care of the family but also restricting the movement of teenage Laotian girls. Sixteen-year-old Blia, a graduating senior and a gifted artist who had contributed her drawings to publications at Richmond High School and AYA, said that she argued with her parents about how late she could stay out, which college to go to, and whether she could go on the senior trip to Hawaii.[3] As in other families, Blia's parents wanted her to remain under their protective wing while her two older brothers enjoyed much greater freedom and mobility. Blia had gained admission into one of the University of California campuses to major in graphics and art, but her parents wanted her to stay at home and go to the local community college. She eventually complied with their wish. Of the other respondents who were pursuing higher education while I was in the field, all but one chose to go to a college that was close enough for them to stay at home.

Second-generation Laotian young women are very aware of the educational and career opportunities in the United States. Moreover, most of my respondents acknowledged that their parents supported their desire for acquiring an education and expected them to participate in the workforce. Even though these public arenas embody different cultural constructions of femininity and sexuality than those in immigrant families (Maira 2002), expectations of "good" Laotian womanhood remain. Parents' control of their adolescent daughters' interactions and movements served to ensure that their daughters maintained an unsullied reputation as well as interdependence with the families. And given the high degree of poverty and welfare dependency in the Laotian community, these parental pressures to stay at home and attend a local college also reflected an economic decision.

Dating, Marriage, and Sexual Practice: "I Don't Wanna Marry a Mien Person"

Some of the young women in the study rebelled against patriarchal gender relations and asserted dating and marriage preferences to gain control over their social lives. Laotian parents, however, attempted to exert some control over their daughters' marriage preferences as a way to maintain ethnic/racial boundaries[4] and cultural difference in the face of strong assimilative demands in the United States.[5] Almost all the young women said that their parents would prefer them to marry someone from the Laotian community, though Gain's parents would not "say anything if it's an Asian person" even if she did "marry someone out of my race." Two of my respondents who had African American boyfriends reported parental disapproval. The young women understood their expected role in keeping cultural boundaries through in-group marriage, as sixteen-year-old Cuo, of Group 2, said: "If I was to, like, marry a white person, then I would be oooohh a traitor, or whatever, you know."[6] Cuo's father tried to ensure that she remained within the fold of Laotian community and culture by strongly disapproving of her mobility and interactions outside school, by restricting her television viewing and limiting music choices to Mien music, and by expecting her to attend the

Mien church in Richmond on a regular basis. Among my respondents, only three stated that their parents would not mind if they dated or married someone outside the Mien community. Fifteen-year-old Cept noted that while her dad liked her white boyfriend, he would prefer her to be dating a Mien. On the other hand, her mom had told her "that it doesn't matter what color as long as you are happy with each other." Fifteen-year-old Tsiet and sixteen-year-old Lily, of Group 2, were the only girls who said that their parents would not mind if they dated an African American.

The second-generation Laotian young women in this study, who read magazines aimed at teenage girls, such as *YM, 17, Teen,* and *Essence,* and who participated in school homecoming events and senior prom nights, had adopted the ideology of romantic love and American ideals of freedom, choice, and individualism promoted in popular culture. Thirteen-year-old Lisa, of Group 4, explained: "If you fall in love with somebody beyond your race, you know, you can't help yourself. And then in a way I don't think we have to please our parents because it's our choice, you know." Lisa and some of the other Mien girls in Group 4, all of whom were born in the United States, particularly noted that they did not believe in the tradition of consulting the "marriage book,"[7] which would indicate whether or not two people were suited for each other.

The dating preferences and actual dating patterns of my respondents indicate that many deviated from parental expectations and refused to be responsible for keeping cultural boundaries. Of the girls who had boyfriends during the time I was in the field, eight were dating Laotians, three or four were dating African Americans, one was dating an Asian of different ethnicity, and one had dated a mixed-race white/Latino man. During focus group discussions almost two-thirds of the young women stated adamantly that they would not marry a Mien or Laotian person. Fifteen-year-old Gain was emphatic that she "don't wanna marry a Mien dude," because of

> all the thing about the reputation and stuff, I don't know. It's like if you do something wrong, they'll, like, talk bad about you behind your back and stuff. I don't want that. I mean, I'd rather have, go on with my life, you know.

Gain's comment highlights the ways in which Laotian adults and elders use gossip to monitor ethnic authenticity of Laotian girls. Even the youngest members of AYA, in Group 4, echoed this displeasure with community gossip and their refusal to fulfill these expectations:

BINDI: Yen, why do you think you would not marry a Mien person?
YEN: Um. Don't want to [*raised voice*]. I mean, just like Lisa said, like if you marry a Mien person and something goes wrong, if you burned the rice or something, then they go tell their friends.
LISA: I know. "Oh, that's a bad daughter."
BRYANNA: Especially the mother [who would say that she is a bad daughter-in-law].

Fiey and Tsiet, both fifteen years old, also mentioned that they did not know how to cook, especially rice. "I'll forget about the rice and then it burns," Fiey recounted. Burning the rice, to my respondents, was a metaphor for a daughter who did not pass the test of authenticity and therefore was unacceptable to future in-laws. When I asked if they would consider marrying a Laotian person who had grown up in the United States and thus might not have the same expectations as their parents, they rejected that possibility. Bryanna, Lisa, and Yen reminded me that they would still have to learn to "cook the food," look after the husband's parents, and perform "traditional" roles during ceremonies. These second-generation Laotian girls struggled under patriarchal gender relations within Laotian families. Rather than conform to parental expectations and fulfill the role of maintaining ethnic boundaries, they hoped that through interethnic and interracial dating and marriage they would acquire autonomy and the freedom to pursue their desires, including marital relations characterized by respect and a more equal partnership.

Parent-Child Communication: "Why You Talking Back to Me?"

In a context in which Laotians and their children are exposed to a range of ideological discourses on gender, control of women is one of the primary means of maintaining ethnic boundaries and a distinct Laotian culture. But this strategy is not without emotional costs for second-generation Laotian young women. In interviews and focus group discussions my respondents' faces conveyed stress and extreme frustration from being caught betwixt and between multiple expectations. And they found it difficult to resolve conflicts arising from competing sets of values.

Schools, media, peers, and informal settings such as APEN and AYA expose Laotian children to the American ideal of independence and self-assertion. Yet in a discussion on Laotian culture at the 1998 AYA summer retreat, Gabriela, a self-confident seventeen-year-old, noted: "I can't make eye contact with my mom because it's a sign of disrespect. It's like challenging her." In interviews other young women described how parents interpreted the expression of opinion as "talking back" rather than a need to communicate. Lon, a peer of Gabriela's, preferred not to get into a big argument but "just leave it the way it is." Blia talked about how her parents take the expression of feelings and opinions as a challenge to their authority:

> I don't really talk to them about how I express my feelings because at home we don't do that. But then if I did, then, I mean, if I did express my feelings and opinions and I looked at them, they will have, like, a face on like, "What you say that for?"

Thirteen-year-old Angela, of Group 4, did not "really communicate" with her dad and was "kind of scared" of her mom. At the time of the study "even though she [her mom] gets mad at me, if I have something to say 'cause she's wrong," she would say it. Angela noted that as a result "we are always arguing with each other." Cuo, of Group 2, was one of the few girls who said that she talked back to her dad, but the consequence was that he would then "start getting mad and he'll start telling my mom about how [she] raised me." Cuo regarded her dad as "too Mien," expecting obedience and not encouraging open communication. My respondents' comments suggest that second-generation Laotian women still avoid conflict and maintain respect for elders, especially parents (see Anderson 2005) regardless of the length of their involvement in AYA. Even the oldest girls—Gabriela, Lon, and Blia, who had been involved in the youth program for four years—described their parent-child relationships in this manner. The APEN staff placed an emphasis on cultivating a new generation of young women leaders in the Laotian community. To that end, the staff stressed learning good communications skills and resolving conflicts immediately through group discussions and peer counseling sessions in an effort to build a strong group identity among the girls. The girls were encouraged and expected to participate actively and express their opinions all the time. When I asked them if they thought APEN was teaching them to be "outspoken, loud, and rebellious," this is how Seng, an active and ambitious seventeen-year-old, responded:

> No! No! [*Emphasizes it and raises her voice slightly.*] I mean, we just stand up for what we believe in, you know. It means, you know, all my life, from elementary school through junior high school, I've been really, really quiet. Even when I didn't understand a problem, I wouldn't ask the teacher who taught me. I never asked them or anything. And then, after I joined APEN, I was still shy the first year and stuff. But after a little while, like, you know, I started to, like, sit up, you know . . . like asking questions and stuff because that was the only way that I was gonna, you know, get through it, school and stuff so. And also because that was the only way that I could be heard at our school.

Like Seng, the majority of my respondents felt that AYA had taught them to be visible and to demand their due. Seng also talked about how silence makes her invisible and perpetuates a culture of oppression, which she attempted to overcome. But it is noteworthy that she mentioned only one social context, that of school. In the school environment she was able to navigate her way using the communication skills and growing self-confidence acquired through her participation in the youth program. As we learned in Chapter 1, she also displayed leadership when she formed a school club to address racism and prejudice among the students at Richmond High. Yet these skills and confidence had failed to cross over to the private sphere of parent-child relationships.

MacDonald (1997) notes that in "traditional" Mien families, children would never make their own decisions; rather, the household head, usually an elder male, would make decisions for the family and its individual members. In this hierarchical order older males are accorded respect and authority while young women and girls are expected to abide by their decisions. Moreover, in Iu Mien and Lao culture, family and ancestral relationships are emphasized rather than individual independence (MacDonald 1997; Anderson 2005). Within the context of the United States, maintaining hierarchical parent-child relationships conferred power, respect, and influence on parents in the private, domestic sphere. However, lines of authority were upset and roles reversed in other arenas when parents had to rely on their children, who gained English proficiency and cultural knowledge of American institutions faster.[8] Thus parents were unwilling to negotiate and may have simply commanded and expected obedience. For the most part, my respondents were resigned to the fact that in the context of the home culture, which emphasized respect for elders, solidarity, politeness, and hierarchical parent-child relationships in which Laotian girls were placed at the bottom of the hierarchy, their opinions remained unheard and their personal desires unfulfilled. Second-generation Laotians felt obliged to abide by patterns of respect and authority in Laotian families. While these different styles of communication in different contexts can be interpreted as another instance of "code-switching" (Ballard 1994:31), such a strategy does not come easily or without emotional costs. Laotian teenagers often felt that their parents did not care about them or their needs but simply expected them to perform the tasks of nurturing the whole family.

A lack of understanding of the ways in which American institutions function may also hinder communication; the majority of Laotian parents had rural backgrounds, and few had received a formal education. While some were able to speak a basic level of English, they often did not have English facility at a higher cognitive level. Bouakhay Siripanyo, a psychological counselor who worked in the West Contra Costa County Unified School District with Laotian youth who had been referred to her by probation officers and Child Protective Services, believed that the "biggest issue is parenting"; she felt that "parents find it hard to connect with their children" (conversation with Siripanyo, 5 May 1999).[9] In addition, communication with parents was difficult when they themselves were dealing with the trauma of war and escape as well as marginalization and subordination in the United States. A Laotian community activist who worked with Laotian at-risk youth in Richmond and San Pablo observed that during family visits she met parents who had been diagnosed with post-traumatic stress syndrome, were addicted to drugs and gambling, and were aloof. Moreover, parents were often working long hours and odd shifts, creating little opportunity for parent-child communication (conversation with Anousone Karncharanwong, 23 October 1998).

The Family: "I Like the Family Gatherings"

Despite difficult parent-child relationships and contestations around in-group gender, marriage, and child-bearing practices that maintain ethnic identity and community, the family remained important in the young women's lives. When asked how they would characterize their family relationships, almost all my respondents described their families as close or fairly close. When asked whom they spend their free time with, many said they "hang out" with cousins and other relatives during the weekends. Then, when I asked, "What do you like about Laotian culture?" fifteen-year-old Fiey highlighted both food and "the family gatherings" when cousins, relatives, and friends come over during birthday or wedding celebrations or ceremonies. Seventeen-year-old Rachel liked "getting together [with family] and then, like, listening and talk a lot." Fifteen-year-old Tsiet echoed what a third of my respondents liked about Laotian culture: "When we kick it with the family." In other words, spending time with the family, a valued part of Laotian culture, also defined their worldview.

Valuing family and family relations was what made them Laotian, in contrast to "Americans," who are "too caught up with . . . making the money," according to Lisa, or who "just value money," and for whom acquiring money for personal consumption takes a priority, according to Sarah and Seng.[10] Maya further elaborated on the different values placed on money among Laotians and among Americans:

> Like my mom says, American people can work for money. They work to buy a new car; they work to buy a house. But then it's like, we're working to, like, she's, like, "We're working to just survive," you know. "And we ain't got time to go out and, like, go to parties or go south to the boardwalk or something." . . . So they teach us that if we make money, we have to save some money just in case something happens.

Getting together with extended family members, cooking together and speaking in Lao or Mien, and learning from elders about values and ways of life were not only affordable pleasures but also key elements of Laotian culture that my respondents cherished. Other Laotian communities in the United States also demonstrate these patterns of social life, which revolve around the extended family and lineage, and families characterized by strong loyalty, cooperation, and interdependence (MacDonald 1997; Anderson 2005). Mien social worker Moung Saetern (1998) observed that the Laotian community continues to value collective social activities and traditional practices that allow them to construct community in the United States. Collective social relations and strong community links not only aid in the settlement process but also shield Laotians from the assimilative and alienating demands of U.S. society (Anderson 2005). Families can provide strength and resources for adolescent girls of color who experience the challenges of uncertainties, conflicting expectations, and rejection based on color, culture, language, and class. For second-generation Laotians, "the family" plays a central role in their lives and gives meaning to their ethnic identity. The hierarchical family system, and the protection it confers, appear to be more important than complete independence and individualism for my respondents.[11] However, when second-generation Laotian women acknowledge the importance of family life, they do not necessarily accept as legitimate the hierarchical organization of the household or the exercise of male power (Glenn 1986; Brah 1992b).

The dilemma facing many immigrant women is how to defend and hold together the family while inducing changes in the gender ideologies that subordinate women (Glenn 1986:193). I turn next to the ways in which the young Laotian women in AYA learned to contest two dominant norms within the Laotian community and in the process acquire greater power and control over their lives without rejecting their ethnic ties.

Teenage Pregnancy: "You Have to Commit to That Baby 24/7"

Laotian families uphold the intrinsic value of children and large families. Saetern (1998) writes that in the United States, many Iu Mien parents enforce the cultural practice of marriage and having children at a young age. Other studies confirm this trend among Laotian communities in other parts of the United States (MacDonald 1997; Dunnigan et al. 1997). According to my respondents, parents understood having a child during adolescence as normal practice if the teenage girl was already married or engaged. If the young woman is pregnant but not married, parents agree to a hasty marriage or arrange for the girl to move in with her boyfriend and his family in order to save face for the girl's family.[12] I argue that in the context of the United States, these practices represent another attempt to control young women's sexuality and enforce women's role as the keepers of culture and ethnic boundaries. Having a daughter marry at young age is a sign that she is both "pure" and "properly" trained, confirming her authentic status. A University of California study confirms traditional courtship, marriage and fertility patterns among Laotians in the United States.[13] However, according to Jeffery MacDonald (1997), younger community leaders understand the consequences of large families and dependency on welfare. They believe that if young women and men cannot avail themselves of the educational opportunities in the United States, the long-term economic success of the community and the individual will be threatened. Similarly, the young women in this book, who experienced a discourse within AYA that actively discourages teenage motherhood, also reflect changing family ideals.

APEN staff took the position that poverty and lack of support rather than the availability of welfare contributes to teenage pregnancy.[14] But they also adopt a middle-class liberal ethos when they suggest that teenage motherhood undermines a young woman's economic situation and educational opportunities, preventing her from leading a stable and productive adult life. Thus, together with a broader agenda of improving the environmental and economic health of the community in which Laotians live, APEN believed that information on reproductive health and protective behavior would enable second-generation Laotians to make healthy choices.

A focus on reproductive health also provided the AYA staff opportunities to highlight the impact of the environmental health of Richmond on the young women's reproductive health. This link surfaced close to home for AYA staff when one of the girls, recruited in 1995 as a member of Group 1, could not come on the first day of the youth program because she had to accompany her mother to the hospital. Her mother was later diagnosed with cancer, as Peggy Saika recalled (interview, 21 October 1998). Moreover, there is growing evidence of the direct correlation between age at exposure to environmental toxins and the incidence of certain kinds of cancers or reproductive health problems later in a woman's life. Those young Laotian women born in Thailand were also likely to have been exposed in utero or as young children to environmental toxins because of DDT spraying programs in the refugee camps or because of Agent Orange, sprayed in Laos during the Vietnam War (APIRH 1997). A recent study found elevated levels of vanadium in the indoor and outdoor air of Richmond homes, suggesting ongoing exposure to environmental toxins. Vanadium is an indicator of oil combustion and a reproductive and developmental toxicant (Morello-Frosch 2008; Domingo 1996, both cited in Communities for a Better Environment 2009). These trends underscored not only that "we really needed to do more education and training at a much younger age," as Peggy observed (interview, 21 October 1998), but also the unique framing of reproductive rights in Laotian and other Southeast Asian communities, according to Chit, a 1.5-generation AYA youth organizer:

> Like, for us it's more than just a legislative barrier. It's, like, a health barrier. You know, if you have an economic barrier and if you have all these industries polluting your body, you can't have a baby. That's infringing your rights. (Interview, 21 September 1998)

Not only did the APEN staff view the girls as the main conduit for disseminating information to members of their families and community; the staff also firmly believed that knowledge of the reproductive system and reproductive health was vital if they were to become advocates for their community. Each summer AYA worked in partnership with Asian Pacific Islanders for Reproductive Health (APIRH) to engage the newly recruited group of thirteen- and fourteen-year-olds with the HOPE (Health, Opportunities, Problem-solving, and Empowerment) for Girls Curriculum. Through a popular education approach the girls participated in activities that introduced them to women's reproductive cycle, male and female reproductive organs, and contraception, as well in-depth discussions of teenage sex, relationships, peer pressure, the economics of teen pregnancy, body image, diet, gender stereotypes, and links between their health and their physical environment. Toward the end of the summer the girls visited a local Planned Parenthood clinic and other clinics. In other words, APIRH staff discussed reproductive health in the context of factors such as wealth, cultural norms, self-esteem, and the physical environment. During subsequent summers and retreats APIRH staff continued the emphasis on sex education, prevention of pregnancy, and safe sex. At the summer 1998 retreat Carol, from APIRH, facilitated a review session on contraceptives. She split the thirty-one girls into groups, gave each a specific contraceptive with an information sheet on it, and asked the girls to devise a commercial on the benefits and hazards related to the contraceptive. After the skits Carol reviewed the different types of contraceptives available, how to use each of them, and the benefits and problems associated with each. Though some of the girls were embarrassed to talk about contraception, Carol created a safe space that allowed them to ask questions such as where they can purchase condoms, the purpose of spermicide, and the side effects of abortion. At the end of that session Carol also handed out a folder that included information on female and male reproductive systems, pelvic exams, the menstrual cycle, contraceptive options, HIV/AIDS, and sexually transmitted diseases. Carol hoped that this would provide a refresher on the material each group had covered in the first summer at AYA. Also included were two cards displaying the addresses and phone numbers of free clinics and other resources for teenagers.

The message of making healthy choices was carried through in discussions of teen sex and role-plays on peer pressure and teenage pregnancy, in which the teens developed their own solutions to given scenarios. For example, in the final scene of Group 4's graduation skit on teen pregnancy, peer pressure, and trust, the young women presented three options to the audience: abortion, adoption, and keeping the baby. In the skit Mercedes, a Laotian high school girl, had had unprotected sex with her boyfriend, Benz. In the final scene she cried out: "What should I do? There are so many options." Then she froze, and the speaker narrated the following:

> Mercedes has a big decision to make. Decision making is hard in life, but Mercedes went to the clinic to find out all her options. The skit was also about the importance of friends supporting and trusting each other and about needing education on reproductive health.
>
> Laotian teen women have one of the highest teen birth rates. One out of four sexually active teens will get an STD by the age of 21. Half of all HIV infections occur in individuals under the age of 25.
>
> Through learning good decision-making skills, reproductive health, and the importance of supporting and trusting each other, we can all strive in lowering these statistics. (Excerpt from Group 4 graduation skit, July 1998)

Through skits, statistics, and information on the prevention of pregnancies, AYA and APIRH staff aimed to create an awareness of the issues facing teenage Laotian girls as well as to give them tools to make healthy choices. They presented all this information in terms of choice, resisting peer pressure, and reproductive health. In subsequent years there was a subtle but strong undercurrent pushing the girls to stay in school, do well, and go to college or get a job. In other words, APEN staff encouraged the girls to set future-oriented life goals, and in so doing they directly challenged traditional fertility patterns and gender ideologies in the Laotian community.

APEN's position on teenage motherhood, though it opposed conservative discourses that link teenage pregnancy to welfare, also represented support of the view that women on welfare, who cannot support their families, are not considered full citizens.[15] For APEN, citizenship implied active participation in the political process. Early motherhood would hold back the second-generation Laotian girls from becoming leaders and active shapers of their community's future and prevent APEN from reaching its goal of changing the leadership landscape of the Laotian community. What were the outcomes of APEN's attempts to transform cultural understandings and create new cultural practices within the collective context of AYA? While engagement or marrying young were not challenged by my respondents, almost all of them indicated that they did not support having children in their teens. When asked how they would advise a close teenage friend who was thinking about having a baby, most of my respondents adopted a pragmatic position. Seventeen-year-old Gabriela would support her if it was an informed decision rather than an emotional one:

> I would give her a book that APEN has given me with all those valuable health information. You know, before she goes in and, you know, treats herself, I'd give her all those stuff, you know. Tell her what her options are and then think. You know, after that, if she decides to go through with it, you know, "Hey, go for it," you know, but it's at your own risk, you know.

Julia and Marn, both fourteen-year-olds from Group 4, knew an eighth grader who had a baby at age twelve with a twenty-one-year-old man who subsequently went to jail. This young woman was unable to take care of the baby and often left the child with her parents while she went out. While they would support a friend who was thinking about having a baby, they too would tell her to "go ask a friend or relative how it's like before she has it" or "enter this program where they give you a fake baby. It will cry, act, and so you can see how it is," as Julia stated. Sixteen-year-old Blia said that she would tell her friend not to have a baby because "it destroys your whole life," and the full-time responsibility of caring for the baby will mean "then you can't go out, you can't go to the prom." Leah also highlighted how teen motherhood would affect a young woman's future:

> She's gonna lose all the opportunity that's coming at her because she has to do other stuff for her baby and she won't have time to do other stuff that will help her future. Or that will help her life to get down or whatever.

Fourteen-year-old Alison, of Group 3, had friends who were teen mothers, and when she saw them she realized that "when they take care of their child, it's hard." She too would advise a friend against becoming a teen mother because "you can't go nowhere and all you can do is stay home." A variety of factors contributed to the pragmatic position that the majority of my respondents took: their families' experiences of poverty and continuous economic struggle, their knowledge of cousins and friends who are unable to enjoy teenage pursuits and are stressed out, and their awareness of opportunities for women in the United States.[16]

However, seventeen-year-old Seng unhesitatingly adopted a strong moral stance against teen pregnancy:

> Well, I say *No!* I say, "Oh my gosh!" 'cause I have all these relatives and all these friends, they got pregnant, all when they're too young and all that stuff, and they, like, all have to carry the baby to school and stuff. I think that's like the biggest embarrassment that you get, you know, pregnant, that, you know, young and stuff. It seems that you don't have any values or any morals and stuff.

Seng's comment indicates that she has adopted the moral rhetoric embodied in the public debates on welfare and teenage pregnancy. Whether the young women regard teenage pregnancy as deviant and immoral or oppose it on more pragmatic grounds, their positions contrast with trends in the Laotian community. Within the context of AYA the second-generation Laotian young women in this book were not only exposed to discussions on teenage sex, peer pressure, and consequences related to teenage pregnancy; they also had their opinions and desires affirmed and validated by staff. As Chittraphone, a 1.5-generation AYA youth organizer, commented, AYA staff not only emphasized "being healthy, having a healthy life," but also helped the girls "be on track in terms of where they want [to go], in terms of achieving"(interview, 17 August 1998).

The girls who joined and stayed in APEN were partly self-selected, in the sense that they were interested in what the program had to offer and viewed it as a good opportunity. And in part the APEN staff selected them for their interest and commitment to community issues. Almost all my respondents stated in interviews that they would like to go to college and get a job. Of the girls who wanted to delay marriage and had ambitions to go to college, all said that their parents supported them, at least emotionally even if they did not have the financial means. Toward this end, the coethnic and interethnic relationships formed through participation in AYA increased their cultural capital regarding success in education and provided a social milieu where friendship bonds as well as their individual commitments to academic achievement could be strengthened. AYA staff not only exuded a form of authority and norms that reflected middle-class values prevalent in the dominant culture but also acted as "authentic carers" (Valenzuela 1999:157) who provided help and support.[17]

Thus I was very surprised to learn that three of my respondents had become pregnant during the 1999–2000 school year. Out of my sample of thirty-one, I knew of five who had had children or were pregnant before age seventeen. These three young women had become pregnant during their final year at APEN. I had already completed my research by then and heard about their pregnancies from other respondents I encountered at the local mall. All of them were performing very well at school and aspired to go to college, and two were active members of the youth program. And all of them had mentioned practical reasons for not becoming teenage mothers when I had asked for their opinion during interviews.

Fifteen-year-old Tsiet, of Group 3, who had wanted to become a lawyer or a police officer, had said that she would dissuade her friend from having a baby by pointing to practical concerns:

> I think she should, like, get everything first. Like, get an education, get a career, ahead of herself so that when the baby comes, it seems, like, I don't know, a better place for the baby instead of, like, just living with parents or something.

The other two young women had been part of Group 2 but had dropped out of AYA and school during the 1999–2000 school year. Perhaps the disjunction between their words and actions means that they told me what they thought they should say; after all, I was a non-Laotian adult attached to but not an official part of AYA. If this is indeed the case, then their strategy demonstrates that young people have the power to control social research and provide selective access to their worlds. In any case, I do not believe that the choices and actions of these three teenagers point to individual failings; rather, they demonstrate the structural powerlessness that the children of immigrants and other young people of color experience in deprived, inner-city neighborhoods. The AYA staff's discussion of choice, resisting peer pressure, and reproductive health in terms of individual actions and behaviors becomes meaningless without the enabling conditions through which they can be realized. Despite their performance at school and participation in AYA, the gender, race, and class subordination these second-generation Laotian young women experienced within the wider society and within their ethnic community left some of them with few options for attaining social prestige, as well as love and dignity.[18] It appears that AYA staff could not help the young women acquire enough cultural capital and the power and resources to overcome race and class subordination in the wider society. Nor could the staff influence cultural practices in the Laotian community. Like young Hmong women in the Midwest, my respondents drew on a practice available in Laotian social relations for their own purposes of escaping parental authority and alienation due to structural inequalities in society (Ngo 2002; see also Horowitz 1995). In this context, teenage pregnancy does not appear irresponsible but makes sense in an environment that offers few opportunities. Having a child increases a young woman's status, at least in the Laotian community. The outcome of this choice may, however, reinforce her marginal position within the wider society.

The life choices of these three young women also indicate that second-generation Laotian girls are constructing a variety of Laotian femininities in the U.S. context. Tsiet had moved out of state to live with her African American boyfriend and his family and was working. The other two, who had stayed close to their families, were working and continuing with their education at the local community college while parents and grandparents helped take care of the children. Their actions challenge the logic of linear development of progress and change (Mohanty 1992:87; Ong 1995). Particularistic self-understandings, which are anchored in complex and multiple relations of power, govern their practices and actions; the multiple subjectivities produced through gender, class, ethnicity, and race give rise to discontinuous and often fragmented experiences, and therefore ambivalent outcomes.

Gender, Power, and Political Leadership

The importance of family, discussed earlier, illustrates the emotional dependency of second-generation Laotians on their families and communities. This dependency can work in reverse, too. The faster pace of acculturation into U.S. culture among the children of immigrants thrusts them into acting as cultural brokers and bridge builders.[19] As we saw in Chapter 4, Laotian children, with their rapid English-language acquisition, quickly take on the role of translators and cultural intermediaries for parents who are bewildered and intimidated by the ways of American institutions and society in public contexts as well as in daily life. For example, seventeen-year-old Gabriela explained the reason she had to keep me waiting when I went to pick her up one afternoon:

> Gabriela tells me that her mom had asked her to help make a PIN number for her new ATM card. Gabriela told her that she didn't have time at that moment. Then her mom asked her when she would be back. Gabriela replied "around 10" as she ran out the door. Gabriela noted that her mom would be mad with her when she gets home because she will already be in bed and therefore it will be too late to help her create a PIN number. (Field notes, 10 December 1998)

Gabriela's father died fighting the Pathet Lao. Thus, as the oldest child, Gabriela had the responsibility of helping her mother navigate the financial system in the United States and balance the family finances. Her brother, as the firstborn son, will take over this role when he is old enough. But until then Gabriela bore the responsibility because she is the one with the knowledge and English facility. The children of immigrants serve as cultural brokers, reading documents and letters written in English, communicating with various authorities, and interpreting in public settings such as hospitals, schools, and welfare offices. Such role reversals bestow both power and independence on the second generation (Kibria 1993).

The mediatory role these girls played also occurred within a context of Laotians lacking visibility and voice at federal, state, and local levels of government. Given this material reality, second-generation Laotians were vital in making the needs of Laotians visible and in securing resources for the community, as we saw in Chapter 4. Over the four years that the girls were expected by APEN staff to remain involved in AYA, they had a range of opportunities to develop community-organizing and leadership skills around critical issues that directly affected them, and to gain knowledge for navigating American institutions and making the voices of Laotians heard. In the summer of 1998 the Group 1 girls, who were sixteen to seventeen years old, shifted their role in the program from youth participants to paid staff members for about two months. Each Group 1 teen became a Lead Youth Intern (LYI) and worked as a counselor with the younger cohorts or as an organizer for the first ever Environmental Health Festival in the city of Richmond, sponsored by APEN that summer. The three girls organizing the festival took on responsibilities for developing media coverage, garnering donations, arranging food booths, and securing the participation of other community, city, and county environmental and health programs. The goals of the festival were to celebrate the work of groups in Contra Costa County that address environmental and health issues and to educate members of the Asian Pacific Islander, Latino, African American, and white communities on these issues, as well as make them aware of the available resources (Lon, Group 1 member, interview, 7 December 1998). The three who worked as counselors alongside adult staff were responsible for planning and implementing the summer curriculum of education, training, games, and field trips for the younger cohorts of girls.

In these ways second-generation Laotian girls participating in APEN's Asian Youth Advocates program were acting as cultural brokers as well as contributing to the gradual expansion of opportunities for Laotian women to become public leaders. In this effort they were joining other young Laotian women in social service and law enforcement agencies, schools, community organizations, and medical clinics who combined traditional skills and roles with good English, American education, and professional training to represent and advocate for the Laotian community (MacDonald 1997; Magagnini 2000c; Anderson 2005; Lee 2005; Hein 2006). The public speaking, group communication, and organizing that my respondents learned at AYA gave some of them confidence to run for leadership positions at school, as we saw of Seng in Chapter 1. Seng was junior class president and senior class president at Richmond High. Seventeen-year-old Rachel, also of Group 1, was senior class vice-president at Middle College High School, and fifteen-year-old Cept of Group 2 was junior class treasurer at Richmond High. When the young women take leadership positions, engage in community activism, and act as representatives of the Laotian community, they are directly challenging the traditional position of girls and young Laotian women. In Laos, leadership and community politics is a male domain (Julian 1998), and this practice had continued in the United States until the mid-1990s (MacDonald 1997:136). Saetern (1998), speaking of the Mien community in Oakland, California, stated that when community leaders elect a "mayor" in the different cities where Iu Mien reside, the criteria for mayoral candidacy include being well known and respected by everyone in the community, as well as being male.

Leadership in the public arena does not necessarily enhance the status of my respondents within their families. Involvement in AYA may have added to the rapid pace of acculturation that second-generation Laotians experience and increased the distance from their parents. A girls-only program, the level of support for individual girls, the nurturing of self-confidence and skills, staying "on track," and the opportunities for public leadership all convey implicit messages of independence, women's rights, and the importance of fulfilling individual aspirations for education and work. However, most of the young women disclosed that their parents approved of their participation in AYA because it kept the girls off the streets and because they perceived AYA as helping the girls negotiate school expectations, a role that parents felt unable to play because of their lack of time, education, and knowledge of the American school system.

Conclusion

The acts of immigration and settlement produce seismic crises in family, intergenerational, and gender politics. Ethnicities become the sites for negotiating power relations and maintaining ethnic group integrity. In the context of the United States, immigrant Laotian parents were dealing with the emotional trauma of war and escape, as well as marginalization and subordination along race and class relations of power. Laotian parents reaffirmed their self-worth by holding onto power in the only arena where they had a modicum of control: parent-child relationships in the private sphere. In addition, because policing women's bodies is one of the main means of maintaining ethnic boundaries and cultural difference, second-generation Laotian women faced numerous restrictions on their autonomy, mobility, and personal decision making.

But this strategy imposed emotional costs on daughters. Many young Laotian women experienced stress and alienation in trying to negotiate and express their personal desires and to resolve conflicts with parents from their marginal position in the intergenerational hierarchy. For other young Laotian women, traversing multiple cultural worlds was constraining and difficult. But this betwixt-and-between position also enabled them "to read domination differently and to remake their agency" (Ong 1995:363). They drew on different discourses, such as the ideology of romantic love, freedom, choice, opportunities for education, and equal rights, to resist family control in the arenas of dating and marriage preferences, to negotiate the multiple pressures of teenage motherhood, and to actively transform Laotian gender and generational relations in the public arena. When the young women took leadership positions, engaged in community activism, and acted as representatives of the Laotian community, they directly challenged the traditional position of Laotian girls and young women. This is not simply a process of acculturation and "Americanization" but also a case of young Laotian women actively responding to the social, economic, and political conditions in the United States and, in so doing, changing Laotian gender ideals. As Virinder Kalra et al. (2005:58) observe, new contexts "provide fertile, if fraught, sites from which to resist practices that oppress women." In these ways second-generation Laotian young women were not "naturally passive" (Puar 1996), trapped between the mutually exclusive and opposing poles of Laotian/American, but exercised their agency and constructed resistance within specific social contexts.

At the same time, second-generation Laotian girls and young women remained anchored in the Laotian community in the United States. Despite having American middle-class aspirations and desire for gender equality, they were kept rooted in Laotian families and Laotian collective social practices by the race and class subordination they and their parents experienced in the dominant society. The participation of the Laotian girls in AYA heightened their interdependence and solidarity with their families and community. The leadership and organizing skills they gained through the program enhanced their role as cultural intermediaries and positioned them to work collectively for social change to benefit the whole community. APEN endowed second-generation Laotian women with social capital and provided them with the tools to better negotiate American society not for individual gain but on behalf of all Laotians. The process of mobilizing group efforts to gain access to larger social, material, and political resources for the Laotian community served to strengthen second-generation Laotian girls' membership in that community and affirm their Laotian ethnic identity.

The construction of community, kinship, and identity is fluid and rooted in everyday practices of exclusion and inclusion (Ong 1996:741) experienced in the interconnections between primary and secondary social relations. For second-generation children of immigrants, social meanings of gender, generation, and ethnicity are produced, appropriated, disrupted, and contested through social interactions inside and outside ethnic communities (Nagel 1994), thus challenging the notion of a public/private dichotomy and reiterating the intimate linkages between private lives and larger sociopolitical structures. The experiences that teenage Laotian girls have in specific local, state, national, and class contexts in the United States help to transform the meaning of the category Laotian and to nurture new gendered subjects. But ethnic reconstruction does not only involve transformations in ethnic social relations, institutions, and cultural practices; it also challenges dominant narratives in the United States which equate ethnic identity with a foreign national identity. Thus culture is central to the enterprise of nurturing critical incorporation, and has concomitant implications both for creating collective self-understandings in the fight for social rights and in intergroup relations, which I discussed in Chapters 4 and 5, and for redefining dominant ideas of what it means to be an American, which I explore in the next chapter.

7

Building Community, Crafting Belonging in Multiple Homes

APEN is like another family to turn to. It's like a home where we not [only] talk about our own needs but other community and family needs. We are like a super girl who find crime and find smart ways to make it right. Like a family we also comfort each other because we express our feelings. . . . So APEN is very important to me, like my family is important to me.

—Lai, Group 3 (Journal entry, summer 1998)

"Home" is "that which we cannot not want. It stands for a safe place, where there is no need to explain oneself to outsiders; it stands for community."

—Dorinne Kondo (1996:97), rephrasing Spivak (1987)

We all need to know who our friends and foes are, where are the safe spaces we can rest, and who are the supports we can rely on and whom we should distrust. For those of us on the margins, we need to know where we fit in and where is "home" (Afshar 1994:127). In this chapter I move from discussions of the politics of belonging in previous chapters to address constructions of belonging and community that reflect emotional investments and the desire for attachments. As Yuval-Davis, Anthias, and Kofman (2005:526) argue, how individuals feel about their location in the world is relational and in part shaped by their experiences of exclusion rather than inclusion. The range of spaces, places, and communities in which we feel we do not or cannot belong generates a recurring question: Where do I belong? "Belonging therefore involves an important affective dimension, the emotional attachment to important social bonds and ties" (Yuval Davis et al. 2005:528). As members of an environmental justice organization working with a new immigrant community, the staff at APEN is cognizant that emotional investments and attachments to both place and institutional space will facilitate community engagement with a range of environmental and social justice issues. Not having a sense of belonging acts as a barrier to creating political efficacy and a sense of confidence that one is worthy of participating in the polity and has the right to demand social equality. As APEN staffer Miya Yoshitani observed:

> This community is like so many other immigrant and refugee communities that really they don't feel like they have rights. And don't really feel like they have the right to challenge some of the inequities that their community is

living with. You know, there are some other problems, like people are facing great poverty and lack of opportunity. Those are huge barriers to organizing in the community, of course, but there's some level of just, like, building desire or building, like, the vision. That is building the possibility in people's minds that you have the right to do this, and you have the right to demand a better life for the community and for your children. (Interview, 22 September 1998)

At the time of the study, the Laotian Organizing Project had a three-year presence in the community and many Laotians were supportive of the initiative. Miya recounted the type of comment the APEN staff had heard from several community members: "I really believe in what you are doing. It's really important and we pray for you. But I have three jobs and I can't always come on Sundays.... I will do, like, whenever you need something, ask me and I'll probably be able to do that." However, individuals in the community were unable to become involved in ongoing discussions about LOP's work. Furthermore, Miya acknowledged that, in 1998, "there's not a sense of ownership of LOP and the vision and the work." She attributed the lack of identification with LOP to an "absence of confidence" and recognized that "it's so hard for someone who has only real fears about what will happen if they do that [engage in community activism]. And this is not natural, to come into this situation and be kind of confident of keeping the leadership." Miya also noted that this lack of confidence was prevalent among the girls: "They have grown up feeling like they don't deserve what other people may have" (interview, 22 September 1998). Yet as the first bilingual generation, these young women played an important role in the community as bridge builders and generators of new social capital. If they were to become leaders and advocates for their community, as APEN hoped, the staff had to focus on generating a sense of ownership of both AYA and LOP among the young women. In this chapter I examine constructions of belonging among the young women and their emotional investments in AYA, their families, the ethnic community, and the nation.

The sense of belonging has two facets: first, identification, both individual and collective, or membership in a distinctive bounded group, whether place-based or ethnic, racial, national, cultural, or religious; and second, the affective dimension, or emotional feelings of belonging in a space where one does not have to explain oneself, a sense of location (Anthias 2002). These two senses of belonging, the emotional and the identificatory, commingled and became explicit for second-generation Laotian girls who were negotiating formal and informal experiences of exclusion. In my respondents' narratives and writings, the terms "home" and "family" were often used to describe their feelings about AYA/APEN staff and the youth program in general. Therefore, I use the notion of home to understand the spaces in which second-generation Laotian girls felt an emotional sense of belonging and a sense of solidarity and identification with fellow group members. I examine feelings of being "at home" among second-generation Laotians in relation to their families, the APEN youth program, the ethnic community, and the nation. This multiscalar focus, and the practices and relationships that help create a sense of belonging or exclusion within these spatial scales, reveal the connections between "homes" in different and overlapping spaces for second-generation Laotians.

The term "home" is invested with contradictory meanings, emotions, experiences, and relationships, and it resonates with multiple associations (Blunt and Varley 2004:3). Feminist and cultural studies scholarship indicates that homes imply different scales and spaces: the private and the public, and from the national to the local community. "Home" or "feeling at home" refers not only to a literal sense of place but also to the imagining of a collectivity, whether it is based on ethnicity, nationality, gender, sexuality, or class (Anthias 2002; Martin and Mohanty 1986). Some feminists have focused on the home as a private domestic sphere but view "home" either as signifying control and imprisonment for women (see, for example, Oakley 1974) or as a space and place both to affirm one's culture and community and to resist racism and prejudice in the larger community (hooks 1990; Brah 1992a; Grewal 1988). In literature concerned with notions of location and dislocation, belonging and displacement, and migration and exile, cultural theorists have been interested in the associations of home with origins, identity, attachment, and settlement, and with its frequent use as a metaphor for nation (Espiritu 2003; Blunt 2005; George 1996). In these writings home represents a way of establishing difference and that which determines who can belong to the nation, whose boundaries are fixed. Rosemary Marangoly George (1996:9) asserts that homes "are built on select inclusions," which are "grounded in a learned (or taught) sense of kinship that is extended to those who are perceived as sharing the same blood, race, class, gender or religion."

These multiple understandings of home challenge the view of home as fixed, bounded, and confined to a location; rather, as Blunt and Varley (2004:3) assert, "geographies of home traverse scales from the domestic to the global in both material and symbolic ways." Drawing on Doreen Massey (1994), who writes that homes are created by external relationships as much as they are by internal relations, I argue that everyday experiences and social relations that influence feelings of home on a domestic scale resonate far beyond the family. Emotions and associations generated in the private sphere are intimately bound up with experiences and relations in the public arena at local and national levels. The operation of multiple relations and differentials of power suggest that homes are not stable; they are always a work in progress. Home not only has to be continually negotiated, but individuals and groups cannot be linked to only one home; rather, power relations differentially situate (Espiritu 2003) individuals and groups with respect to specific collectivities. At the same time, attention to place and space suggests the "historicity of identity" (Dirlik 1999:47), or the idea that ethnic and national identities are associated with specific places and historical moments. This allows for the possibility that homes at multiple scales can coexist; one can be both "Laotian" and "American." Moreover, home at one spatial scale can lead to a sense of agency and possibilities for constructing homes at other spatial scales.

APEN as Home

My respondents' narratives suggest that they saw APEN[1] as a refuge where one is accepted, respected, supported, and nurtured, and as a place and space one can navigate with ease and comfort. During interviews, in journals written during the summer programs, and in evaluations of AYA,[2] almost 42 percent of the young women in the study described APEN as home, as a second family.

When asked what APEN came to mean to her, seventeen-year-old Gabriela, who had been in the program for four years, said:

> It's like a, like a family now . . . I was, like, having problems the first year . . . so I always thought of APEN as, like, an organization, you know, a group of people, you know, there to help me. . . . But like, through the years, I've come to think of APEN more like family. More, I guess, more like a second home that, you know that . . . like, I have, you know, away from home, you know, when I come, when I need it or whatever.

For Gabriela, the staff members at APEN cared for her, guided her, and were there for her when she needed them. Fourteen-year-old Lai, a shy member of Group 3 who also participated in her church youth group, thanked APEN "for giving me a comfortable second home!" in her end-of-summer 1998 evaluation, a year after she had joined the program. Gain, of Group 2, thought of APEN as family because "it's like a part of my life now." Gain, who had been in the program for three years, felt close to everybody in APEN and able to "talk to anybody," the counselors and other girls alike. Eight months after she joined the program, I interviewed Angela, of Group 4, who also described APEN as "like my next home" because she felt comfortable talking to the counselors if she had any problems. Angela's peer in Group 4, Marn, wrote this message at the end of her first summer to the following year's new recruits into the APEN program: "You will never be by yourself. You will always have someone by your side to trust." Both thirteen-year-old Angela and fourteen-year-old Marn had joined AYA after hearing about it from older sisters or friends, and they had settled in quickly, not only accepting the expectations AYA staff set for them but also enjoying its benefits as articulated by the older girls.

Another 26 percent of the girls also articulated these themes of trust, support, understanding, dependability, there when you need them, and strong friendships even though they did not specifically describe APEN as a second home or family. These positive emotional feelings extended to both the other girls in the program and the youth organizers at AYA, as I witnessed in August 1998 during a sad and tearful session when Chittraphone, one of the 1.5-generation Laotian youth organizers, announced to Group 3 that she was leaving. Pham wrote in her journal after Chittraphone's announcement: "I tell her things that I could never tell my parents." To other girls she was like an older sister, and they felt as if a close member of their family was leaving them. Many of the girls in

Groups 2 and 3 had grown attached to her during the year that she had worked at AYA.

Not all the girls saw APEN as a second family, however. Two respondents from Group 2, who had been with APEN for three years at the time of the interview, said that while they thought the counselors were supportive, they did not feel able to talk to them. Caryn wrote in her end-of-summer evaluation:

> I feel kinda uncomfortable sharing my problems with the counselors or the other AYA staff because I don't really communicate with them and when I do it's hard for me to talk 'cause I don't know what to say.

Ruby also did not feel she could approach APEN staff with her problems, nor did she feel she could rely on her peers in Group 2. During my time in the field, neither sixteen-year-old Caryn nor fifteen-year-old Ruby was an active or regular member of AYA, and both had more tenuous relationships than other girls with other members of Group 2 and AYA staff. Two members of Group 4 also said that APEN had no special meaning for them. Both left APEN before the end of their first year there.

Nevertheless, the majority of the young women saw APEN as a refuge; they cast APEN as a home, and in so doing, my respondents conveyed both that they are visible and that they feel secure in this space. APEN was a place of safety and comfort in the context of growing up as the daughters of immigrants in urban multiracial neighborhoods. These feelings, emotions, and possibilities of belonging, acceptance, and community were not always present in other spaces that my respondents traversed. Anousone Karncharanwong, a community activist working in Richmond and San Pablo, characterized Laotian young people as being "lost," not fitting into mainstream society or the parents' culture because "it's way too strict" (conversation with Karncharanwong, 23 October 1998). Grace Kong likewise observed that while the young women appeared "so hip" and connected to urban pop culture, they were "totally disconnected from the broader society" in terms of their family and community experiences (interview, 9 October 1998). In Chapter 6 I discussed the often fraught and tense intergenerational and gender relationships within Laotian families in the United States in detail. I suggested that we could interpret teenage motherhood as a way for some second-generation Laotian girls to deal with feelings of alienation and lack of a sense of belonging within their parental families. For several of the young women in the study, family life was unstable and required them to move to another city to live with relatives. Other Laotian young people dealt with the pressures of adaptation by joining gangs and doing "crazy things," according to Anousone (23 October 1998).[3]

The young women experience the pressures of adaptation both within the family and in the wider society, in the everyday encounters that structure their lives in California. Assumptions of "foreignness" and "otherness" were among the meanings of "Asian" that shaped both the informal and formal encounters for second-generation Laotians. School is a setting where the Laotian girls in this study spent significant amounts of time. It is in this setting that peers frequently questioned their ties and relationship to U.S. society and culture. Through archival research at AYA, I discovered that second-generation Laotians experienced racial name-calling such as "rice," that Laotian languages and food were disrespected, and that peers perceived Laotians as unclean. A skit created and performed at the 1998 summer retreat portrayed some of these practices of exclusion at school:

> The first scene is a classroom full of students and one teacher. The teacher asks who has done their homework. Several people raise their hands, and the teacher asks two of the students to read their essays. The first is a Laotian student who has written about going to her cousin's house for a ceremony. As she is reading this, another student shouts, "They probably eat dogs." In the next scene the Laotian student goes home and tells her parents what happened. Her father tells her to ignore that person. The student says that she can't and writes an essay about stereotyping and being proud of who she is.

All these stereotypes denote Laotians as "foreign," as "other," yet this skit ends on a positive note, reflecting the many discussions on Laotian history and culture and affirmation of ethnicity that the young women experienced in AYA and APEN. Grace, the youth program coordinator, reported that when the young women asked for clarifications on a school assignment or activity, teachers often responded with, "What's your problem, don't you understand English?" This is perhaps surprising since the majority of my respondents were performing well at school, and none of them mentioned such experiences to me. However, if such retorts were prevalent, they mark Laotian students, many of whom were born in the United States, as perpetual foreigners (Tuan 1998).

Other Laotian adults also observed that schools do not meet the needs of many Laotian students.[4] Anousone pointed to a cultural gap between teachers and second-generation Laotians, which often leads to the racialization of young Laotians as "at risk" in Contra Costa County:

> One of the main problems with the kids is that a lot cut school because they don't like teachers, or they can't understand class and teachers are not patient enough, so they cut class and do poorly, which makes the teachers even more inconsiderate. Counselors at school are also very inconsiderate; all they do is discipline and give class schedules. They do not take time to understand what's happened at home, why they are late. (Conversation with Anousone Karncharanwong, 23 October 1998)

Disillusionment with school and the curtailment of opportunities when teachers and officials perceive them as "at risk" may in part explain juvenile delinquency and gang-related activity among Southeast Asian youth (Walker-Moffat 1995; Um 2003; Lee 2005). These experiences were particularly common for male friends of my respondents. As Maya recounted in an interview, her male friends often told her there was not any point in working hard and going to school because the teachers did not care about them. All the young women knew of Laotian peers who were involved in gangs, and many had experienced the effects of gang violence when brothers or friends were shot or incarcerated.

Like other students of color, Laotian students also experienced marginalization and invisibility at school.[5] Dean Saechao, of Richmond High School, noted that Laotian students often complained about the lack of Laotian history and culture in the curriculum. They also preferred to learn Mien rather than Spanish as a second language since English was already their second language (conversation with Dean Saechao, 29 April 1999).[6] As the only Laotian faculty at Richmond High at the time of the study, Dean Saechao assumed the burden to help Laotian students understand their community's history and place in U.S. society. It is in the context of feelings and experiences of displacement, exclusion, and invisibility within the family and at school that the APEN youth program initially became important for adolescent Laotian girls at a critical point in their lives. Within APEN, and specifically AYA, my respondents did not experience patriarchal oppression and racial marginalization but rather enjoyed intimacy, comfort, positive relationships, and a sense of location. What were the specific practices and relationships that helped to constitute APEN as home?

Creating APEN as Home

For many of my respondents, APEN was a second family because the counselors there and the peer counseling sessions that were part of the program provided a "safe" space where they could share feelings, discuss problems, and get advice from other teens. The peer counseling sessions were particularly precious because it provided time for the girls to reflect and express their feelings and experiences without the responsibilities of home or school. As Blia stated, "It gives a chance to, like, just tell how our life is going because that was the only time we got to spend with each other." She remembered these sessions as "pretty good because we all had, like, stress from school and from family and stuff and we got to RC [reevaluation counseling[7]], and we got to, like, you know, take it off our chest and stuff." Maya, a Group 3 member, valued these sessions because since it was all girls, "we get to talk about anything, you know, even our periods and all that stuff."

AYA provided both structured and informal opportunities to talk about personal, emotional, and other issues particularly important to young women at the adolescent stage of life. As Miya noted, "We're trying to have a program that people who don't have perfect lives can be a part of." Staff viewed the peer counseling sessions and provision of support as an avenue to ensure that the young women "really thrive and grow as leaders and to be organizers" (interview, 29 September 1998). In addition to the opportunity for addressing personal issues, these spaces were "safe" because the interactions were confined to 1.5-generation Laotian women youth organizers, second-generation Laotian girls, and young Asian American women activists. Fifteen-year-old Cept, of Group 2, who was born in the United States, stated that while she was close to her mom and talked to her, "it's nothing like what I talk to my best friend and my APEN counselors." For Sarah, APEN was like a family because "it's like you say whatever you want and they respect what you're saying," experiences that she did not have in other social spaces in her life.

Moreover, the staff was always available when the young women needed emotional support or someone to talk to. According to Sarah, "they [the AYA staff] are always there, no matter what. I think they are always there. And, like, they are so tripped [busy], but they are still looking out for you." Seng noted:

Like every time we go there, like, they're always smiling, they're always, if you're, like, they know that you're sad or whatever they always ask you and stuff. And they're always, like, willing to take out their time and, you know, spend it with you and help you and stuff.

However, this emotional sense of belonging was built on select inclusions and exclusions (George 1996:2). While all the girls in the study would have joined AYA even if it had been open to girls of all races and ethnicities, and in fact some would have preferred that, for many of the girls it was important that APEN was a place and space for just Laotians and just girls.[8] Gain, of Group 2, said, with conviction. "I like it a lot, like, because there's girls, all different [in terms of personality] girls, and we can, like, communicate with each other better." Lon, of Group 1, commented, "There's a kind of closeness between women" that would not have occurred if young Laotian men had also been part of the program. She remarked that she didn't think "the outcome would have turned out as good either," nor would "the girls would be as into and as committed to the program" if boys had been involved in APEN.

Anousone Karncharanwong, quoted earlier, highlighted another selection criterion. She noted that while APEN "is excellent for girls who are college-bound," it should recruit more at-risk girls, who are "better" for the APEN program since they analyze the "system" in a way that college-bound girls do not (23 October 1998). This community activist was perhaps suggesting that at-risk girls might become more committed community activists if they had access to APEN's training and resources, but she also may have been referring to the class backgrounds of the APEN and AYA staff. As I noted in Chapter 5, most of my respondents were performing well at school and aspired to attend college. However, they also came from very low-income families and were surrounded by vulnerabilities. They all had siblings or friends who were engaging in at-risk behaviors such as involvement in gangs or teenage motherhood, and so we cannot assume that they were immune to such behaviors or that they would be able to acquire a higher education. In Chapter 6 we saw that Tsiet, of Group 3, who aspired to become a lawyer or a police officer at the time of my interview with her, had become a teen mother a year later. Moreover, they and their families, like other Laotian families in Contra Costa County, also suffer the inequities of class and race in the United States.

In these safe spaces, which were not available in any other arena of their lives, the young women learned to navigate the competing gender ideologies to which they are exposed and to develop strategies to challenge racism and alienation in schools and neighborhoods. However, perhaps what was more important for second-generation Laotian girls was that the AYA staff understood the demands of growing up in America. In my interview with seventeen-year-old Gabriela, she described her time at high school as the "four toughest years" she had ever had. She stated that if it had not been for APEN/AYA, she would not have made it. The staff

> know what it's like to grow up, you know, just in America, they know all those stuff, you know. And they're the ones who, like, tell you about it, you know, like the pressure of it and everything, you know.

Gabriela thought of APEN as family because

> I think it's the nourishment that I need, you know, like not in the sense that inner strength, but also like intelligence as well, you know. The information, the communication, and what you learn as well. I mean at home, like, we get nourishment and stuff, you know, like from my mom and stuff, but it's not, like, the same, you know, it's different, you know. It's very different when it's based at home and you learn anything that you just know. 'Cause at home, half the time my mom doesn't even understand what I'm doing, you know. And at APEN, like I do something and they'll be, like, oh okay, you know. Like they get it, you know. And at home I'm like, I sit there and just explain it over and over again, you know, to my mom 'cause she questions that, she doesn't know.

Gabriela referred to the knowledge about community issues that the girls learned through APEN, as well as the organizing and communication skills. Nevertheless, as a young woman, what was more important to her about APEN was that the staff understood her actions and opinions within the context of the demands and pressures of growing up in America, unlike her mother.

APEN was home, a safe space where second-generation Laotian girls had a sense of location and inclusion, also because they could acknowledge their multiple subjectivities. They could be both Laotian and American. When I asked my respondents what identity they feel most while at APEN, to my surprise they said that at APEN they feel "everything," or as fifteen-year-old Pham said, "Fifty-fifty." At APEN the staff would not judge them for such a mundane practice as eating with their hands or for expressing their opinions. As sixteen-year-old Cuo said:

I feel both like Laotian and American 'cause the things that we are learning and stuff is towards the American side. It's like we are learning how to, like, do campaigns and whatever, and how to, like, public speak and stuff. And Laotian because, like, we are all Laotian, and, like, when we eat or something, we share food and we use our hands.

APEN was a space where second-generation Laotians could practice specific cultural practices freely. Leah, of Group 2, commented that APEN allowed her to be Laotian: "I am surrounded by Laotian girls, and sometimes we speak our own language. It's nice to share that with young girls our age." At APEN the cultural practices of Laotians were not ridiculed or judged as alien and "other"; rather, the young women were encouraged to value their cultural heritage. In these different ways the young women could fully express Laotian cultural difference in the United States. But APEN also represents a mode of incorporation into America, and the specific activities and experiences that my respondents encountered socialized them into American political cultures and systems. Fifteen-year-old Gain described the sense of efficacy and of feeling "more in control, helping your community" when working on campaigns or protesting initiatives such as Proposition 187 as "American stuff." Sarah pointed out that "in Laos we don't do stuff like this . . . they don't organize the community . . . like, we don't have officers, we don't sit here in meetings," but "just go in the house and talk." Thus she defined "American" as learning to become political subjects, taking control, and working to improve material conditions for the community.

Sarah added two other characteristics to an "American" identity when she described the moments that she felt American:

I mean, once I got, when I'm around the girls, I don't know what I felt. But once I am around the staff and, like, working, I feel like too Americanized. Everything has to go right, duh duh duh duh [in order and efficiently]. Everyone's competing with each other.

During their final summer Sarah and the other five members of Group 1 had taken on more responsible roles at APEN and had worked as paid interns in the capacity of counselors or organizers, as noted in Chapter 6. Sarah had worked as a counselor, and when she was around the other APEN staff, she felt she had to be more formal, organized, and efficient, even competitive, all qualities that denoted Americanization to her. Seng, who had worked as a counselor that summer as well, also demarcated when she felt American and when she felt Laotian:

Well, it's like the whole, just the whole idea, like, you know, of being a counselor or whatever is, makes me feel more, like, American. But then, like, when you are actually in the group, because, like, they [the other girls in the program] are all Laotian and stuff, makes me feel more, you know, culture and stuff.

For Seng, when she was a counselor she was being American because "it was a new experience," which "you wouldn't get if you were over there in Thailand." But when she was just a participant in the youth project and "hanging out" with the other girls, she felt more Laotian.

The narratives of second-generation Laotian girls and young women reveal their marginal position within the Laotian family and community, and within the dominant society. It is in this context that APEN becomes home, a second family. AYA staff members act as "authentic carers" (Valenzuela 1999) who are critical to the lives of these young women. Through the multidimensional program activities and support systems, the young women are able to create "a comfort zone," as Gabriela described APEN, and an emotional sense of belonging and location. APEN enables the girls to interpret, understand, and navigate the different cultural worlds they encounter, and it nurtures a sense of efficacy. In these ways, not only does APEN allow these young women to acknowledge their complex multiple subjectivities, but as one girl put it, "They are teaching us how to survive."

The Fragility of APEN as Home

The feeling of being at home or a sense of belonging in a space or place is fragile, however, and open to disruption; constant work is required to maintain it as home. Two episodes that occurred while I was in the field indicate that the notion of APEN as home was not absolute, with any fixity or singular meaning or understanding. The rules and requirements, the "passport" (Sagar 1997:237) to involvement and participation in AYA, changed, and with that, the feeling of security and safety diminished.

In September 1997 the particularity of the structural relations at APEN changed in a way that induced discomfort, insecurity, and the possibility of "homelessness" (Sagar 1997:237). The staff decided to shift from what it called "youth programming" to "youth organizing" (Peggy Saika, interview, 21 October 1998). The goal was to build the Laotian Organizing Project by recruiting and developing girls as leaders, as well as to use the leadership of those in the youth program to do actual base-building work in the community. The decision to shift to youth organizing reflected a desire to harness the energy of the girls as well as the realization that no other group in the Laotian community was in a position to build LOP. The implementation of this strategy had consequences both for the type of program activities in which the girls would primarily participate and for the expectations for each girl. While the staff retained the peer support groups, they decided to focus the school-year and summer program activities on training for community organizing and to conduct actual campaigns and organizing activities on specific issues.

Expectations for each girl also changed. Some AYA staff believed that in order to develop leadership among the young women, AYA had to require a firm commitment to the group from the girls throughout the year. In addition to attending meetings and planning events, there were many opportunities during the school year for the girls to participate in field trips, interact with other youth groups, or talk to people about APEN's and AYA's work and about their experiences in AYA. The staff saw these opportunities as ways to develop communication and organization skills among the girls. Thus they decided to tighten requirements for attendance and participation in AYA during the school year and make meetings more focused and structured.

The focus on structure, regular and active participation, and visible leadership development among *all* the young women during the school year signaled not only a shift in goals and strategies but also changes in the resources available to run the youth program. Beginning in the 1997–1998 school year, there were only two staff members, Grace and Chittraphone, working with twenty-two girls, compared with higher staff-youth ratios in previous years. More favorable ratios in the early years of the youth program had allowed the staff to convey to the girls that the staff was not there just to teach the organizing skills or writing skills, but "we're here because we really care about you," as AYA staff member Ming recounted (interview, 12 October 1998). This comment suggests that while power differentials between adults and young people in AYA were still prevalent, they were perhaps significantly reduced and the young women felt safe and secure within AYA. However, at the time of the study, both Ming and Miya expressed concern that the ability of staff to develop deep relations with the young women, to act as authentic carers (Valenzuela 1999), and to help the young women address their immediate needs, as well as carry out the leadership development goals of the program, would become increasingly difficult as more girls joined the program and staff capacity decreased.

In the eyes of my respondents, these assessments and expectations signaled a change in the norms of the program; it was no longer voluntary. They had to attend a specified number of individual group meetings and whole group meetings, as well as the spring retreat, to earn the privilege of the paid summer program. When I interviewed the young women at the end of 1998 and early in 1999, these changes in the program requirements were still weighing on the minds of girls in Groups 1, 2, and 3, who were most affected. A few of the girls who were active participants, such as Fiey and Seng, were nonchalant about the requirements. Fiey asserted: "For the people who, like, who don't come a lot, I think it was a good idea for them to do that. 'Cause, you know, most people have to come, 'cause they signed up for it." Seng perceived these requirements as a way to winnow out "the people who really wanted to be there, you know, to like, you know, show up and stuff," from the girls "who didn't really want to be there." But several other girls, who themselves attended regularly and participated fully, noted that the changes had generated resentment. Sarah, of Group 1, recounted that many members of her group as well as all the girls in Group 2 felt that the expectations from Grace and Chittraphone were unreasonable:

I'm going to say it; I know a lot of people want to say it. There is problems, the expectations are too hard, they get so much stuff to do, they expect just too much from, like, and we're, like, you know, we need to have, like, our time off too, you know.

While many of the girls understood the rationale behind these new requirements, others still questioned why participation was mandatory, as Tracy, of Group 3, recounted: "Why are they forcing us, you know? Like, why are they becoming so strict?" Pham, also of Group 3, said, "I didn't think that was necessary to make us, to make us feel obligated to go to the meetings, you know." Cuo, of Group 2, understood why "they had to, like, lay down something" but also believed that "it [AYA] is, like, you know, kind of the program where they don't kick us out, we kick ourselves out."

The resentment and resistance that the shift generated, and in particular Cuo's comment, suggest that before this moment there were minimal power differentials between staff and the girls. The young Laotian women had been made to feel both valued and "important . . . involved in everything [in all of APEN's community organizing work]," according to Grace (interview, 9 October 1998). For the girls, the change signaled the reintroduction of adult authority and a new regime, one that was formal, rule-oriented, and tightly structured. The conditions, the "passports," for belonging to AYA had altered, and that raised the possibility of "homelessness" for some. Fifteen-year-old Biet, of Group 2, recalled that Grace had imposed restrictions on her, and if she did not meet the requirements, she was "going to be kicked out." Biet was angry about this possibility because, "like, I've been at APEN longer than her [Grace]." Biet was invoking the notion of family here. She believed that she had seniority based on her length of time at APEN and was suggesting that Grace, a junior in this case, had no right to challenge her participation. Yet Biet, along with Ruby and Caryn, had not been an active or regular participant in AYA and often came for social reasons rather than taking part in the leadership development and peer counseling activities.

The changes in the rules and mechanisms of inclusion that occurred in early 1998 represented a departure from unconditional belonging in APEN, which heretofore had not required members to satisfy obligations and responsibilities. These changes altered power relations between the staff and the young women, with the effect that my respondents no longer felt that they could influence the AYA program in ways they had done in previous years. Perhaps because of the strong resistance to these changes from the young women, and realization among the staff that an emotional sense of belonging and location within the youth program was in danger of dissipating, the formal rules and requirements were abandoned in the subsequent school year (1998–1999).

The conditions for belonging also changed for the first group of young women who "graduated" from the program in June 1999, at the end of their senior year at school. While they were still welcomed and the staff was available to talk with them and advise them, the opportunities they had over their four years were no longer automatically available to them. Their relationship with APEN and its staff was no longer informal and certain. Rather than the flexible peer relationships they had enjoyed previously, and which had created a secure and trusting atmosphere, their relationship had become structured and rigid. APEN had represented a place of safety and security for the young women in Group 1, who had enjoyed close, positive relationships with APEN and AYA staff. But now that they had "graduated" from the program, they felt abandoned, no longer valued as central to APEN's organizing work; there was the fear of loss of a second family.

These shifts and turns reflected an attempt to address the practical concerns of resources and staff availability and the desire of some staff to reorient the conditions for membership in AYA so that they more directly met APEN's goals of changing the leadership structure of the Laotian community. This strategy led to a more formal and structured program, and in the process the strength of emotional ties and bonds diminished for some girls, and the young women who had been part of Group 1 were set adrift. These reactions and feelings among the teens suggest that for those on the margins, the conditions of feeling "at home" are not stable; they require constant production and negotiation if second-generation Laotian women are to maintain self-confidence and a sense of personal and collective efficacy.

The Creation of a Collective Laotian Identity

Despite the fragility of APEN as home, for the most part the youth program represented a place and space where second-generation Laotian women could overcome the alienation and exclusion experienced in other arenas of their lives, and nurture affective ties with each other and with the Asian American and 1.5-generation Laotian staff. I argue that this emotional sense of belonging acted as a springboard for consolidation of a home within the broader Laotian community and a sense of feeling at home in the place where the young women resided. In Chapter 6 I showed that ethno-national identities were important to the young women in this book. Here I discuss the reinforcement of the symbolic boundaries of a collective Laotian identity, as opposed to a sub-ethnic Laotian identity, and the cultivation of an identificatory sense of belonging to the Laotian community among second-generation Laotian girls.

My respondents had plenty of informal opportunities to develop friendships with other second-generation Laotians living in Richmond and San Pablo. All but four of the young women said they "kick it" with Laotian friends and cousins outside school. Even those four spent time with Laotians but also had Latino and African American friends. And in school half my respondents mainly spent free time with Laotians, while the other half spent time with Laotians, other Asians, Latinos, and African Americans. However, the intensive summer program, the end-of-summer graduations, and semiannual retreats that were part of the youth initiative, as well as the meetings throughout the school year, provided a more formal environment in which the specific goal was to nurture bonds among Laotian girls from all the sub-ethnic groups living in west Contra Costa County. During interviews I asked the girls, "What has been the most memorable moment at APEN so far?" Fourteen mentioned the retreats without any hesitation. Sarah's comments capture the reasons why the retreats made an impression on at least half my respondents:

> **SARAH:** I think all the retreats that we've had. Some of them can be successful; some of them can't, you know. And it's just that that's when everyone hangs out. Mostly we don't; they talk about different issues during the day, and you know how, you know how it is at the retreat, during the day it's all different issues, but then in the afternoon and stuff you spend doing games and things. So that's what sticks out for me.
> **BINDI:** At the retreat you have the time.
> **SARAH:** Yeah, now at the retreat it's, like, where you hang out with other people, so that's what sticks out mostly, the retreat.

Other girls mentioned that the retreats were a chance to get away from their everyday urban environments. Lily remembered her first retreat in the following way:

> We saw a waterfall, we went hiking. And we got to, like, 'cause we were with the first group, we got to know them. We were in teams . . . with different people. And after that, I don't know, everybody just cling together.

While the retreats were a mix of minivacation and summer camp, they overwhelmingly made an impression because they provided space and time for the girls to develop relations with each other as well as with the staff. Ten teens mentioned that the end-of-summer graduations were most memorable for them. The planning for the graduation involved the girls working in their individual cohorts as well as together with all the groups to create presentations, performances, skits, speeches, and so on to show family, friends, and community members what they had learned during the summer. For some girls, the graduations provided an opportunity to overcome their fears of public speaking as well as to learn a variety of other skills. But the graduations were also memorable because, as Maya said, "Everybody was in it." For Seng, the graduations were

> really fun because then we all come together in, you know, 'cause, like, during the summer we do our own individual thing in our own individual groups. Then at the end, we all come together, and even though we haven't, like, been together for that long, you know, we still perform together and put our feelings aside and, you know, just do what we need to do.

It was a time to share in the camaraderie developed during the summer, the school year, and at the retreats. But more than that, ethnic institutions such as

APEN are important because they provide a setting for Asian Pacific Americans to establish social ties and to discuss their common problems and experiences; in so doing, they have an opportunity to develop a racial/ethnic consciousness out of their shared history of discrimination (Espiritu 1992). In addition to providing a safe physical space, free of drugs and violence,[9] AYA created an institutional space within which the teens could understand their common experiences as young Laotian women, of various ethnic affiliations, growing up in immigrant Laotian families in the U.S., and where they could form a cohesive interpersonal network as well as mobilize the collective power of Laotians.

In story after story in the newspaper the repeated theme was one of Laotians remaining invisible, lacking representation, and not having their needs met (see Lee 1998; Lochner 1997; Sandosham 1999). Laotians lacked visibility and voice even at federal, state, and local levels of government. For example, Tom Lochner (1997) noted that San Pablo was the "most Hispanic and Laotian city in Contra Costa County," judging by the number of grocery stores and restaurants along the city's main streets. In fact, in the late 1990s San Pablo was 27 percent Hispanic, 17 percent Asian, 21 percent black, and 35 percent white, according to Lochner, yet there were no Latinos or Asians on the San Pablo city council, which was four-fifths white. Inh Sooksampan, of Lao Family Community Development, Inc., which provides social-service, crime-victim, and employment referrals and counseling to Laotians from San Pablo and neighboring cities, remarked that he didn't "have any direct contact to the city [of San Pablo]" (quoted in Lochner 1997).[10] Through APEN, second-generation Laotian women were involved in many different efforts to make the needs of Laotians visible and to gain access to resources to meet these needs. For example, in 1996, the year before I entered the field, two of my respondents accompanied APEN staff to urge California's senators to vote no on the Personal Responsibility and Work Opportunity Act. This bill made all immigrants, including permanent resident aliens, ineligible for Medicaid (if states choose to exclude them) and food stamps, and cut Supplemental Security Income (SSI) for elderly, blind, and disabled immigrants.

In Chapter 4 we learned about another opportunity to put Laotians on the "local" map when an accident at the Chevron refinery in Contra Costa County released sulfuric gas into the atmosphere on 25 March 1999. This instance of environmental injustice presented APEN an opportunity to mobilize the Laotian community and campaign for a multilingual phone alert system in Contra Costa County. Throughout the campaign diverse strands of the Laotian community, including second-generation girls, worked together to voice the needs and concerns of the Laotian community. I believe my respondents' desire and willingness to work across generations and ethnic affiliations in this campaign stemmed from two sources: their own experiences of the effects of the accident and the ongoing effort by APEN staff to inform the Laotian teenagers about the environmental hazards in their community.

The skills and knowledge that second-generation Laotian girls acquired through AYA allowed them to understand the needs of the community and give voice to them. More importantly, the shared experiences of structural oppression, together with the perspectives and relationships nurtured by the APEN staff, generated solidarity between different generations of Laotians as well as Laotians of various sub-ethnic groups. As seventeen-year-old Gabriela noted, a key aspect of APEN's youth program that she liked was

> when we really go out to the community and do work. You know, like, talk to community members, you know. And how they respond to us and how they listen. It's what I really like . . . that attention that we get. You know, also the attention that we can give them.

Thus the multipronged youth program not only enabled the young women to create a sense of emotional belonging in APEN but also created a space where adults took them seriously and where they had a role in actively working for social change in their community. As Miya remarked to the young women during the summer 1998 AYA retreat, "You all are part of this trip that we are on. Our goal is to build a healthy, strong, unified, powerful Laotian community."

Within AYA a range of activities allowed my respondents to explore and affirm valued aspects of Laotian culture and history, generating an identificatory sense of belonging to the Laotian community. Discussions and writing on Laotian culture and identity enabled my respondents to explore who they were as second-generation Laotians. For example, the Oral History Project, which Group 2 carried out in the summer of 1998, provided an opportunity for the girls to build an understanding of both their family's history and the experiences of other Laotian ethnic groups. At the end of the summer 1998 program, Cept wrote in her evaluation, "It helped me learn more about my mom's life in Laos." In her evaluation Gain noted that "this was the most valuable activity because I learned more about other people's experiences in Laos." Most of the teens had little knowledge of their family history, and for many parents and grandparents it was difficult to talk about the painful period of their lives in Laos, escape from Laos, and life in refugee camps in Thailand. The Oral History Project was a vehicle through which parents could begin to share aspects of their history and through which the young women gained an interest in and a better understanding of the conditions that brought their parents and grandparents to the United States and their struggles in the new homeland.

While I was in the field, Group 3 conducted a writing project for the 1997–1998 school year for which each member had to select and write on three essay topics. Fourteen-year-old Alison wrote an essay titled "Culture & Family," in which she described how hard it was to live in multiple cultural worlds but also how hard it was "living in a world where you feel you are not wanted." Alison referred to name-calling and other exclusionary practices that she experienced because of her culture and who she was. She wrote, "Everyday I think of why we get disrespected because of our culture." Over time she realized "how important my culture means to me. My culture represents who I am. My culture also is my pride." Through this writing project Alison, a shy but studious young woman who aspired to be a pediatrician, was able to reflect on her experiences of exclusion and displacement in the larger society and identify positively as a Laotian despite the fraught and tense gender and generational relationships within Laotian families described in Chapter 6.

Activities such as the Oral History Project and the writing project emphasized cultural similarities, common histories, and similar fates of being categorized as Laotians, thus creating ties between the different Laotian ethnic groups. Such activities affirmed aspects of Laotian culture that were disallowed in the dominant culture. Additionally, opportunities to represent Laotians in the public arena and to struggle for social rights nurtured a collective Laotian identity with a concomitant sense of groupness and solidarity among the second-generation Laotians in this book. APEN fostered sharper symbolic boundaries around the Laotian community and my respondents' membership in that community, despite the acute alienation that many experienced in their natal families, their decreasing command of Laotian languages, and the devaluation of specific cultural practices and norms, as I discussed in Chapter 6. In the context of AYA/LOP, the sub-ethnic Laotian identities—Lao, Mien, Hmong, Khmu, Lue—were subordinated to the collective Laotian identity. In this sense, a collective Laotian ethnic identity became socially and politically relevant not simply because state classificatory systems imposed this category but because it was actively constructed through struggle and resistance. In view of the exclusion, marginalization, and invisibility that Laotians experienced in the larger society, APEN served as a space and place where dignity and integrity could be restored and confidence in a new homeland could be fostered. The alternative arena of APEN nurtured a meaningful and empowering construction of the Laotian community in the United States, and conveyed the message that Laotians are both visible and belong. However, the danger is that it also served to reinforce the distinctions between Laotians and other racial groups in Contra Costa County. Perhaps at that point in Laotian history in the United States, it made sense to defend a politics of location (Crenshaw 1995:375) in order to make Laotians visible and assert claims on the nation for which they fought.

Asserting Cultural Difference and Claiming Membership in the Nation

Common perceptions of the nation assume that a natural link exists between people and places, and that people with the same blood, race, or religion belong to clearly demarcated, bounded territories, which shape their distinctive cultural identities (George 1996; Espiritu 2003). The young women's informal and formal encounters, discussed earlier, as well as the experiences of other Asian Pacific American groups, whether recent immigrant communities or those several generations old, suggest that these groups are perceived as alien and foreign and are still considered outside America's national imaginary (Tuan 1998; Gotanda 1999;

Ancheta 1998; Kibria 2000; Espiritu 1997; Ong 1996). In other words, the inclusions and exclusions to the nation have been based on particular conceptions of a place—as fixed, singular, and bounded—with a cultural identity based on whiteness and in which racially different others are distanced (Espiritu 2003:13). Massey (1994) points out that a particular set of social relations, which interact at a particular location, shape the identity of a space as a "place":

> The singularity of any individual place is formed in part out of the specificity of the interactions which occur at that location (nowhere else does this precise mixture occur) and in part out of the fact that the meeting of those social relations at that location (their partly happenstance juxtaposition) will in turn produce new social effects. (Massey 1994:168)

With this formulation of space, "the identity of any place, including the place called home, is in one sense forever open to contestation" (Massey 1994:169), and feeling at home at one scale can create a sense of agency and efficacy in constructing home at other scales. As we saw in previous chapters, the young women defined APEN as an "American" space; yet as we have seen in this chapter, APEN was also a place of relative safety and security, a home. This sense of belonging enabled the young women to challenge dominant ideas about who can and cannot belong to the nation and to create a community of resistance (hooks 1990) to dominant images of Laotians in mainstream society. A few years after the welfare reform bill became law, one of the young women felt compelled to write about how welfare had helped her family rebuild their lives in the United States when they first arrived, and about her fears that this support would not be available to other new arrivals. As sixteen-year-old Fam Linh Saechao, a member of AYA, wrote in *Youth Outlook* in 2001, "We didn't come to the United States to get welfare. We came because we had no choice." (Saechao's father and grandfather were killed by land mines while fighting with U.S. forces during the Vietnam War.) For Saechao, democracy meant

> that the government cares about us and represents us. But now I'm confused. It looks like the elected government officials care more about rich people who give money to their campaigns, but those people don't make up most of our society. People like me and my family make up most of this country, yet we don't have a voice. We don't get to tell our side of the story.
>
> My hope is that these politicians hear my story. I hope that they listen with their hearts, and understand that a life preserver is often the only thing that separates life and death. (Saechao 2001)

In fact, Saechao's grandmother, who was not a U.S. citizen, had lost her Supplemental Security Income because of the 1996 welfare reform bill. In this article Saechao underscored the fact that Laotians have no representation in the United States; they are excluded from the nation. Espiritu (2003:47) uses the term "differential inclusion" to refer to the fact that at times some Asian Americans have been forcibly included in the American nation and at other times excluded. Saechao recognized that Laotians and their children experience symbolic and material exclusion despite being differentially *included* when the CIA recruited Laotian men to fight alongside U.S. forces in the Vietnam War. However, here in the United States, Laotian refugees and their children, like Cambodian refugees (Ong 1996), were excluded from the nation and placed closer to African Americans on the bipolar racial model of the United States. The dominant society perceived Laotians as having little economic or cultural capital, and therefore as less desirable, less worthy of becoming Americans than Vietnamese refugees, who came with more human and cultural capital. By telling her family's story and lobbying U.S. politicians, Saechao hoped to influence dominant perceptions of Laotians but also voice the specific needs of the Laotian community in the United States. At the same time, in noting that people like her and her family make up most of the country, Saechao acknowledged the ties that Laotians have to other racially and economically marginalized communities.

At an individual and personal level, the second-generation Laotian women in this book also resisted dominant perceptions of Laotians as forever foreign. When I asked my respondents what they would like others to know about them, Bryanna said:

> That, you know, we are just like any other people, you know. We can do what anybody else can do, you know; we adapt quickly too and I don't know. That's it. Just don't judge us for what we look like 'cause that's not what's inside.

Sarah's response to my question about how they would like a newspaper reporter to write about them was passionate:

> That we are nice. We ain't dirty. First of all, we are not dirty. We may be, like, might not be rich now, but we are not poor. Like everybody thinks that we are poor, we eat dog, we eat cat [*Seng makes an "ugh!" sound*]. That need to get straightened up.

Bryanna and Sarah wanted to erase stereotypes that cast them as "un-American" and wished that the dominant society would perceive them like "anybody else" in the United States. Gabriela, too, wanted a reporter to not just write about "sympathy and stuff, and, you know, like it's all pain and like it's all sad and gloomy and everything," nor write about them as a model minority, "the story that we are so successful, you know, that it's beyond reach. Why can't other immigrants do the same thing, you know?" Gabriela wanted "a combination, a mixture" that portrayed the reality in the Laotian community. Being cast either as refugees or as the model minority projects Laotians as fundamentally opposite to what is American (Kibria 2000).

Even as second-generation Laotian women in this book wanted to maintain cultural difference and identify in ethno-national terms,[11] as I discussed in Chapter 6, they wanted to erase the taint of "otherness" and inassimilability. They wanted to imagine possibilities that other Americans can imagine. They vividly expressed this desire to belong, the yearning for identification and participation in the nation on equal terms, on a "story cloth," a traditional Laotian art form that uses textiles and quilting to document village and family history. Over a period of a year the girls in Groups 1 and 2 created a semiautobiographical story that they embroidered in the center three panels of the story cloth. The story depicted a young Laotian girl growing up in the United States after arriving from a Thai refugee camp following the Vietnam War. The journey ended with the young woman becoming president of the United States. Twenty-three of my thirty-one respondents were born in the United States, so this was a theoretical possibility, leaving aside the race, gender, sexual, and class politics of becoming president. Through the story cloth my respondents were able to imagine a more empowering construction of Laotians, a construction that portrayed them as located in the nation that is America.

An indication that Laotians have entered the nation and claimed visibility and a sense of belonging at the local level, if not yet at the national level, was evident at a community event in August 2000 to celebrate the victory on the pilot teacher advisory program and the multilingual emergency warning system. Elderly Laotians, girls in AYA and their friends, some parents, and staff were in attendance as well as assorted other guests, including a member of Contra Costa County's Board of Supervisors. This supervisor was going to present an award to LOP for its work on the multilingual emergency warning system. He was sitting at the front of the room and, on recognizing fourteen-year-old Bryanna standing at the back of the room, walked over to shake her hand. He asked her how she was, and Bryanna shyly replied, "Fine." Later, when I commented to Bryanna how impressive it was that he had recognized her and had come up to say hello, she shrugged it off and noted that she had met him a few times. Bryanna had been active in both campaigns at LOP and had participated in meetings with this supervisor either as a translator for elderly Laotians or as a representative of Laotian girls in AYA.

Conclusion

The experiences of second-generation Laotian girls in this book have demonstrated that for those of us on the margins, home is that which we cannot not want, to reiterate Kondo's argument. We cannot dismiss the desire or yearning for emotional attachments to important social bonds and ties, and the role these attachments play in creating community and a sense of belonging. Given the multilayered and cross-cutting individual and collective identities of second-generation Laotian women, the location of belonging, or home, is not fixed, bounded, and stable; rather, it is contingent and immanent, and requires ongoing negotiation and construction. This chapter has illustrated the relation between embodied subjectivity, place, and belonging. For second-generation Laotian women, it was their experiences of exclusion and invisibility in the United States and marginalization within the family and community that provided a backdrop for their self-definition and identity. And it is against this backdrop that we can understand APEN and its youth program as a creative response to the specific circumstances and positioning of second-generation Laotians in the United States. If second-generation Laotians are to actively participate in achieving social change for the community, social justice organizations must also address the teenagers' experiences of growing up in immigrant families and in urban multicultural environments.

While second-generation Laotian women experienced exclusion in the larger society and marginalization in the Laotian community, their placement within APEN, at specific moments, was secure. From this solid ground, even if temporarily so, they developed intimate and trusting personal ties and a strong emotional sense of belonging. These feelings of community and support allowed second-generation Laotians to resist the alienating demands of complete assimilation into American culture and to negotiate practices that oppress them as young women. APEN was thus a fertile though fraught site from which to create home at various scales. APEN served as a trusted space where the young women were able to generate meaningful and empowering constructions of Laotians in the United States. Through political engagement, second-generation Laotian women were able to create an identificatory sense of belonging to a collective Laotian identity. This Laotian ethnic identity illustrates the "historicity of identity" (Dirlik 1999); it became socially and politically relevant within the context of the needs and interests of the Laotian community in the late-1990s United States. The individual and collective sense of efficacy and agency thus generated enabled the young women to assert difference as well as construct a different claim to be an American. Thus homes, both material and symbolic, can coexist at different scales and remain connected through social practices and power relations.

Placement and visibility in APEN was a way to express placement and belonging in the nation, at the local level, in west Contra Costa County, and by extension in the United States, rather than remaining forever excluded and invisible. The two meanings of home—as a private space and laden with affective ties, and in its broader signification as nation—are thus closely intertwined. Staking out moral claims as racial and economic minorities and challenging dominant constructions of Laotians enabled Laotian girls to both define Laotian collective identity and community and redefine who can and cannot belong in the nation. In all these ways, they were working to subvert the dominant constructions of Asians and Asian Americans as inassimilable aliens and claim full citizenship. The coexistence of multiple homes thus opposes the linear trajectory of assimilation, integration, and citizenship. More importantly, this chapter has demonstrated that environmental justice organizations working with new immigrant communities must address multiple planes. APEN also represents a cultural project that performs the necessary task of "correcting histories, shaping legacies, creating new cultures, constructing a politics of resistance, and opening spaces for the forcibly excluded," as Espiritu (1997:98) so aptly puts it. Generating bonds to a community space and encouraging emotional attachments to the place in which they live is a key element in facilitating community engagement on a range of environmental and social justice issues and, in the process, fostering a sense of inclusion and belonging in the nation for new immigrants and their children.

8

Becoming "American"

Remaking American National Identity through Environmental Justice Activism

This story of second-generation Laotians in Asian Youth Advocates, a youth leadership development program, focuses on how new immigrants and their children engage with environmental and social justice activism, conceive of citizenship, and create new spaces of citizenship both materially and symbolically at multiple spatial scales. The book shows that immigration is a generative site for shaping what it means to be "American." The unprecedented and massive mobilization of immigrants protesting immigration legislation in spring 2006 highlighted the ongoing struggle for legalization, participation, and citizenship among immigrant groups and their children (Pantoja et al. 2008). These events also drew attention to the politics of belonging, the maintenance and reproduction of boundaries of the community of belonging by dominant political powers, as well as to their contestation and challenge by those considered outside the community of belonging. This case study of second-generation young Laotian women and the spring 2006 protests testify to the continuing debates about the nature of citizenship and national identity in the United States in the late twentieth and early twenty-first centuries.

While political mobilization among immigrants has revealed the contradiction between the liberal ideology of universal citizenship and the collective boundaries of race, nationality, gender, and class that defines substantive citizenship, or a sense of belonging, participation, and equal access to rights and opportunities, for the most part scholarly research on the new second generation has remained within an assimilationist paradigm. Researchers have argued that it is important to understand the prospects for socioeconomic integration for the new second generation because, in the next fifty years, the culture and quality of life in America will be shaped by the experiences of today's children of immigrants. Echoing this concern, Portes and Rumbaut (2001:xvii) assert: "Whether this new ethnic mosaic reinvigorates the nation or catalyzes a quantum leap in its social problems depends on the forms of social and economic adaptation experienced by this still young population." However, what this concern fails to capture is that even when new immigrants and their children achieve socioeconomic mobility, social citizenship continues to elude them. A strict focus on socioeconomic adaptation in which "race" is simply a matter of color or ethnic differences, and racism is seen as merely the consequence of individual prejudices, ignores the question of the potential for symbolic belonging in the nation for new immigrants and their children.

The main argument I make in this book is that there is another story to be told—what the experiences of adaptation and incorporation among the new second generation reveal about contemporary understandings of national identity and membership in the nation, and how these play a role in the incorporation of immigrants and their children and in the formulation of their claims for citizenship and belonging. Such a focus illuminates the distinction between formal and substantive citizenship (Glenn 2004). I find that the racial positioning of new immigrants in the United States, as well as laws, policies, and programs implemented in a range of institutional and public arenas such as schools, social service providers, local and state agencies, employers, and churches, influences their economic, social, and cultural incorporation. Through such daily encounters they undergo a process of sociopolitical incorporation, becoming subjects of dominant rules, norms, values, and systems. This ethnographic case study of second-generation Laotian girls participating in Asian Youth Advocates focuses attention on the role that actors such as social justice organizations play in the dynamic of immigrant sociopolitical incorporation. It considers how interactions structured through a social justice organization help to form their political and social identities and shape their ideas about what it means to be an "American," as well as what resources they acquire to make claims at local, state, and national levels. I discover that in order to successfully empower and mobilize Laotians against the environmental and social injustices prevalent in their community, APEN had to first focus on political socialization and the lack of political efficacy within the Laotian community in Contra Costa County. In other words, the struggle for ecological justice, environmental rights, and beneficial corporate-community relations had to go hand in hand with developing autonomy and self-determination, along with social movement building, some of the key components enshrined in the Principles of Environmental Justice adopted at the First National People of Color Environmental Leadership Summit, held in October 1991 (Taylor 2000). This was a new immigrant community that lacked structures to mobilize for social change, was linguistically isolated, and continued to have fearful memories of the way politics was conducted under authoritarian and Communist regimes in Laos. Within this context the bilingual second generation played a vital role in generating new social capital and nurturing a sense of individual and collective efficacy to participate in social change. However, if second-generation Laotian women were going to become advocates for their community,

APEN also had to address their experiences of growing up in immigrant families and urban multicultural environments. Thus the APEN staff created a broad, integrated youth program that addressed the multiple goals of leadership development and community organizing as well as issues of adolescence experienced by young Laotian women. The book demonstrates that APEN engaged in the cultural politics of *critical incorporation,* or a set of practices in the cultural political realm that challenged, accommodated, or transformed power relations within civil society and the nation as well as within Laotian families and community. What is revealed is the contradictory impact of contemporary racial politics on the children of immigrants; the ways in which second-generation Laotians negotiate majority-minority, interminority, and gender relations; and the resources they acquire to challenge their simultaneous positioning as immigrants, young people of color, poor, and teenage girls and transform the social world around them. In so doing, this book is one answer to Brulle and Pellow's (2005) call for a dialogue between environmental justice studies and other relevant fields, in this case migration and youth studies within sociology, critical Asian American studies, and feminist studies.

Young Women of Color Forge Social Citizenship

This book has focused on one institutional site, that of a youth initiative within an ethnic identity–based social justice organization, which is representative of the new politics in immigrant communities. It can also be interpreted as a struggle to "'win' a sense of citizenship *from below*" (Mac an Ghaill 1999:98; emphasis in original). Citizenship is generally understood as an adult experience. Rarely do we hear of young people engaged in politics in its widest sense or involved in alliances with other subordinated groups to achieve social transformation. As Henry Giroux (1998:24) observes, young people are restricted from speaking in those arenas where "public conversations shape social policy, and refused the power to make knowledge consequential with respect to their own individual and collective needs." And I would add that this is even more true for Asian American young people, who are often portrayed as the overachieving "model minority," uninterested in, or unwilling to engage in, political activism. The daughters of one of our newest immigrant groups display a wide range of responses to life in poor, multiracial cities. But they can give us the beginnings of a practice and a vision that uses difference as a resource to transform wider frameworks of social justice, rights, and citizenship through political struggle. I do not wish to privilege this institutional space or to suggest a differentiated category of immigrant young people as a source of social change. There is no self-evident equation between social location, knowledge, and identity (Moya 1997). For young people of color, however, the collective context of a social justice organization provides space to interpret individual experiences of oppression or marginalization and construct alternatives to the dominant representations of young people as "at risk" (Kelly 2000), drawing on their wider social environments and emphasizing collective solidarity. Immigrant young people and young people of color can struggle for an expanded notion of citizenship that encompasses both adults and young people, and for a more inclusive nation.

My findings also demonstrate that social rights are racialized, thus prompting a reevaluation of the concept of citizenship. Ong (2003:7) reminds us that American notions of the ideal citizen are rooted in the bourgeois individual and reflected in both official programs and unofficial practices that participate in subject making. The 1996 Welfare Reform Act, which was aimed at the long-term unemployed and those relying on public assistance such as Southeast Asian refugees, is one of the most recent manifestations of this ideal citizen, who is self-reliant and economically independent. Through Asian Youth Advocates, APEN provided opportunities for second-generation Laotians to lobby local politicians and remind them that while Laotians were differentially included (Espiritu 2003) during the Vietnam War, they are now not only excluded from the nation but also seen as less desirable and less worthy than others of becoming Americans (Ong 2003). Through such acts second-generation Laotians resisted neoliberal discourses of citizenship. Healthy physical environments, language access to public institutions such as schools and social service agencies for new immigrants, and the availability of high-quality education are also governed by race and ethnicity in the United States. The political implications of these findings point to a reinstatement of the role of the state in ensuring access to social rights for all, at a time when the state is withdrawing from this role and becoming confined to protecting individual rights rather than society in general. The three campaigns that the second-generation young women were involved in—for a multilingual emergency warning system, against the abolition of bilingual education in schools, and for improved academic counseling services in schools—call attention to a larger role for the state, not a smaller one, to ensure social rights in order to create the enabling conditions for new immigrant groups and their children to be full and active members of the nation.

The Durability of Ethnicity in American National Identity

This book also demonstrates that ethnicity is an ongoing durable force in the everyday lives of second-generation Laotian girls, as well as in the formation of group identity, the struggle for a multicultural democracy, and access to social rights. However, in contrast to Jeremy Hein (2006), who argues that the ongoing significance of ethnicity stems from continued immigration, I argue that its durability is due to negotiations at two levels: interactions at the individual level and negotiations of group identities within wider meanings associated with race and nationhood. Like other new Asian immigrants and their children (Kim 2008; Espiritu 2003; Kibria 2002), second-generation Laotians do not wish to abandon their ethnic identity and become absorbed into the white category, and they resist blending into the collective black group. Nor do they wish to assimilate into a more homogenized "Asian" racial grouping that will erase their difference and uniqueness. Ethnic and wider cultural affiliations are important to the construction of individual identities among second-generation Laotian girls. When they self-identify in terms of ethno-national categories, this desire to maintain ethnic distinctiveness is a reaction to racializing processes that group all Asians together as well as an affirmation of their membership in the Laotian community.

This study has also demonstrated, however, that the meanings attached to particular ethnic identities are subject to contestation and change. Particularistic self-understandings and multiple subjectivities produced through generation, gender, class, ethnicity, and race generate an array of cultural practices and multiple meanings attached to a Laotian identity. Thus, as academics and researchers, we must guard against conflating ethnicity with culture, and against the tendency to assume that a particular ethnic identity delineates cultural practices that privilege ethnic constructs, at the expense of those that embody gender or class or other social relations (Solomos and Schuster 2000:91). Even as second-generation Laotian girls affirm their Laotian ethnic identity, their social and cultural practices reveal a desire to transform the meaning of such an identity. The narrative and social practices of Laotian adolescents in this book do not represent the deliberate preservation of immigrant cultures through selective acculturation (Portes and Rumbaut 2001). It is not a nostalgic definition of being Laotian, which, in the racializing process of the United States, would cast them as Asian and, therefore, as outsiders and perpetual foreigners. It represents a desire to be ethnic without being foreign.

An examination of the interconnectedness of primary and secondary social relations challenges the public/private duality and unravels the linear and bipolar concepts of ethnic consciousness and affiliation in assimilationist and multiculturalist frameworks in the United States. Asian Youth Advocates acts a vehicle through which second-generation Laotian girls can navigate and negotiate relations of power within Laotian families while remaining connected to their ethnic communities. For new immigrant parents, the acts of migration and settlement often produce marginalization and subordination along racial and class lines. Laotian parents reaffirm their self-worth by holding onto power in the private sphere of parent-child relations and by imposing differential expectations on their daughters that restrict their autonomy, mobility, and personal desires.

Second-generation Laotian girls respond by accommodating gender expectations related to the reproduction of the household and hierarchical parent-child relations at the same time as they draw on prevalent discourses in popular culture and at AYA to resist pressure to maintain ethnic boundaries through family control in the arenas of dating and marriage preferences. In this way they not only negotiate the multiple pressures of teenage motherhood but also actively transform Laotian gender and generational relations in the public arena. In so doing, second-generation young Laotian women are changing Laotian gender ideals. However, this is not simply a process of acculturation and "Americanization" but a case of young Laotian women actively responding to their situation in the United States. Despite American middle-class aspirations and a desire for greater gender equality, the race and class subordination they experience in the dominant society keeps them embedded in Laotian families and collective social practices. Furthermore, participation in AYA enables these young women to not only affirm their cultural identities but also make Laotians visible and advocate for the community's interests and access to social rights, thus heightening their interdependence and solidarity with the Laotian community.

An ethnic identity also becomes salient and durable in negotiations with wider meanings associated with race and nationhood. The experiences of Laotians, like those of other Asian Americans (Lowe 1996) and racial/ethnic groups (Collins 2001), challenge the dominant narratives of the nation that cast America as an inclusive country, open to all who are willing to work hard and who believe in the principles of equality, democracy, and freedom, and can thereby reap the rewards they desire. Thus "America is the place of rebirth, a land in which [any and all] may shed old allegiances and Old World notions" and adopt new ones (Hsu 1996:38). However, in the United States, racial identity has always been the crucial factor in representations of the national culture and in deciding who fully belongs to this nation. The racial identity that has held currency is "white," and as Omi and Winant (1994) have argued, American identity has come to be defined as white, ordering the nation along the black-white axis and placing Asian Americans as the foreigner within.

In the latter part of the twentieth century, both pundits (Schlesinger 1992; Brimelow 1995) and the public have been concerned about the symbolic and cultural issues that the post-1965 immigrants and their children have raised in relation to language, loyalty, and national identity. Despite popular belief that America is a nation of immigrants, concerns about assimilation are mainly directed toward immigrants from Latin America and Asia and center on the perceived tendency of people of color to place ethnicity above individuality, particularism above universalism, and thus thwart the process of assimilation. The fear is that the "cult of ethnicity" (Schlesinger 1992:15) will solidify ethnic group boundaries, leading to the balkanization of a previously united and harmonious nation. These newcomers are perceived to be "space invaders" (Puar 2004) whose presence challenges the perpetuation of national myths of essentialized singular cultures and racial histories. On the other hand, American multiculturalism frames groups in terms of racial categories and expects new immigrants to shed their cultural heritage and blend into panracial groups. Multiculturalists envision a plural society in which cultural rights are a necessary condition of developing civil, political, and social rights and full citizenship (Rosaldo 1994). The construction of cultural citizenship developed by Latino scholars (Rosaldo 1994; Flores and Benmayor 1997), for example, advocates incorporation into U.S. society and the simultaneous development of specifically Latino cultural forms of expression.

I contend that both the nativist sentiments and multiculturalist assertions deny the possibility of holding multiple identities (except oppositionally; May 1999:20), the possibility that one can be both "Laotian" and "American." Arif

Dirlik (1999) has argued that attention to place and space forces us to accept the "historicity of identity" that can lead to the recognition of "homes" at multiple scales. Particularistic and collective self-understandings and collective identities develop and change, and can be contextually and historically specific. Moreover, multiculturalism's demand of blending into panracial groups in the United States erases particular Laotian immigration histories, which shape both the contexts of reception (Portes and Rumbaut 2001) and the racial positioning of Laotians in the U.S. social order. This book has demonstrated that even as second-generation Laotians assert cultural difference and claim a space and rights in the United States, they operate within and negotiate the disciplining constraints of the nation within a range of public arenas such as schools and hospitals.

By focusing on issues of race as well as those of immigration, nativism, and the ethnic-specific and class concerns of Laotians, APEN activists drew attention to the increasing salience of the immigrant experience and ethnicity in political life. By framing the siting of toxic industrial plants in communities of color, monolingual English emergency warning systems, the attempt to ban bilingual education, and inadequate school counseling services in a school in which 95 percent of the students are people of color as evidence of deep-seated societal racism and classism, APEN attempted to build a collective solidarity between racial groups linked by class position. Rather than impose an Asian American pan-ethnic identity on a community that thinks of itself as refugees, immigrants, poor, and low-wage workers, APEN fostered a politicized Laotian identity among Laotians of various ethnic affiliations that also had connections to other communities of color in Contra Costa County. In other words, the category "Laotian" became a means to an end, not the end itself. The campaign for a multilingual emergency system in Contra Costa County also demonstrated that Laotians are beginning to demand greater public recognition of their ethnic and cultural identities. Such demands challenged "English-only" movements and the nativist discourse on national identity more generally. Laotians were asking for participation as full citizens without the cost of losing cultural and linguistic identities and practices, a key component of environmental justice principles in the United States. Scholars have argued that ethnic conflict and lack of political commitment to the nation arise most often when governments and the dominant society avoid, suppress, or ignore such rights, not when ethnic, linguistic, and/or religious rights are accorded some degree of public recognition (May 1999; Bloemraad 2006). My findings suggest that assertions of ethnicity among second-generation Laotians are very much a part of the process of becoming American, not a holdover from primordial origins. However, as this case study has demonstrated, ethnicity is not fixed or stable, nor does it *contain* (May 1999:33) new immigrant groups within a hermetically sealed culture. Through the LOP and AYA, second-generation Laotians learned to demand a new racial formation in the United States, a more fluid and contingent conception of American national identity that will enable new immigrants and their children to acquire substantive citizenship.

The Possibilities and Limits of Social Justice Organizations as Sites for Critical Incorporation

APEN presented a radical perspective on integration and incorporation into American society; through Asian Youth Advocates, second-generation Laotian women became aware of specific political values, such as the belief that whatever the citizenship status of new immigrants and their children, they have social and political rights; the importance of participating in the democratic process; the value of direct collective action; and common struggle with other communities of color. These political values, together with the critical discourses of equality and justice, signaled alternative routes to becoming "American." My findings suggest that attention to the tensions in and limitations of APEN's creativity are equally important for understanding the effects of sociopolitical incorporation enacted by a community organization with a broad social and environmental justice agenda.

Unlike many of their male peers, the majority of Laotian girls in this book were educationally oriented and aspirational, as well as bonded to their families' values that hard work, perseverance, and right values and attitudes will lead to success. They were optimistic that they could fulfill their aspirations and achieve social mobility and acceptance in U.S. society. In this they displayed what Cheng and Espiritu (1989) call an "immigrant ideology." In addition, their attempts to distance themselves from "ghetto culture" indicated an awareness of the racialization processes operating in the United States, where racial power is attributed to whites (Bonilla-Silva 2003) and the positioning of African Americans at the bottom of the racial hierarchy is linked to moral deficiencies and negative values rather than to structural inequalities and barriers to opportunities for success. Such racialization processes privilege assimilation into middle-class white society as a route to gaining social prestige and citizenship. This ideology of assimilation created limits to APEN's goal of nurturing a critical racial solidarity among Laotians and other communities of color in Contra Costa County, and advocacy of alternative routes to becoming "American" that are based on equality and justice for all.

APEN's creativity, as well as the tensions and limitations in its work, calls for an analysis of the power relations that occur within community-based initiatives. In particular, an analysis blind to interethnic power relations provides an incomplete picture of power and resistance in marginalized communities. What did it mean for new Asian immigrants and refugees, such as Laotians, to participate in an organization in which second- and third-generation East Asian American women occupied key staff positions? How did Laotians react to an organization that espouses membership-based democratic political structures that are open to all segments of the Laotian community, rather than hierarchical structures that promote elite leadership? Did LOP, an organization whose impetus came from outside the community, have legitimacy in the Laotian community? When asked about this, APEN staff member Miya Yoshitani said she believed that APEN brought the political value and language of organizing to the Laotian community. APEN saw its role as "building the possibility in people's minds. That you have the right to do this, and you have the right to demand a better life for the community and for your children" (interview, 22 September 1998). However, she emphasized that individuals within the community identified the absence of an organization that could pull the various ethnic groups together. These community members were most likely not those with privilege and status, nor those who held a deferential view of authority (Hein 1995:100). Nevertheless, three years after its inception, APEN staff had difficulties organizing Laotian adults and felt that the broader Laotian community lacked a sense of ownership of LOP (Miya Yoshitani, interview, 22 September 1998), though this was not true of many of the teenage Laotian girls participating in the youth program, as I discussed in Chapter 7. In response to my suggestion that this may be a sign of quiet resistance to APEN's goals and values among elders and adults in the community, Miya was quick to point out that APEN had received "a truly positive reaction from the community" about the work it was doing and had never heard anyone say that "you really should not be doing this." At the same time, it must be acknowledged that there were very real structural limitations to Laotian adults' participation, such as low levels of English literacy, little understanding of American cultures, and working several jobs to sustain their families. But it may be more than just structural limitations or feeling disempowered in a new culture and society. Their experience of the way politics was conducted in Laos under authoritarian and then Communist governments, as well as the negative connotations associated with the very term "politics," may have acted as further disincentives to political participation (Hein 1995).

Openly negative reactions to APEN's work in the Laotian community came from some elders and leaders who felt that an organization whose impetus originated from outside the Laotian community, and which was trying to bring the various factions and ethnic groups together despite their past adversarial relations, would undermine their authority.[1] Ming Chang, an APEN staff member, observed that the position and status of the Laotian political leaders in Contra Costa County during the mid-1990s was based on their "privilege from the home country, and they have language privilege and they have class privilege." With this privilege they have been able to obtain grants and other resettlement monies and hold on to their status and power (interview, 12 October 1998). Ming's comments are ironic, especially in light of Espiritu and Ong's (1994) findings that established that second- and third-generation East Asian Americans have benefited more than newly arrived immigrants because they know how to access financial resources from private and public funding agencies, they participate in advocacy and social service coalitions, they have the ability to negotiate with elected officials and public agencies for social and civil rights, and they have had opportunities for higher education opened up by affirmative action programs. Due to their class privilege, Chinese and Japanese Americans have been most able to assume leadership positions in pan-Asian organizations (Espiritu and Ong 1994:309) and in ethnic-specific organizations that are often initiated by East Asian American activists, as LOP's case demonstrates.

Emerging young community activists in the Laotian community also commented on the dominance of East Asian Americans in key staff positions at LOP. They pointed to the power dynamics that can arise because of the privileged background of some of the staff members, their lack of life experience as members of a refugee community in the United States, and their inability to incorporate parents and families of the teens into the Laotian Organizing Project. Until 1999 the one male Laotian organizer was the only permanent staff member at LOP. One activist commented that because this organizer is male and represents the community to non-Laotians, "he is already in the old structure." She asserted that while this may be revolutionary "to the outside community" (having a Laotian in an Asian Pacific American community organization and representing Laotians to the wider community), it is not seen that way "within the community" because elder males have traditionally held leadership positions (Chit, interview, 21 September 1998). However, she also acknowledged that not many Laotians were ready and willing to take on underpaid jobs as community organizers. Several APEN staff members also discussed the dilemmas and difficulties of having leadership emerge indigenously from the Laotian community and having Laotians take on key organizing roles in LOP. But in the real world of community organizing, these dilemmas had to be balanced by the need to achieve political goals and operate successfully in the U.S. political and funding systems, which require skilled and politically sophisticated individuals.

In creating a youth program specifically for young Laotian women, APEN staff also displayed a feminist impulse. APEN envisioned that the cultivation of leadership skills and a process of politicization among the young women would change the leadership landscape of the community. Grace Kong explained APEN's broad, long-term goal of "nurturing a new generation of leaders, of girl leaders" in the following terms:

> That ten years from now the community is going to look really different because there's gonna be forty-plus or whatever of these girls that, you know, have this experience. And that concretely we want some of them to be staff here and leading organizing efforts in the community. But across the board, when they are having families, and as members of the community, that there's been some value instilled in them through this experience. . . . And it is important, I think, to connect it to the community and that it is worth, you know, trying to make change here. (Interview, 9 October 1998)

APEN staff valued in and of itself women's leadership and girls' leadership and having a space for girls, a political value that APEN brought to the community. However, working with teenage Laotian girls was seen both as filling a need for that age group and as an instrumentalist tactic of reaching the Laotian community through a bicultural generation growing up in America, thus fulfilling APEN's goal of doing base-building work in the Laotian community and creating an Asian Pacific American face in the environmental justice movement. Ming noted that she and Peggy Saika, APEN's executive director, both believed that "if the girls can organize across their many tribal groups, then there's a chance for the community to organize," to overcome past adversarial relations and create a strong community-based organization (interview, 12 October 1998). In other words, they believed that investing resources in young women would lead to a deeper and more extensive impact on the community.

APEN's political orientation, goals, and strategies call attention to interethnic power differentials in community-based organizations but also suggest an expanded analytic focus on the feminist ethos that the staff brought to young Laotian women. The case of AYA, however, illustrates how APEN nurtures the leadership of teenage Laotian girls within the context of achieving social justice for the whole community, rather than promoting narrow, individualistic women's rights. Miya asserted that APEN does not promote a "women's agenda" but "a human rights, community driven agenda, and a social justice agenda" (interview, 22 September 1998). Grace emphasized that "we want these girls to have the skills and knowledge to be able to improve the community and serve their community" (interview, 9 October 1998). Second-generation Laotian young women were nurtured as leaders in the context of benefiting the whole community. While this may be seen as a paternalistic/maternalistic desire to teach new immigrants their rights, I argue that, despite interethnic power differentials, the Laotian Organizing Project offered a broad segment of the Laotian population opportunities to actively participate in making decisions that shaped their lives, as I discussed in Chapters 4 and 6. My respondents' community activism and involvement in APEN's youth program generated new social capital for the Laotian community, the networks, trust, information channels, obligations, and expectations that encourage and facilitate greater community involvement in collectively solving the social problems it faces. In this sense, APEN also emphasized second-generation Laotian girls' interdependence and commitment to Laotian families as well as their role in community building and mediating with American institutions in public spheres. In the process of acquiring substantive citizenship, second-generation Laotians demonstrated that they were involved in a dialogue about the conception of citizenship in the United States. Even as they were becoming "American," they contested the meaning of this national identity. Through contemporary social justice organizations, new immigrants and their children learn to preserve the conditions for a participatory multiracial democracy that enable such dialogues and the continual reconstruction of American national identity.

Epilogue

Twelve years after this research was completed, Asian Youth Advocates no longer exists. The staff continued the youth leadership development program for a further two years after I left the field, recruiting teenage Laotian girls to form Groups 5 and 6. However, in 2002 it was decided to abandon the program because of a lack of staff and financial resources. The Laotian Organizing Project continues to focus on environmental justice issues, and the male Laotian is still the lead organizer, supported by Tracy, originally a member of AYA's Group 3, as a full-time organizer, and by Yen, originally of AYA's Group 4, as a part-time administrative assistant. Through their family and community networks these three Laotian staff members provided news on some of the young women who had been members of Groups 1 to 4.

Of the four young women portrayed in Chapter 1, Bryanna had not stayed in touch, and no one had news of her. Seng had finished second in her graduating class at Richmond High School and had secured a place at the University of California–Berkeley. Miya Yoshitani, now an acting director at APEN, believed that Seng was unlikely to have completed college, however, because of financial constraints. Seng was in Atlanta, working as a nanny and planning to marry an African American man. Leah was working for Bayer and completing an undergraduate degree in a science-related subject. Pham was married with a two-year-old child and completing a nursing program while working as a phlebotomist. Tsiet partially fulfilled her ambition by completing a degree in criminal justice and is now working as a legal secretary while raising her eight-year-old daughter. Many of the other young women were still living in Contra Costa County, going to school and working part-time, as well as raising families.

Among the thirty-one teenage Laotian girls in this book, three have continued to work in community organizing in some way. Gabriela, of Group 1, had wanted to work at Chevron when she first joined AYA but subsequently became passionately involved in social and environmental justice issues. Her future career was perhaps predicted when she was selected as one of "20 teens who will change the world" (cited in Chao 1999b) for her work on environmental justice issues in APEN. Since graduating from AYA, Gabriela has focused on both broad Asian American activism as well as Southeast Asian American social justice issues. She is also an accomplished author. Tracy, married and with a nine-year-old son, has worked with LOP in various roles: first in an administrative position, then as a youth organizer with AYA, and most recently as a community organizer for LOP. Before taking up the last position, she had worked with a community organization focused on reproductive justice in the Asian American community. Yen, also married and with a four-year-old son, was supplementing her part-time position at LOP by working as a phlebotomist. She was also responsible for contributing to LOP's organizing work.

During the first decade of the twenty-first century, LOP joined a growing progressive coalition in Richmond to work on the politics of land use, environmentalism, and development (Schafran and Feldstein 2009). In 2006 LOP joined the Just Cause Rent Control Campaign, which aimed to resist gentrification. In this campaign LOP worked in coalition with other social justice organizations as part of the Richmond Equitable Development Initiative, a multiorganization coalition instituted by the Oakland-based Urban Habitat to address a range of equity issues in Richmond. Schafran and Feldstein (2009) characterize LOP's involvement in the campaign as a shift from protest-demand politics to electoral politics. More recently, Chevron has continued to be the focal point of LOP's environmental justice concerns. In 2009 LOP/APEN, the West County Toxics Coalition, and Communities for a Better Environment filed a lawsuit to prevent the company from activating licenses granted by the Richmond City Council on the grounds that the environmental impact review did not address whether Chevron would be able to process dirtier crude oil, the impact of resulting pollution on Richmond residents, or plans for mitigating increased greenhouse gas emissions. Dirtier crude oil could increase the release of highly toxic mercury, selenium, and sulfur flare gases, and greenhouse gas emission could increase by almost 900,000 tons per year.[2] The Contra Costa Supreme Court upheld the challenge and ordered Chevron to halt expansion plans until a valid environmental impact review was completed. Chevron appealed this decision at the California State Court of Appeals, but in April 2010 the company lost the appeal when this court also ruled against the expansion.

APEN's current work focuses on a statewide Climate Justice Campaign to mobilize Asian Pacific Islander communities around the state of California for green jobs and green homes. In 2010 it launched the Asian Pacific American Climate Coalition to act as a vehicle for this work.[3] At the local level, LOP will continue to work within the Laotian community to ensure that its voices are heard in climate justice policies crafted at the state level. In this work LOP is supported by its Leadership Group, which became an intergenerational committee in the fall of 2009. Four former AYA members—Rachel of Group 1, Leah of Group 2, Maya of Group 3, and a young woman from Group 5—joined the first-generation adults and elders already in the group. Rachel, Leah, and Maya were part of this study. Since graduating from AYA, Rachel completed college and has been working for the Social Security Administration. She is married with a two-year-old daughter and expecting a second child. Maya also graduated from college and is working for Social Security. She is married and has two children. Involvement in the Leadership Group requires the young women to participate in leadership development training, meet monthly to discuss LOP's campaigns and activities, and identify the roles they play to support staff through both acting as representatives of the Laotian community at public events and meetings and facilitating deeper involvement among Laotians in addressing environmental and community injustices.

APPENDIX

Socio-demographic Information on Second-Generation Laotians Who Participated in the Study

Name*	Age in June 1998	Ethnic Self-Identification	Country of Birth	Age at Migration	Languages Spoken	No. of People in Household
Bryanna	14	Mien, Asian, Asian American, American	USA		Mien, English	8
Lisa	13	Lao, Mien, Asian, Asian American	USA		Mien, English	9
Julia	14	Lao, Mien, Asian, Asian American	USA		Mien, English	5
Marn	14	Mien	Thailand	2–3 yr	Mien, English	11
Karouna	14	Lao	USA		Laotian, English	5
Huk	14	Khmu	Thailand	1–2 yr	Khmu, English	9
Koy	14	Mien	USA		Mien, English	3
Yen	14	Mien	USA		Mien, English	6
Angela	13	Lao	USA		Laotian, English	6
Paeng	15.5	Asian	Thailand	2 yr	Khmu, English	
Tracy	15	Lao, Mien, Asian, Asian American	Thailand	3 mo	Mien, English	
Lai	14	Mien, Asian, Asian American	USA		Mien, English	7
Pham	15	Mien, Asian	Thailand	6 mo	Mien, English	4
Alison	14	Mien	USA		Mien, English	6

Name*	Age in June 1998	Ethnic Self-Identification	Country of Birth	Age at Migration	Languages Spoken	No. of People in Household
Tsiet	15	Mien	Thailand	6 yr	Mien, English	7
Fiey	15	Mien, Asian American	USA		Mien, English	6
Maya	15.5	Lao, Asian, Asian American	USA		Laotian, English	10
Biet	15	Mien	USA		Mien, English	6
Ruby	15	Lao, Lue, Asian American	USA		Laotian, English	6
Lily	15.5	Lao, Asian, Asian American	USA		Laotian, Thaidam, English	
Cept	15.5	Mien, Asian American	USA		Mien, English	
Cuo	16	Mien, Khmu, Asian American	USA		Mien, English	8
Caryn	16	Khmu	USA		Khmu, English	3
Gain	15	Mien, Asian, Asian American	USA		Mien, English	6
Leah	16	Lao	USA		Laotian, English	6
Seng	17	Mien	Thailand	2.5 yr	Mien, English	8
Lon	16	Mien	USA		Mien, English	4
Sarah	16	Lao	USA		Laotian, English	8
Blia	16	Hmong, Asian American	USA		Hmong, English	5
Rachel	17	Lao	USA		Laotian, English	5
Gabriela	17	Mien	Thailand	6 yr	Mien, English	6

* All names are pseudonyms.

NOTES

Chapter 1

1. This event, which brought together more than three hundred delegates and four hundred observers and supporters from environmental, civil rights, and community groups for three days in Washington, D.C., provided opportunities for participants to make conceptual linkages between ostensibly different struggles, imagine alliances not imagined before, and identify common themes of racism and economic exploitation of people and land (Cole and Foster 2001:32).

2. The Principles of Environmental Justice, which were ratified 27 October 1991 at the First National People of Color Environmental Leadership Summit, Washington, D.C., are available at http://www.ejnet.org/ej/principles.pdf.

3. See Cole and Foster (2001:chap. 1) for a detailed history of the environmental justice movement in the United States. Rather than use a single event or date to mark the beginnings of the movement, Cole and Foster apply the metaphor of a river fed by many tributaries to argue that the environmental justice movement has sources in several other social movements of the 1960s, 1970s, and 1980s.

4. A recent example is Das Gupta's *Unruly Immigrants* (2006).

5. I have used pseudonyms to identify some APEN and AYA staff, all the young Laotian women in the study, all the teachers at Richmond High School, the Laotian community organizer who worked in Richmond and San Pablo, and the mental health specialist who provided psychological services in Richmond schools.

6. Saika described these girls and subsequent recruits as neither the "whiz kids" who had access to resources and support structures nor teens involved in drugs, gangs, and dropping out of school, who would have programs to help them. The Laotian girls who joined the program were "on the edge of all that" and therefore "there would be nothing for them" (Peggy Saika, interview, 21 October 1998).

7. When I entered the field in September 1997, one of my first tasks was to acquire informed consent from all involved in the study. All the staff and all the girls consented in writing to be part of my research study. I also sought written consent from the girls' parents by sending a letter to them in Lao and English and offering to discuss my project with an interpreter. All the parents of the girls consented to their daughters' participation in the study.

8. "Check-in" was a time at the beginning of each meeting when we would say a few words about our emotional and physical well-being, how the day had gone, or respond to a lighthearted question posed by the meeting facilitator. The staff used this activity to focus everyone's attention on the agenda at hand and on the people attending.

Chapter 2

1. Trueba et al. (1990:xxiii–xxiv) describe the interview process and some of the circumstances the refugees endured while decisions were made about resettlement.

2. Other states with sizable Laotian populations include Texas, Washington, Minnesota, Wisconsin, Michigan, Illinois, Pennsylvania, New York, and Massachusetts.

3. In a study of Sacramento's new immigrants and refugees, Smith and Tarallo (1993) found that two-thirds of Mien male heads of households were unemployed and dependent on food stamps, Medi-Cal, general assistance, AFDC (Aid to Families with Dependent Children), and SSI (Supplemental Security Income).

4. The category Laotian includes Lao, Mien, and Hmong, though Hmong teens are more common (California Youth Authority Information Systems Bureau, personal communication, 6 March 2002). However, a review of newspaper reports on Richmond and San Pablo indicate that there are Asian gangs operating in west Contra Costa County, and the names of those standing trial suggest that they are young Mien men (see, for example, Fulbright 2001). A 1993 study by Waters and Cohen found that in 1991 Mien young people were being committed to the CYA at a higher rate than not only other Asian groups but also all groups in California.

5. Ima (1995) notes that between 1988 and 1992 the number of Asian refugee youths with delinquency records increased approximately 500 percent and refugee gang membership rose fivefold. Southeast Asians had the highest rate of gang-related homicide among all ethnic groups.

6. The lure of gangs for young Laotian boys is poignantly illustrated in *Caught Up*, a play about a boy involved in gang activities and unable to get out, written by Laotian boys from San Pablo and Richmond while at Byron Boys Ranch in 1999, a CYA facility (Esquibel 2001).

7. The West Contra Costa Unified School District averted financial bankruptcy in the late 1980s with a multimillion-dollar state loan. District schools still struggle with the deterioration of existing facilities, and a lack of investment in new facilities, and persistently low student achievement (Shire 2001).

8. See Walker and the Bay Area Study group (1990) for a review of the political economy of the Bay Area since the 1950s.

9. National Park Service, http://www.nps.gov/rori (accessed 4 April 2010).

10. National Park Service, http://www.nps.gov/rori.

11. See http://www.ci.richmond.ca.us/index.aspx?NID=112 (accessed 24 October 2008).

12. "Environmental Justice Case Study: West County Toxics Coalition and the Chevron Refinery," available at http://www.umich.edu/~snre492/sherman.html (accessed 20 April 2010).

13. See http://www.apen4ej.blogspot.com/2008/02/chevron-among-top-3-polluters-in-bay.html (accessed 5 May 2010).

14. See http://www.pslweb.org/liberationnews/news/06-03-01-organizing-against-oil-companies.html (accessed 4 April 2010).

15. "Environmental Justice Case Study: West County Toxics Coalition and the Chevron Refinery," available at http://www.umich.edu/~snre492/sherman.html (accessed 20 April 2010).

16. See http://www.ci.richmond.ca.us/index.aspx?NID=112 (accessed 24 October 2008).

17. See http://www.ci.richmond.ca.us/index.aspx?NID=112 (accessed 24 October 2008) for 1980 population figures. A comparison of census figures for 1980, 1990, and 2000 reveals that these demographic trends in Richmond are mirrored at the county and state levels. The state as a whole experienced tremendous growth in the Latino and Asian populations.

18. The ways in which Latinos are cast as "newcomers" and "foreigners" are another example of these racialization processes in American society (Sanchez 1997:1018). George Sanchez argues that such racialization processes can explain the invisibility of Latinos as both victims and victimizers during the 1992 Los Angeles riots in both popular and academic accounts. Latinos have been ignored in these accounts "because it disturbs strongly held beliefs in notions of community, belonging, and race in this country" (Sanchez 1997:1018).

19. The blue-ribbon Commission on Immigration Reform in 1997 embraced the need to encourage "Americanization" of immigrants (U.S. Commission on Immigration Reform 1997:vi).

20. Scholars have noted that the rise in nativism represents a profound sense of the decline of the American nation. Paralleling the increase in anti-immigrant sentiments is a fundamental restructuring of the U.S. economy, involving rapid deindustrialization, the growth of the service and high-tech sectors, and the worldwide movement of capital (Sanchez 1997:1021).

21. See http://www.onenation.org/.

22. Jonas (2006) identifies three laws in particular, all passed in 1996, that treat immigrants as a threat to U.S. national security, broadly defined to include concerns related to jobs, population growth, and cultural values and norms. The Illegal Immigrant Reform and Immigrant Responsibility Act of 1996 removed many basic legal rights for immigrants and asylum seekers and increased the grounds for exclusion and deportation. The Anti-Terrorism and Effective Death Penalty Act of 1996 also contained several punitive anti-immigrant provisions. The Personal Responsibility and Work Opportunity Reconciliation Act of 1996 denied public services and benefits to all noncitizens, thus greatly extending the exclusions implemented under California's Proposition 187.

23. The events of 11 September 2001 and the subsequent USA Patriot Act (H.R. 3162) heightened suspicion of immigrants, particularly sections of Asian American and Arab American populations, as potential terrorists. A more recent manifestation of anti-immigrant sentiments was encapsulated in H.R. 4437 (the Border Protection, Anti-Terrorism, and Illegal Immigration Control Act), a bill that passed in the House of Representatives in December 2005 and would criminalize undocumented immigrants. In May 2006 the Senate passed a "compromise" bill, S.B. 2611, that included security and deportation measures, militarization of the border, a border fence, English as the "national language," a temporary guest worker program, and the possibility of a very conditional "earned" legal status (Jonas 2006:7).

24. See "Environmental Justice Case Study": West County Toxics Coalition and the Chevron Refinery, http://www.umich.edu/~snred492/sherman.html; http://www.pslweb.org/liberationnews/news/06-03-01-organizing-against-oil-companies.html; and http://www.stratsolve.net/West_about_us.htm (all accessed 4 April 2010).

25. See http://www/apen4ej.org (accessed 4 April 2010).

Chapter 3

1. Headlines such as "We're All Minorities Now" (*West County Times*, 30 March 2001), "New Asian Diversity by the Bay" (*West County Times*, 15 August 2001), and "Suburban Melting Pots" (*West County Times*, 23 April 2001) illustrate the increased racial and ethnic diversity in metropolitan areas of California.

2. Sanchez (1997:1016), however, notes that Asian Americans and Latinos continue to be seen as only the latest of immigrant groups to America despite their active presence in American society and involvement in nation-building processes since the mid-nineteenth century.

3. Winant made these comments in his response to the papers presented at the "Reconstructing Race in the New Millennium" panel at the Annual Meeting of the American Sociological Association, 20 August 2001.

4. Neckerman, Carter, and Lee (1999) also critique the segmented assimilation model for associating minority cultures simply with the oppositional culture of the minority underclass and ignoring the culture of mobility among middle-class American minority groups. This minority culture of mobility is not simply a reflection of mainstream white middle-class culture but possesses distinctive cultural elements that provide strategies for managing economic mobility in the context of racial discrimination and group disadvantage.

5. I borrow this phrase from West (1993).

6. Lowe (1996:178) defines the U.S. orientalism of the twentieth century as the institutional, scholarly, and ideological representations of "Asian" and of "Asians in the United States."

7. The model-minority and yellow-peril/foreigner representations can exist together. While Asian Americans' success can induce nativist racism, the (feminized) model-minority image can tame fears of a (masculinized) yellow peril (Okihiro 1994; see also Espiritu 1997).

8. Indeed, community activists in the San Francisco Bay Area believe that a war on young people, particularly young people of color, has been waged since the late 1980s, culminating in the Gang Violence and Juvenile Crime Prevention Act, approved by California voters in 2000.

9. An exception is Angela McRobbie's work, which examines gendered relations to mass cultural images, and the construction of femininity through pleasure, tastes, and "enterprise culture" (Gelder 1997:86).

10. Ong (1995:350) argues that dominant assessments in the West of Chinese women fleeing China and coming to the West assume that they are leaving behind an oppressive society and entering the point of full emancipation. Indeed, many Asian American discussions also portray immigration to the United States in terms of a "loss of the 'original' culture in exchange for the new 'American' culture" (Lowe 1996:62).

11. The burgeoning literature on transnational migrants (see, for example, Basch, Glick Schiller, and Szanton Blanc 1994; Smith and Guarnizo 1998; Guarnizo, Portes, and Haller 2003; Purkayastha 2005; Levitt 2007) has also pointed to immigrants maintaining multiple national identities and multiple geographical locations of "home."

12. Sze (2004) observes that APEN is the only organization in the United States that addresses environmental justice issues within Asian Pacific American communities.

Chapter 4

1. In 1996, before I entered the field, several of the Group 1 youth were involved in protesting and lobbying against the so-called welfare reform bill. This bill, which was signed into law by President Clinton, directly affected the almost 60 percent of Laotians who relied on public assistance for their survival.

2. This explosion was followed by two more leaks in June and July of that year (Kong 2001:4). As discussed in Chapter 1, there has been a long history of fires and accidents at the Chevron Richmond refinery.

3. "Shelter-in-place" alerts warn residents to seek shelter, close the doors and windows, and shut off ventilation systems (Kong 2001:17).

4. In addition, Laotians have more than sixty-two dialects (Kong 2001:13), further complicating efforts by state agencies and social service providers to reach all the residents of Contra Costa County.

5. Ferris (1999) reports that more than one thousand people went to area hospitals, and one young person broke out in a rash after the accident.

6. Given that almost 60 percent of Laotians in Contra Costa County are on public assistance, many families rely on Medi-Cal or emergency care and are unlikely to receive adequate health care for the long-term effects of such ailments.

7. By early 2000 Contra Costa County had not begun to implement the multilingual warning system, citing the need to secure resources. APEN/LOP began a second campaign to press the county to commit resources for the new system. LOP also developed a model pilot program to reach the Laotian community and enroll households into the new system, and identified potential outside funding for the work. On 24 July 2000, the County Board of Supervisors Internal Operations Committee agreed to the following demands from LOP: (a) secure outside funding sources for the implementation of the Laotian languages pilot program (with the commitment to set up other languages after the pilot); (b) investigate the potential of using the Chevron fine from the March 1999 explosion toward funding the multilingual phone alert system; and (c) launch a new program to help Laotian families get access to low-cost health care programs (Kong 2001:20). It was not until 2006 that the county launched a Lao-language pilot telephone warning system and agreed to create separate databases in the existing system that would make calls in three of the sixty-two Laotian dialects. The county hopes to eventually add Spanish, Vietnamese, and Hmong (Platoni 2007).

8. This was not the first time APEN's work in the Laotian community had come under attack, as I discuss in the Chapter 8.

9. Over time some ethnic organizations were willing to participate in the campaign by writing letters of support to county officials (Kong 2001:30).

10. Nevertheless, Hein (1995:104) also cites instances of grassroots activism around the United States related to issues of inadequate social welfare services, rent increases, and segregated school facilities (also see Somekawa 1995).

11. The staff spent resources and time on removing or minimizing structural barriers that prevented elders, women, and poor and working people in the community from participating in grassroots social change. LOP provided childcare, transportation, and food and snacks and endeavored to hold meetings during evenings and weekends to accommodate those who were working. In addition, the staff had to devise ways to conduct multilingual and interactive community meetings that ensured the participation of all, not just the established leaders in the community who had political experience or those with a good command of English (Kong 2001:26–29).

12. Smith and Tarallo (1993:98) observe that in Laos, the Laotian population remains divided between the dominant, relatively urbanized, and nationally integrated lowland Lao and more than forty different ethnic minorities, many of which reside in the mountain regions, such as the Iu Mien. The historical isolation of these villages, their limited integration into the nation's economy, and their ethnic and linguistic diversity have all hindered the development of a unified Laotian national identity. As noted in Chapter 1, in Contra Costa County there are a number of informal community organizations, each representing a specific ethnic group. These organizations have not built alliances or worked collectively for the benefit of all Laotians in the county.

13. In *The Unmaking of Americans,* John Miller (1998:239–249) delineates a contemporary "Americanization" program that would, among other things, eliminate bilingual education, allow employers to adopt English-only rules, end exemptions to the English-language

requirements for elderly people seeking naturalization, abolish affirmative action, and deny welfare to noncitizens.

14. It is worth noting the divisions in the nativist sentiments of the late 1990s. Ron Unz, the creator and sponsor of Proposition 227, saw it not as an anti-immigrant proposition but rather as an immigrant's ticket to "the American Dream of economic and social advancement" (English Language in Public School 1998, cited in Crawford 1999). However, Crawford (1999) argues that Unz's attempt to dismantle bilingual education represents a "broader, neoconservative agenda" of rolling back the social programs and civil rights reforms of the 1960s, an effort that casts him as both "pro-immigrant" and "pro-assimilation."

15. At Richmond High School, where the majority of the girls in the APEN youth program went to school, there were seven hundred students in the Bilingual Program in 1999, and 50 percent of them were Asian (interview with resource teacher for the Bilingual Program at Richmond High, 19 May 1999).

16. APEN and AYA staff had encouraged Groups 1 and 2 to get involved in the campaign against Proposition 209 in 1996. Seng had become a precinct leader, Rachel and Gain had worked some precincts, and Gabriela had accompanied the staff on a demonstration against the proposition (field notes, 6 April 1998).

17. Twenty-four Laotian Mutual Assistance Associations sponsored the 1998 Lao New Year Festival celebration in Richmond, which has been organized annually since 1996.

18. Bill Ong Hing (1996:17–18) has noted that immigrants entering the United States in the 1990s learned English at the same rate as other immigrant groups before them. Demand for English as a Second Language classes was high, and immigrant parents encouraged their children to learn English. Even among Latinos, whom cultural assimilationists often accuse of not wanting to learn English, many regularly spoke English, particularly those who had lived in the United States for fifteen years. In addition, about 93 percent of all Mexican immigrants agreed that U.S. residents should learn English.

19. A considerable body of research supports Seng's experience, showing that on average, academic proficiency in a second language takes four to seven years to develop (Collier and Thomas 1989, cited in Crawford 1999:8).

20. This link is also recognized by academics; in reference to second-generation Vietnamese and Mien young people in Sacramento, California, Smith and Tarallo (1993:xiii) assert that access to appropriate bilingual teaching assistance is particularly important and may help prevent problems such as involvement in gangs.

21. Also see Lopez 2004; Lee 2005; Kwon 2008.

22. According to Crawford (1999), most of the more than six hundred newspaper articles, as well as countless radio and television broadcasts, that appeared on Proposition 227 in the six months before election day framed the debate in terms of an either/or decision and did not ask questions about ways to improve bilingual education.

23. On 2 June 1998, Californians approved Proposition 227 by a vote of 61 percent to 39 percent (Crawford 1999). Crawford (1999) provides a detailed analysis of the role of the proposition's backers, the media, and bilingual educators in framing the issues in ways that were bound to deliver a "yes" vote.

24. In 2001 a report by the Superintendent of Schools Fiscal Crisis and Management Assistance Team used professional and legal standards to assess the West Contra Costa Unified School District (WCCUSD) in five areas: community relations, personnel management, pupil achievement, financial management, and facilities management. On a scale of 0 to 10, where 10 represented not only full implementation of standards but also sustaining them with high quality, the report gave the district a 6.27 for community relations, 5.30 for personnel management, 5.26 for facilities management, and 4.38 for financial management, but

only 2.76 for pupil achievement (Superintendent of Schools 2001). Annual California Schools Safety Assessments indicated that in the WCCUSD, crimes in certain categories (assault with a deadly weapon, possession of weapons, property crimes) decreased over the period 1997–1999, but crimes in other categories such as battery increased dramatically, while those related to sex offenses, robbery, and drugs/alcohol increased slightly (Shafer 2000).

25. For example, in April 2001 California governor Gray Davis approved $3.3 million for juvenile crime prevention in Contra Costa County. Among other things, these funds financed a program that places probation officers in selected high schools and middle schools to provide supervision and services to students with problems ranging from truancy to major criminal offenses (Jokelson 2001). Federal law also mandated that any public school receiving federal funding institute a "zero-tolerance" policy for certain weapons offenses. Though schools and school districts implemented such a policy differently, studies by community organizations around the country found that zero-tolerance policies disproportionately affected students of color (ERASE Initiative 2000).

26. Trueba et al. (1990:75) found that Hmong students' attempts to belong and participate fully in class were undermined by teachers who remained firmly in their own training and cultural values and demanded compliance with American cultural norms of performance. When the teachers' expectations were not met, the Hmong children were judged to be performing at low levels of achievement and exhibiting learning disabilities.

27. However, as I discuss in the next chapter, both teachers and African American students perceived Asian students at Richmond High as being the smartest.

28. APEN staff members carried out a great deal of research in all these areas before presenting the options to the girls.

Chapter 5

1. Kao (2000) found that white, Asian, and Hispanic students at a high school in Chicago held similar group images and racial stereotypes of their black peers.

2. Discussing the relegation of mainly African Americans to ghettos in contemporary times, Bernasconi (2002) argues that despite the abolition of legal segregation in the mid-twentieth century, a de facto racial segregation continues. Residential segregation together with a hollowing out of jobs from the cities and white flight, which left cities with a declining tax base to address the problems of poverty and a deteriorating infrastructure, has led to the formation of ghettos. Some academics, such as Clark (1965), have argued that the persistence of ghettos has created a "ghetto culture" or a "culture of poverty" characterized by a poor work ethic, welfare dependency, a propensity for crime and drugs, and a rejection of middle-class values. Twenty years later Wilson (1987) also attacked the "culture of poverty" but believed that it stemmed from social isolation and created the "truly disadvantaged." Wilson argued for programs to create opportunities for economic mobility that would allow residents to leave the ghetto.

3. Paralleling my findings, Lopez (2003) reports that Dominican and Haitian second-generation girls in New York are far more educationally oriented, have middle-class aspirations, and are more tied to their families' immigrant communities than their brothers, who are much more influenced by a street culture that is in large part African American and Puerto Rican.

4. Also see Lee 1996:101; Waters 1999:319–321.

5. Also see Jeung 2002. Smith-Hefner (1999:195) reports that in the late 1980s, when she conducted research, young Khmer men also experienced alienation from school and were embarrassed to ask for help. She also notes that most preferred to dress in the "gangsta" or "hip-hop" style associated with urban black and Latino males.

6. In a 1992 survey of more than five thousand teenage children of immigrants in the San Diego and Miami metropolitan areas, Rumbaut (1994) found that Laotians and Cambodians had the lowest scores in English-language proficiency and on Stanford reading achievement tests. Among Asian students, Hmong and Cambodian students were also well below national math norms, followed by Lao. Rumbaut (1995) cites a 1986–87 study by the Indochinese Health and Adaptation Research Project of a representative sample of Indochinese refugees in San Diego which found that Cambodian and Lao students showed the lowest levels of attainment in GPAs and test scores in math and reading, with Vietnamese and Chinese having the highest scores and Hmong in an intermediate position. And in a survey of eighth and ninth graders in San Diego schools, Hmong and Lao, as well as Cambodians and Mexicans, expressed lower occupational aspirations than other groups (Rumbaut 1995).

7. During the 1998–99 school year the ethnic makeup of a total of 1,587 enrolled students at Richmond High was as follows: 49.8 percent Latino, 26.0 percent African American, 17.9 percent Asian, 3.6 percent white, 0.2 percent Native American, 2.5 percent Filipino, and 0.0 percent Pacific Islander, according to the California Department of Education (2002d).

8. There are two perspectives on the dramatic rise in gang activity among Southeast Asian youths. Ima (1995) argues that the increase in juvenile delinquency and gang-related activity reflects schools' inability to retain Southeast Asian students in classes, and an increasing number find themselves in trouble with the law. Walker-Moffat (1995) offers a racial analysis, arguing that the rise in these statistics reflects the youths' disillusionment with school and a realization that the kind of education they are receiving in inner-city schools will not equip them for entrance into college and the white-collar jobs that would lead to social mobility.

9. It is interesting to note that Ms. Collins did not perceive the Laotian students as American. As I noted in Chapter 3, 23 out of my 31 respondents were born in the United States.

10. The image of a "model minority" was fashioned by the media in the 1960s in the wake of the civil rights movement. See Petersen 1966 and *U.S. News and World Report* 1966.

11. Kao (2000) has found that group images and stereotypes of Asian Pacific American (APA) students as smart, hardworking, and excelling in math and science had the effect of creating high educational expectations for APA students among their black, white, and Hispanic peers, and compelled APA students to meet these high expectations of them as well as avoid disappointing their parents.

12. The percentage of white people in this community is very small, as noted in Chapter 2.

13. Sarah's comments underscored Espiritu and Ong's (1994:303–304) observation that the managerial and professional class dominates most pan-Asian organizations.

14. Zhou and Xiong (2005:1141) report that both Asian-origin and non-Asian high school students believed "Asian" or "Asian American" referred to East Asians.

15. Dotbusters was a gang in Jersey City, New Jersey, that attacked and threatened South Asians in 1987. Their name alludes to the *bindi* (red dot) that some Hindu women wear on their foreheads.

16. However, Kibria (2000) finds little evidence of pan-Asian ethnicization among Asian Pacific Americans attending college.

Chapter 6

1. Puar (1996) makes the important point that the focus on cultural conflict among the children of immigrants ignores the fact that generational conflict exists in all cultures.

2. Parent-child conflict centered on gender ideals is a recurring theme in studies of the second generation (see Wolf 1997; Espiritu 2003; Smith-Hefner 1999; Butler 1999; Valenzuela 1999; Waters 1996; Rumbaut and Ima 1988; Lopez 2003; Lee 2005).

3. High school seniors at Richmond High often plan and attempt to raise funds for a trip to Hawaii, Mexico, or Disneyland as a way to celebrate their graduation at the end of the school year.

4. Trueba et al. (1990:69) report that the clan linkages resulting from marriage are still very important in Hmong life.

5. I concur with Espiritu (2003:173) that immigrant communities are not the only ones in which parents police these arenas. Feminist research has documented the construction, containment, and exploitation of women's sexuality in various societies.

6. Similarly, MacDonald (1997:123) reports that in Portland, Oregon, when a young Mien woman married a white man, a community leader told her that she would lose face and be sanctioned by the community.

7. The "marriage book" that my respondents referred to is the *Book of Days*, which indicates whether the marriage will be harmonious, based on the birthdates of the couple (Moore-Howard 1989:48).

8. Kibria (1993:149–151) likewise reports a waning of parental authority in the context of the United States and the transformation of intergenerational relationships among Vietnamese immigrants and their children.

9. Trueba et al. (1990) found that second-generation Hmong youth expressed confusion and ambivalence because at home they couldn't talk about school activities, since parents did not understand them. Conversely, at school they couldn't talk about their cultural traditions because non-Laotians would not understand them.

10. Espiritu (2003:161) reports that Filipinos also characterized their family relationships as close-knit, in contrast to the distant and impersonal ties that American families were perceived to have.

11. Research on other second-generation groups (Wolf 1997; Espiritu 2001; Kibria 1993; Lopez 2003) also demonstrates the importance of the "family." Rumbaut (1994:770) reports that in a 1992 survey of five thousand teenage children of immigrants, all Indochinese groups scored higher than Mexican respondents on familism, the deeply ingrained sense of obligation and orientation to family.

12. Moore-Howard (1989) reports that the Mien disapprove of abortion and express ambivalent attitudes toward family planning.

13. The University of California study on teenage pregnancy rates from 1989 to 1998 was reported in a newspaper article ominously titled "Asian Teen Mothers, a Quiet State Crisis" (Kim 2001; see Weitz et al. 2001 for the original study). This headline reflects national anxieties around the complex relationship between teen motherhood and poverty, minority status, and welfare (Piven and Cloward 1997; Horowitz 1995).

14. In adopting this position, they concur with scholars such as Horowitz (1995) and Males (1996).

15. Ruth Horowitz (1995:241) argues that a model of citizenship in which it is linked solely to an individual's relationship to the marketplace is congruous with a commitment to mandatory work requirements and implies that people have a duty, regardless of their situation, to provide for themselves and their dependents. Dominant society greatly stigmatizes and excludes from full citizenship those who receive welfare to remain at home to care for their children.

16. Ngo (2002) reports that second-generation Hmong women in the Midwest are also challenging gender norms by postponing early marriage and pursuing higher education and work outside the home. Similarly, Smith-Hefner (1999) found that some young Khmer

women in Boston have delayed marriage in order to pursue education and career opportunities. Moreover, many of those who dropped out of school to marry and have children have returned to school to get their degrees so they can support their families. Anecdotal evidence from my respondents suggests that among Laotian teenage mothers, those who can find relatives to care for their children have also returned to school.

17. In her study of U.S.-Mexican youth, Valenzuela (1999) found that students who had positive attitudes toward school possessed great social capital, defined as "social ties that connect students together, as well as levels of resources (for example academic skills and knowledge) that characterize their friendship groups" (116).

18. Also see Ngo 2002. Dietrich (1998) found that Chicana adolescents who become pregnant are seeking a more conventional, domestic route to achieving some semblance of self-determination and adulthood. They see teenage motherhood as a means of attaining love, dignity, and social prestige in a world that offers them limited ways to achieve these goals.

19. See also Kibria 1993:151; Chan 1994:56.

Chapter 7

1. When the young women use the term "APEN," they are referring to AYA. For the most part, my respondents' interactions were confined to AYA-related activities and AYA staff. In the early days, however, several APEN staff worked as AYA staff, and so the boundaries between the different entities were not clear-cut.

2. At the end of each summer program the AYA staff had the teens complete an evaluation of the program. The written comments on the youth program, and how the girls thought it affected them, were quite candid even though they were not anonymous and were read by all staff members.

3. Studies on second-generation Filipinos have found that the pressures of adaptation lead many to suicidal ideation. Wolf (1997) found that almost one-third of the female Filipino university students she interviewed acknowledged having suicidal thoughts. Rumbaut (1994) also found lower self-esteem and high depression scores among young Filipinas.

4. Also see Trueba et al. 1990.

5. Valenzuela (1999:172) notes that the fact that the formal curriculum only occasionally incorporates courses on Mexican American history, reflects Mexican American students' marginal status.

6. Similarly, in 2000 there were 7,934 Hmong-speaking students in Sacramento County, California, making up 22 percent of the student body (Magagnini 2000a). But local activists pointed out that few school districts had any materials in Hmong to help students maintain their cultural identity, and there was little communication between parents and school officials (Magagnini 2000d). Tsia Xiong, a Hmong activist in Sacramento, asserted that "each school should have a minimum of one Hmong-speaking staff member in the office" (quoted in Magagnini 2000a).

7. Reevaluation counseling, also known as co-counseling, assumes a peer relationship between two people in which they take turns being the counselor and being the client. Thus peer listening is a key concept in reevaluation counseling.

8. Two respondents wished that APEN had created a separate but similar program for boys. Both these young women had brothers who were involved with gang activity in their neighborhoods. The girls believed that such a program would have been able to help their brothers deal with these pressures as well as the pressures from their families.

9. In the cities of Richmond and San Pablo there are very few safe places for young people to gather, as many of the girls remarked during the time I was in the field. APEN also provided an alternative to staying at home.

10. In the state of Minnesota the needs in the Hmong community came to light only after a series of violent tragedies in the Twin Cities Hmong community, including the slaying and sexual assault of a thirteen-year-old Hmong girl by five white youths in the fall of 1998. Thirty Hmong educators, human service providers, and community organizers met with Minnesota legislators to explore state policy solutions (Lee 1998). Ilean Her, executive director of the Council on Asian-Pacific Minnesotans, noted that the Hmong "never had a strong voice [at the capitol] on youth issues, domestic violence, mental health issues" (quoted in Lee 1998), in part due to Hmong community preferences for dealing with issues internally. Other Hmong leaders described how welfare reform had affected the Hmong, who had a desperate need for public housing, more child-care respite, and some relief from strict welfare rules (Lee 1998).

11. Portes and Rumbaut (2001:160) also found that 66.7 percent of Lao teenagers surveyed identified by a foreign national origin. They argue that groups experiencing racial discrimination and derogation of their national origins are likely to embrace immigrant origin identities even more fiercely (187). In other words, those who have experienced discrimination are less likely to identify as American. And those who expect discrimination no matter the level of education are more likely to maintain a national-origin identity (Rumbaut 1994). Selection of ethno-national categories in the face of exclusion and marginalization is termed "reactive ethnicity" by Portes and Rumbaut (2001:160). I have argued in Chapter 5 and in this chapter that my respondents felt genuine pride in being Laotian, Khmu, Mien, or Lao and in certain aspects of Laotian culture. However, as I noted, while second-generation Laotians choose to self-identify in terms of unhybridized national labels, they reconstruct the meanings and practices that these ethnic identities represent within local contexts. Thus identification with "foreign national identities" is not an indication of "less acculturation," as Portes and Rumbaut (2001:158) argue, but the active cultural construction of Laotian identity in the United States, a construction that embodies multiple and complex subjectivities.

Chapter 8

1. In 1995 some of the men in the Laotian community personally threatened APEN's executive director, Peggy Saika, and the male Laotian organizer who had worked in the community previously and now worked with the Laotian Organizing Project. Attempts were also made to mar the reputation of the Laotian organizer, whom APEN considered key to its work in the Laotian community (Peggy Saika, interview, 21 October 1998, and Ming Chang, interview, 12 October 1998).

2. See http://www.earthjustice.org/our_work/cases/2008/protecting-global-climate-and-community-health-from-oil-refinery-impacts.html (accessed 20 April 2010).

3. See http://www.apen4ej.org (accessed 4 April 2010).

REFERENCES

Afshar, Haleh. 1994. "Muslim Women in West Yorkshire: Growing Up with Real and Imaginary Values amidst Conflicting Views of Self and Society." Pp. 127–147 in *The Dynamics of "Race" and Gender: Some Feminist Interventions,* ed. Haleh Afshar and Mary Maynard. London: Taylor & Francis.
Agrawal, Shantanu. 2008. "Immigrant Exclusion from Welfare: An Analysis of the 1996 Welfare Reform Legislative Process." *Politics and Policy* 36 (4): 636–675.
Alarcon, Norma. 1990. "The Theoretical: Subject(s) of This Bridge Called My Back and Anglo-American Feminism." Pp. 356–369 in *Making Face, Making Soul: Haciendo Caras; Creative and Critical Perspectives by Women of Color,* ed. Gloria Anzaldúa. San Francisco: Aunt Lute.
Alba, Richard, and Victor Nee. 2003. *Remaking the American Mainstream: Assimilation and Contemporary Immigration.* Cambridge, MA: Harvard University Press.
Alexander, Claire. 2000. *The Asian Gang: Ethnicity, Identity, Masculinity.* Oxford: Berg.
Alexander, Jacqui M., and Chandra Talpade Mohanty. 1997. "Introduction: Genealogies, Legacies and Movements." Pp. xiii–xiii in *Feminist Genealogies, Colonial Legacies, Democratic Futures,* ed. M. Jacqui Alexander and Chandra T. Mohanty. New York: Routledge.
Allport, Gordon. 1958. *The Nature of Prejudice.* Boston: Beacon.
Ancheta, Angelo N. 1998. *Race, Rights, and the Asian American Experience.* New Brunswick, NJ: Rutgers University Press.
Anderson, Wanni W. 2005. "Between Necessity and Choice: Rhode Island Lao American Women." Pp. 194–226 in *Displacement and Diasporas: Asians in the Americas,* ed. Wanni W. Anderson and Robert G. Lee. New Brunswick, NJ: Rutgers University Press.
Anthias, Floya. 2002. "Beyond Feminism and Multiculturalism: Locating Difference and the Politics of Location." *Women's Studies International Forum* 25 (3): 275–286.
Anthias, Floya, and Nira Yuval-Davis. 1989. "Introduction." Pp. 1–15 in *Woman-Nation-State,* ed. Nira Yuval Davis and Floya Anthias. Basingstoke, U.K.: Macmillan.
APEN (Asian Pacific Environmental Network). 1999. Video recording of meeting with Mr. Walker, director of Contra Costa County Health Department, April 8.
———. 2002. "From Refugee Camps to Toxic Hot Spot: About the Laotian Community in Richmond, CA." Available at http://www.apen4ej.org/lop_history.htm (accessed 24 October 2008).

———. 2008. "Environmental Justice Groups Sue City of Richmond over Approval of Chevron Refinery Expansion." Available at http://www.apen4ej.org/chevron.htm (accessed 24 October 2008).

APIRH (Asians and Pacific Islanders for Reproductive Health). 1997. "A Proposal for Action." Oakland, CA.

Avalos, George. 2001. "City Beleaguered by the Past Looks to Rebuild Future." *West County Times* (3 November): 6.

Ballard, Roger. 1994. "Introduction: The Emergence of Desh Pardesh." Pp. 1–34 in *Desh Pardesh: The South Asian Presence in Britain*, ed. Roger Ballard. London: Hurst.

Basch, Linda Green, Nina Glick Schiller, and Cristina Szanton Blanc. 1994. *Nations Unbound: Transnational Projects, Postcolonial Predicaments and Deterritorialized Nation-States*. Langhorne, PA: Gordon & Breach.

Benmayor, Rina, Rosa M. Torruellas, and Ana L. Juarbe. 1992. *Responses to Poverty among Puerto Rican Women: Identity, Community, and Cultural Citizenship*. New York: Centro de Estudios Puertorriquenos, Hunter College of the City University of New York.

Bernasconi, Robert. 2002. "The Ghetto and Race." Pp. 340–347 in *A Companion to Racial and Ethnic Studies*, ed. David Theo Goldberg and John Solomos. Malden, MA: Blackwell.

Bhavnani, KumKum. 2004. "Tracing the Contours: Feminist Research and Feminist Objectivity." Pp. 65–77 in *Feminist Perspectives on Social Research*, ed. S. N. Hesse-Biber and M. L. Yaiser. New York: Oxford University Press.

Bloemraad, Irene. 2006. *Becoming a Citizen: Incorporating Immigrants and Refugees in the United States and Canada*. Berkeley: University of California Press.

Bloemraad, Irene, and Christine Trost. 2008. "It's a Family Affair: Intergenerational Mobilization in the Spring 2006 Protests." *American Behavioral Scientist* 52 (4): 507–532.

Blunt, Alison. 2005. *Domicile and Diaspora: Anglo-Indian Women and the Spatial Politics of Home*. Malden, MA: Blackwell.

Blunt, Alison, and Ann Varley. 2004. "Introduction: Geographies of Home." *Cultural Geographies* 11: 3–6.

Bobo, Lawrence D., and Devon Johnson. 2000. "Racial Attitudes in a Prismatic Metropolis: Mapping Identity, Stereotypes, Competition, and Views on Affirmative Action." Pp. 81–141 in *Prismatic Metropolis: Inequality in Los Angeles*, ed. L. Bobo, M. L. Oliver, J. H. Johnson Jr., and A Valenzuela Jr. New York: Russell Sage Foundation.

Bonilla-Silva, Eduardo. 2003. "'New Racisms,' Color-Blind Racism, and the Future of Whiteness in America." Pp. 271–284 in *White Out: The Continuing Significance of Racism*, ed. Ashley W. Doane and Eduardo Bonilla-Silva. New York: Routledge.

———. 2004. "From Bi-racial to Tri-racial: Towards a New System of Racial Stratification in the USA." *Ethnic and Racial Studies* 27 (6): 931–950.

Brah, Avtar. 1992a. "Difference, Diversity and Differentiation." Pp. 126–145 in *"Race," Culture and Difference*, ed. J. Donald and A. Rattansi. London: Sage.

———. 1992b. "Women of South Asian Origin in Britain: Issues and Concerns." Pp. 64–78 in *Racism and AntiRacism*, ed. Peter Braham, Ali Rattansi, and Richard Skellington. London: Sage Publications in association with Open University.

———. 1996. *Cartographies of Diaspora: Contesting Identities*. London: Routledge.

Brah, Avtar, Mary Hickman, and Martin Mac an Ghaill. 1999. "Thinking Identities: Ethnicity, Racism and Culture." Pp. 1–21 in *Thinking Identities: Ethnicity, Racism and Culture*, ed. Avtar Brah, Mary Hickman, and Martin Mac an Ghaill. Basingstoke, U.K.: Macmillan.

Brimelow, Peter. 1995. *Alien Nation: Common Sense about America's Immigration Disaster*. New York: Random House.

Brubaker, Rogers, and Frederick Cooper. 2000. "Beyond 'Identity.'" *Theory and Society* 29: 1–47.

Brulle, Robert J., and David Naguib Pellow. 2005. "The Future of Environmental Justice Movements." Pp. 293–300 in *Power, Justice, and the Environment: A Critical Appraisal of the Environmental Justice Movement,* ed. David Naguib Pellow and Robert J. Brulle. Cambridge, MA: MIT Press.

Bryant, Bunyan, and Paul Mohai, eds. 1992. *Race and the Incidence of Environmental Hazards: A Time for Discourse.* Boulder, CO: Westview Press.

Bullard, Robert. 1992. "Environmental Blackmail in Minority Communities." Pp. 82–95 in *Race and the Incidence of Environmental Hazards: A Time for Discourse,* ed. Bunyan Bryant and Paul Mohai. Boulder, CO.: Westview Press.

Bulwa, Demian. 1999. "Police Say New Arrest Will Curb Youth Gang." *West County Times* (9 October): A3.

Burawoy, Michael. 1991. "Introduction." Pp. 1–7 in *Ethnography Unbound: Power and Resistance in the Modern Metropolis,* ed. Michel Burawoy et al. Berkeley: University of California Press.

Butler, Charlotte. 1999. "Cultural Diversity and Religious Conformity: Dimensions of Social Change among Second-Generation Muslim Women." Pp. 135–151 in *Ethnicity, Gender and Social Change,* ed. Rohit Barot, Harriet Bradley, and Steve Fenton. London: Macmillan.

California Department of Education. 2002a. English Learners by Language and Grade. Available at http://dq.cde.ca.gov/dataquest/LEPbyLang4.asp?cYear=1995-96&cChoice=LepbyLang4&cSelect=RICHMOND%5EHIGH%5E%5E%5E%5E%5E%5E%5E--WEST%5ECONTRA%5ECOS--0761796-0735902&cTopic=LC&cLevel=School, and http://dq.cde.ca.gov/dataquest/LEPbyLang4.asp?cYear=2000-01&cChoice=LepbyLang4&cSelect=RICHMOND%5EHIGH%5E%5E%5E%5E%5E%5E%5E--WEST%5ECONTRA%5ECOS--0761796-0735902&cTopic=LC&cLevel=School (accessed 5 March 2002)

———. 2002b. English Learners by Language and Grade. Available at http://dq.cde.ca.gov/dataquest/LEPbyLang4.asp?cYear=1998-99&cChoice=LepbyLang4&cSelect=RICHMOND%5EHIGH%5E%5E%5E%5E%5E%5E%5E--WEST%5ECONTRA%5ECOS--0761796-0735902&cTopic=LC&cLevel=School (accessed 5 March 2002).

———. 2002c. 12th Grade Graduates Complete All Courses Required for U.C. and/or CSU Entrance. Available at http://dq.cde.ca.gov/dataquest/SchGrad.asp?cSelect=RICHMOND%5EHIGH--WEST%5ECONTRA%5ECOS--0761796-0735902&cChoice=SchGrad&cYear=1997-98&cLevel=School&cTopic=Graduates&myTimeFrame=S&submit1=Submit (accessed 5 March 2002).

———. 2002d. 1998–99 Enrollment by Ethnicity, Richmond High. Available at http://dq.cde.ca.gov/dataquest/SchEnr.asp?TheName=Rich&cSelect=RICHMOND%5EHIGH--WEST%5ECONTRA%5ECOS--0761796-0735902&cChoice=SchEnrEth&cYear=1998-99&cLevel=School&cTopic=Enrollment&myTimeFrame=S&submit1=Submit (accessed 5 March 2002).

California Department of Education, Fiscal Crisis and Management Assistance Team. 2001. *West Contra Costa Unified School District Assessment and Improvement Plan.* Sacramento: California Department of Education.

Camarillo, Albert M. 2004. "Black and Brown in Compton: Demographic Change, Suburban Decline, and Intergroup Relations in a South Central Los Angeles Community, 1950–2000." Pp. 358–376 in *Not Just Black and White: Historical and Contemporary Perspectives on Immigration, Race and Ethnicity in the United States,* ed. N. Foner and G. M. Fredrickson. New York: Russell Sage Foundation.

Carman, John. 1998. "Laotian Kids' Woes Captured on 'P.O.V.'" *San Francisco Chronicle* (30 June): E1.

Chan, Sucheng, ed. 1994. *Hmong Means Free: Life in Laos and America*. Philadelphia: Temple University Press.

———, ed. 2006. *The Vietnamese American 1.5 Generation: Stories of War, Revolution, Flight, and New Beginnings*. Philadelphia: Temple University Press.

Chang, Jack. 2001a. "New Asian Diversity by the Bay." *West County Times* (15 August): A1 and A16.

———. 2001b. "Latinos Changing Neighborhoods." *West County Times* (3 November): 10.

Chang, Jeff, and Lucia Hwang. 2000. "It's a Survival Issue." *ColorLines* 3 (2): 24–27.

Chao, Julie. 1999a. "Mien Girls Straddle Two Worlds." *San Francisco Examiner* (24 January): A1 and A8.

———. 1999b. "Teen Doing a History of Her People." *San Francisco Examiner* (26 December): C1 and C9.

Cheng, Lucie, and Yen Le Espiritu. 1989. "Korean Businesses in Black and Hispanic Neighbourhoods: A Study of Intergroup Relations." *Sociological Perspectives* 32 (4): 521–534.

Chiang, Pamela, and Audrey Chiang. 1999. "The Fight for Multi-lingual Emergency Warning Systems." *APEN Voices* 4 (2): 7–9.

Chung, Angie Y. 2007. *Legacies of Struggle: Conflict and Cooperation in Korean American Politics*. Stanford, CA: Stanford University Press.

Clark, Kenneth B. 1965. *Dark Ghetto*. New York: Harper & Row.

Clifford, James. 1986. "Introduction: Partial Truths." Pp. 1–26 in *Writing Culture: The Poetics and Politics of Ethnography*, ed. J. Clifford and G. E. Marcus. Berkeley: University of California Press.

Cole, Luke W., and Sheila Foster. 2001. *From the Ground Up: Environmental Racism and the Rise of the Environmental Justice Movement*. New York: New York University Press.

Collins, Damien, and Robin Kearns. 2001. "Under Curfew and under Siege? Legal Geographies of Young People." *Geoforum* 31: 389–403.

Collins, Patricia Hill. 1990. *Black Feminist Thought: Knowledge, Consciousness and the Politics of Empowerment*. Boston: Unwin Hyman.

———. 2001. "Like One of the Family: Race, Ethnicity and the Paradox of US National Identity." *Ethnic and Racial Studies* 24 (1): 3–28.

Communities for a Better Environment. 1989. *Richmond at Risk: Community Demographics and Toxic Hazards from Industrial Polluters*. San Francisco: CBE.

———. 2009. *Richmond Health Survey Report*. Oakland, CA: CBE.

Cornelius, Wayne A. 1995. "Educating California's Immigrant Children: Introduction and Overview." Pp. 1–16 in *California's Immigrant Children*, ed. Ruben Rumbaut and Wayne Cornelius. San Diego: Center for U.S.-Mexican Studies, University of California.

Crawford, James. 1999. "The Campaign against Proposition 227: A Post Mortem." *Bilingual Research Journal* 21 (1).

Crenshaw, Kimberle Williams. 1995. "Mapping the Margins: Intersectionality, Identity Politics, and Violence against Women of Color." Pp. 357–383 in *Critical Race Theory: The Key Writings That Formed the Movement*, ed. Kimberle Crenshaw, Neil Gotanda, Gary Peller, and Kendall Thomas. New York: New Press.

Crystal, Eric, and Kaota Saepharn. 1992. "Iu-Mien: Highland Southeast Asian Community and Culture in California Context." Pp. 327–401 in *Minority Cultures of Laos*, ed. Judy Lewis. Rancho Cordova, CA: Southeast Asia Community Resource Center, Folsom Cordova Unified School District.

Dang, Janet. 1998. "Festival Promotes a Better Environment." *AsianWeek* (23 July): 19.

Danico, Mary Yu. 2004. *The 1.5 Generation: Becoming Korean American in Hawaii*. Honolulu: University of Hawaii Press.

Dao, Yang. 1992. "The Hmong: Enduring Traditions." Pp. 249–326 in *Minority Cultures of Laos*, ed. Judy Lewis. Rancho Cordova, CA: Southeast Asia Community Resource Center, Folsom Cordova Unified School District.

Das Gupta, Monisha. 2006. *Unruly Immigrants: Rights, Activism, and Transnational South Asian Politics in the United States.* Durham, NC: Duke University Press

Davis, John, Nick Watson, and Sarah Cunningham-Burley. 2000. "Learning the Lives of Disabled Children: Developing a Reflexive Approach." Pp. 201–224 in *Research with Children: Perspectives and Practice*, ed. Pia Christensen and Allison James. London: Falmer Press.

DeVoe, Pamela. 1997. "Lao." Pp. 107–126 in *Case Studies in Diversity: Refugees in America in the 1990s*, ed. David W. Haines. Westport, CT: Praeger.

Dhingra, Pawan. 2003. "Being American between Black and White: Second Generation Asian American Professionals' Racial Identities." *Journal of Asian American Studies* 6 (2): 117–147.

Dietrich, Lisa C. 1998. *Chicana Adolescents: Bitches, "Ho"s, and Schoolgirls.* Westport, CT: Praeger.

Dirlik, Arif. 1999. "Asians on the Rim: Transnational Capital and Local Community in the Making of Contemporary Asian America." Pp. 29–60 in *Across the Pacific: Asian Americans and Globalization*, ed. Evelyn Hu-DeHart. Philadelphia: Temple University Press.

Dreyfus, Hubert L., and Paul Rabinow. 1982. *Michel Foucault: Beyond Structuralism and Hermeneutics.* Chicago: University of Chicago Press.

Dunnigan, Timothy, Douglas P. Olney, Miles A. McNall, and Marline A. Spring. 1997. "Hmong." Pp. 145–166 in *Case Studies in Diversity: Refugees in America in the 1990s*, ed. David W. Haines. Westport, CT: Praeger.

Ehrkamp, P., and H. Leitner. 2003. "Beyond National Citizenship: Turkish Immigrants and the (Re)construction of Citizenship in Germany." *Urban Geography* 24 (2): 127–146.

ERASE Initiative. 2000. "Facing the Consequences: An Examination of Racial Discrimination in U.S. Public Schools." Oakland, CA: Applied Research Center.

Escobar, Arturo. 1992. "Culture, Economics, and Politics in Latin American Social Movement Theory and Research." Pp. 62–83 in *Making of Social Movements in Latin America: Identity, Strategy and Democracy*, ed. Arturo Escobar and Sonia Alvarez. Boulder, CO: Westview Press.

Espenshade, Thomas J., Jessica L. Baraka, and Gregory A. Huber. 1997. "Implications of 1996 Welfare and Immigration Reform Acts for US Immigration." *Population and Development Review* 23 (4): 769–801.

Espiritu, Yen Le. 1992. *Asian American Panethnicity: Bridging Institutions and Identities.* Philadelphia: Temple University Press.

———. 1997. *Asian American Women and Men.* Thousand Oaks, CA: Sage Publications.

———. 2003. *Home Bound: Filipino American Lives across Cultures, Communities, and Countries.* Berkeley: University of California Press.

Espiritu, Yen, and Paul Ong. 1994. "Class Constraints on Racial Solidarity among Asian Americans." Pp. 295–321 in *The New Asian Immigration in Los Angeles and Global Restructuring*, ed. Paul Ong, Edna Bonacich, and Lucie Cheng. Philadelphia: Temple University Press.

Espiritu, Yen Le, Dorothy Fujita Rony, Nazli Kibria, and George Lipsitz. 2000. "The Role of Race and Its Articulations for Asian Pacific Americans." *Journal of Asian American Studies* 3 (2): 127–137.

Espiritu, Yen Le, and Diane L. Wolf. 2001. "The Paradox of Assimilation: Children of Filipino Immigrants in San Diego." Pp. 157–186 in *Ethnicities: Children of Immigrants in*

America, ed. Ruben G. Rumbaut and Alejandro Portes. Berkeley: University of California Press.

Esquibel, Curtis. 2001. "Teens Caught Up in Real-Life Play." *West County Times* (28 April): A3–A4.

Fernandez-Kelly, Patricia, and Sara Curran. 2001. "Nicaraguans: Voices Lost, Voices Found." Pp. 127–155 in *Ethnicities: Children of Immigrants in America*, ed. Ruben G. Rumbaut and Alejandro Portes. Berkeley: University of California Press.

Fernandez-Kelly, Patricia, and Richard Schauffler. 1996. "Divided Fates and the New Assimilation." Pp. 30–53 in *The New Second Generation*, ed. Alejandro Portes. New York: Russell Sage Foundation.

Ferris, David. 1999. "Criticism for a Late Fume Alert." *West County Times* (3 June): A1 and A16.

Fine, Gary Alan, and Kent L. Sandstrom. 1988. *Knowing Children: Participant Observation with Minors*. Newbury Park, CA: Sage Publications.

Flores, William V., and Rina Benmayor. 1997. "Introduction—Constructing Cultural Citizenship." Pp. 1–23 in *Latino Cultural Citizenship: Claiming Identity, Space and Rights*, ed. William V. Flores and Rina Benmayor. Boston: Beacon Press.

France, Alan. 1998. "'Why Should We Care?': Young People, Citizenship and Questions of Social Responsibility." *Journal of Youth Studies* 1 (1): 97–111.

Frankenberg, Ruth. 1993. *White Women, Race Matters: The Social Construction of Whiteness*. Minneapolis: University of Minnesota Press.

Fujiwara, Lynn H. 2005. "Immigrant Rights Are Human Rights: The Reframing of Immigrant Entitlement and Welfare." *Social Problems* 52 (1): 79–101.

Fulbright, Leslie. 2001. "Teenager to Go on Trial for Murder." *West County Times* (16 June): A3.

Gamson, Joshua. 1995. "Must Identity Movements Self-Destruct? A Queer Dilemma." *Social Problems* 42 (3): 390–407.

Gans, Herbert J. 1992. "Second-Generation Decline: Scenarios for the Economic and Ethnic Futures of the Post-1965 American Immigrants." *Ethnic and Racial Studies* 15 (2): 173–192.

Gelder, Ken. 1997. "Introduction to Part Two: The Birmingham Tradition and Cultural Studies." Pp. 83–89 in *The Subcultures Reader*, ed. Ken Gelder and Sarah Thornton. London: Routledge.

General Accounting Office (GAO). 1983. *Siting of Hazardous Waste Landfills and Their Correlation with Racial and Economic Status of Surrounding Communities*. GAO/RCED-83-168. Washington, DC: U.S. Government Printing Office.

George, Rosemary Marangoly. 1996. *The Politics of Home: Postcolonial Relocations and Twentieth Century Fictions*. Cambridge: Cambridge University Press.

Giordani, Sonia. 1999. "Richmond High Alarmed by Fights." *West County Times* (30 March): A3.

Giroux, Henry A. 1998. "Teenage Sexuality, Body Politics, and the Pedagogy of Display." Pp. 24–55 in *Youth Culture: Identity in a Postmodern World*, ed. Jonathan S. Epstein. Malden, MA: Blackwell.

Glenn, Evelyn Nakano. 1986. *Issei, Nisei, War Bride: Three Generations of Japanese American Women in Domestic Service*. Philadelphia: Temple University Press.

———. 2004. "Race, Gender, and Unequal Citizenship in the United States." Pp. 187–202 in *The Changing Terrain of Race and Ethnicity*, ed. Maria Krysan and Amanda E. Lewis. New York: Russell Sage Foundation.

Gordon, Milton M. 1964. *Assimilation in American Life*. New York: Oxford University Press.

Gotanda, Neil. 1999. "Exclusion and Inclusion: Immigration and American Orientalism." Pp. 129–151 in *Across the Pacific: Asian Americans and Globalization*, ed. Evelyn Hu-DeHart. Philadelphia: Temple University Press.

Grewal, Shabnam, ed. 1988. *Charting the Journey: Writing by Black and Third World Women*. London: Sheba.

Guarnizo, Luis Eduardo, Alejandro Portes, and William Haller. 2003. "Assimilation and Transnationalism: Determinants of Transnational Political Action among Contemporary Migrants." *American Journal of Sociology* 108: 1211–1248.

Gunaratnam, Yasmin. 2003. *Researching Race and Ethnicity: Methods, Knowledge and Power*. London: Sage Publications.

Haraway, Donna. 1991. *Simians, Cyborgs, and Women: The Reinvention of Nature*. New York: Routledge.

Hein, Jeremy. 1995. *From Vietnam, Laos, and Cambodia: A Refugee Experience in the United States*. New York: Twayne.

———. 2006. *Ethnic Origins: The Adaptation of Cambodian and Hmong Refugees in Four American Cities*. New York: Russell Sage Foundation.

Hesse-Biber, Sharlene Nagy, and Michelle L. Yaiser, eds. 2004. *Feminist Perspectives on Social Research*. New York: Oxford University Press.

Hing, Bill Ong. 1996. "Reframing the Immigration Debate: An Overview." Pp. 1–30 in *The State of Asian Pacific America: Reframing the Immigration Debate; A Public Policy Report*, ed. Bill Ong Hing and Ronald Lee. Los Angeles: LEAP Asian Pacific American Public Policy Institute and UCLA Asian American Studies Center.

Ho, Pensri. 2003. "Performing the 'Oriental': Professionals and the Asian Model Minority Myth." *Journal of Asian American Studies* 6: 149–175.

hooks, bell. 1984. *Feminist Theory from Margin to Center*. Boston: South End Press.

———. 1990. *Race, Gender and Cultural Politics*. Boston: South End Press.

Horowitz, Ruth. 1995. *Teen Mothers: Citizens or Dependents?* Chicago: University of Chicago Press.

Hsu, Ruth Y. 1996. "'Will the Model Minority Please Identify Itself?' American Ethnic Identity and Its Discontents." *Diaspora* 5 (1): 37–63.

Ima, Kenji. 1995. "Testing the American Dream: Case Studies of At-Risk Southeast Asian Refugee Students in Secondary Schools." Pp. 191–208 in *California's Immigrant Children*, ed. Ruben G. Rumbaut and Wayne A. Cornelius. San Diego: Center for U.S.-Mexican Studies, University of California.

Isin, Engin F., and Patricia K. Wood. 1999. *Citizenship and Identity*. London: Sage Publications.

Jeung, Russell. 2002. "Southeast Asians in the House: Multiple Layers of Identity." Pp. 60–74 in *Contemporary Asian American Communities: Intersections and Divergences*, ed. Linda Võ and Rick Bonus. Philadelphia: Temple University Press.

Jokelson, Andy. 2001. "Millions to Go toward Youth Crime Prevention." *West County Times* (11 April): A5.

Jonas, Susanne. 2006. "Reflections on the Great Immigration Battle of 2006 and the Future of the Americas." *Social Justice* 33 (1): 6–20.

Julian, Roberta. 1998. "'I Love Driving!' Alternative Constructions of Hmong Femininity in the West." *Race, Gender and Class* 5 (2): 30–53.

Kalra, Virinder S., Raminder Kaur, and John Hutnyk. 2005. *Diaspora and Hybridity*. London: Sage Publications.

Kao, Grace. 2000. "Group Images and Possible Selves among Adolescents: Linking Stereotypes to Expectations by Race and Ethnicity." *Sociological Forum* 15 (3): 407–430.

Karras, Greg. 2000. *Dioxins and Refineries: Analysis in the San Francisco Bay Area*. Report No. 2000-2, 10 August. Oakland, CA: Communities for a Better Environment.

Kasinitz, P. 2004. "Race, Assimilation, and 'Second Generations,' Past and Present." Pp. 278–298 in *Not Just Black and White: Historical and Contemporary Perspectives on Immigration, Race and Ethnicity in the United States*, ed. N. Foner and G. M. Fredrickson. New York: Russell Sage Foundation.

Kelly, Peter. 2000. "The Dangerousness of Youth-at-Risk: The Possibilities of Surveillance and Intervention in Uncertain Times." *Journal of Adolescence* 23: 463–476.

Kibria, Nazli. 1993. *Family Tightrope: The Changing Lives of Vietnamese Americans*. Princeton, NJ: Princeton University Press.

———. 1997. "The Construction of 'Asian American': Reflections on Intermarriage and Ethnic Identity among Second-Generation Chinese and Korean Americans." *Ethnic and Racial Studies* 20 (3): 523–544.

———. 2000. "Race, Ethnic Options, and Ethnic Binds: Identity Negotiations of Second-Generation Chinese and Korean Americans." *Sociological Perspectives* 43 (1): 77–95.

———. 2002. *Becoming Asian American: Second-Generation Chinese and Korean American Identities*. Baltimore: Johns Hopkins University Press.

Kim, Claire Jean. 2004. "Imagining Race and Nation in Multiculturalist America." *Ethnic and Racial Studies* 27 (6): 987–1005.

Kim, Nadia. 2008. *Imperial Citizens: Koreans and Race from Seoul to LA*. Stanford, CA: Stanford University Press.

Kim, Ryan. 2001. "Asian Teen Mothers, a Quiet State Crisis; Problem Will Be Addressed in Oakland Tonight." *San Francisco Chronicle* (7 June): A17.

King, Desmond. 2000. *Making Americans: Immigration, Race, and the Origins of the Diverse Democracy*. Cambridge, MA: Harvard University Press.

Knoll, Tricia. 1982. *Becoming Americans: Asian Sojourners, Immigrants, and Refugees in the Western United States*. Portland, OR: Coast to Coast Books.

Kondo, Dorinne. 1996. "The Narrative Production of 'Home,' Community, and Political Identity in Asian American Theater." Pp. 97–117 in *Displacement, Diaspora, and Geographies of Identity*, ed. Smadar Lavie and Ted Swedenburg. Durham, NC: Duke University Press.

Kong, Maria. 2001. *Fighting Fire with Fire: Lessons from the Laotian Organizing Project's First Campaign*. With Pamela Chiang. Oakland, CA: Asian Pacific Environmental Network; Richmond, CA: Laotian Organizing Project.

Kwon, Soo Ah. 2008. "Moving from Complaints to Action: Oppositional Consciousness and Collective Action in a Political Community." *Anthropology and Education Quarterly* 39 (1): 59–76.

Lee, Jennifer, and Min Zhou, eds. 2004. *Asian American Youth: Culture, Identity and Ethnicity*. New York: Routledge.

Lee, Richard. 1998. "More Deaths Stun Minnesota Hmong." *AsianWeek* (8–14 October).

Lee, Robert G. 1999. *Oriental: Asian Americans in Popular Culture*. Philadelphia: Temple University Press.

Lee, Sara S. 2004. "Class Matters: Racial and Ethnic Identities of Working- and Middle-Class Second-Generation Korean Americans in New York City." Pp. 313–338 in *Becoming New Yorkers: Ethnographies of the New Second Generation*, ed. Phillip Kasinitz, John H. Mollenkopf, and Mary C. Waters. New York: Russell Sage Foundation.

Lee, Stacey J. 1996. *Unraveling the "Model Minority" Stereotype: Listening to Asian American Youth*. New York: Teachers College Press.

———. 2005. *Up against Whiteness: Race, School, and Immigrant Youth*. New York: Teachers College Press.

Levitt, Peggy. 2007. *God Needs No Passport: Immigrants and the Changing American Religious Landscape*. New York: New Press.

Lie, J. 2004. "The Black-Asian Conflict?" Pp. 301–314 in *Not Just Black and White: Historical and Contemporary Perspectives on Immigration, Race and Ethnicity in the United States*, ed. N. Foner and G. M. Fredrickson. New York: Russell Sage Foundation.

Lin, Jennifer, and Howard Greenwich. 2007. *Growing with Purpose: Residents, Jobs and Equity in Richmond, California*. Oakland, CA: Richmond Equitable Development Initiative.

Lipsitz, George. 1998. "The Hip-Hop Hearings: Censorship, Social Memory, and Intergenerational Tensions among African Americans." Pp. 395–411 in *Generations of Youth: Youth Cultures and History in Twentieth-Century America*, ed. Joe Austin and Michael Nevin Willard. New York: New York University Press.

Lister, Ruth. 2003. *Citizenship: Feminist Perspectives*. New York: New York University Press.

Lochner, Tom. 1997. "Diversity Brings Questions to San Pablo." *West County Times* (9 November): A31 and A34.

———. 2001. "Churches Offer Valued Services to Community." *West County Times* (3 November): 10.

Lopez, Nancy. 2003. *Hopeful Girls, Troubled Boys: Race and Gender Disparity in Urban Education*. New York: Routledge.

———. 2004. "Unraveling the Race-Gender Gap in Education: Second-Generation Dominican Men's High School Experiences." Pp. 28–56 in *Becoming New Yorkers: Ethnographies of the New Second Generation*, ed. Philip Kasinitz, John H. Mollenkopf, and Mary C. Waters. New York: Russell Sage Foundation.

Lowe, Lisa. 1996. *Immigrant Acts*. Durham, NC: Duke University Press.

———. 1997. "Angela Davis: Reflections on Race, Class, and Gender in the USA." Pp. 303–323 in *The Politics of Culture in the Shadow of Capital*, ed. Lisa Lowe and David Lloyd. Durham, NC: Duke University Press.

Mac an Ghaill, Martin. 1999. *Contemporary Racisms and Ethnicities*. Buckingham, U.K.: Open University Press.

MacDonald, Jeffery L. 1997. *Transnational Aspects of Iu-Mien Refugee Identity*. New York: Garland.

Magagnini, Stephen. 2000a. "Activists Chart Path for a New Generation." *Sacramento Bee* (10 September): A18.

———. 2000b. "Hmong Teen Builds Future in Two Conflicting Worlds." *Sacramento Bee* (12 September): A1 and A10–A11.

———. 2000c. "Hmong Women Building Bridges." *Sacramento Bee* (11 September): A1 and A6–A7.

———. 2000d. "Trying to Save Hmong Youth." *West County Times* (11 September): A10.

Maira, Sunaina Marr. 2002. *Desis in the House: Indian American Youth Culture in New York City*. Philadelphia: Temple University Press.

Maira, Sunaina, and Elisabeth Soep. 2005. "Introduction." Pp. xv–xxxv in *Youthscapes: The Popular, the National, the Global*, ed. Sunaina Maira and Elisabeth Soep. Philadelphia: University of Pennsylvania Press

Males, Mike. 1996. *The Scapegoat Generation: America's War on Adolescents*. Monroe, ME: Common Courage Press.

Martin, Biddy, and Chandra Talpade Mohanty. 1986. "What's Home Got to Do with It?" Pp. 191–212 in *Feminist Studies/Critical Studies*, ed. Teresa de Lauretis. Bloomington: Indiana University Press.

Martin, Philip. 1995. "Documentation: Proposition 187 in California." *International Migration Review* 29 (1): 255–263.

Massey, Doreen. 1994. *Space, Places and Gender*. Minneapolis: University of Minnesota Press.

Massey, Douglas S. 1995. "The New Immigration and Ethnicity in the United States." *Population and Development Review* 21 (3): 631–652.
May, Stephen. 1999. "Critical Multiculturalisms and Cultural Difference: Avoiding Essentialism." Pp. 11–41 in *Critical Multiculturalism: Rethinking Multicultural and Antiracist Education*, ed. Stephen May. London: Falmer Press.
Metinko, Chris. 2001. "Chevron Refinery Has Been Around Longer Than City," *West County Times* (3 November): 6.
Miller, John. 1998. *The Unmaking of Americans: How Multiculturalism Has Undermined the Assimilation Ethic*. New York: Free Press.
Misir, Deborah N. 1996. "The Murder of Navroze Mody: Race, Violence, and the Search for Order." *Amerasia Journal* 22 (2): 55–76.
Mohai, Paul, and Bunyan Bryant. 1992. "Environmental Racism: Reviewing the Evidence." Pp. 163–176 in *Race and the Incidence of Environmental Hazards: A Time for Discourse*, ed. Bunyan Bryant and Paul Mohai. Boulder, CO: Westview Press.
Mohanty, Chandra Talpade. 1991a. "Cartographies of Struggle: Third World Women and the Politics of Feminism." Pp. 1–47 in *Third World Women and the Politics of Feminism*, ed. Chandra Talpade Mohanty, Ann Russo, and Lourdes Torres. Bloomington: Indiana University Press.
———. 1991b. "Under Western Eyes: Feminist Scholarship and Colonial Discourses." Pp. 51–80 in *Third World Women and the Politics of Feminism*, ed. Chandra Talpade Mohanty, Ann Russo, and Lourdes Torres. Bloomington: Indiana University Press.
———. 1992. "Feminist Encounters: Locating the Politics of Experience." Pp. 74–92 in *Destabilizing Theory: Contemporary Feminist Debates*, ed. Michele Barrett and Anne Phillips. Stanford, CA: Stanford University Press.
Moore-Howard, Patricia. 1989. *The Iu Mien: Tradition and Change*. Sacramento, CA: Sacramento City Unified School District.
Moraga, Cherrie. 1994. "From a Long Line of Vendidas: Chicanas and Feminism." Pp. 34–48 in *Theorizing Feminism: Parallel Trends in the Humanities and the Social Sciences*, ed. Anne C. Herrmann and Abigail J. Stewart. Boulder, CO: Westview Press.
Moya, Paula M. L. 1997. "Postmodernism, 'Realism,' and the Politics of Identity: Cherrie Moraga and Chicana Feminism." Pp. 125–150 in *Feminist Genealogies, Colonial Legacies, Democratic Futures*, ed. M. Jacqui Alexander and Chandra T. Mohanty. New York: Routledge.
Murguia, Edward, and Tyrone Forman. 2003. "Shades of Whiteness: The Mexican American Experience in Relation to Anglos and Blacks." Pp. 63–79 in *White Out: The Continuing Significance of Racism*, ed. Ashley W. Doane and Eduardo Bonilla-Silva. New York: Routledge.
Nagel, Joane. 1994. "Constructing Ethnicity: Creating and Recreating Ethnic Identity and Culture." *Social Problems* 41 (1): 152–176.
Neckerman, Kathryn M., Prudence Carter, and Jennifer Lee. 1999. "Segmented Assimilation and Minority Cultures of Mobility." *Ethnic and Racial Studies* 22 (6): 945–965.
Ngai, Mae M. 1999. "The Architecture of Race in American Immigration Law: A Reexamination of the Immigration Act of 1924." *Journal of American History* 86 (June): 67–92.
Ngo, Bic. 2002. "Contesting 'Culture': The Perspectives of Hmong American Female Students on Early Marriage." *Anthropology and Education Quarterly* 33 (2): 163–188.
Niedzwiecki, Max, and T. C. Duong. 2004. *Southeast Asian American Statistical Profile*. Washington, DC: Southeast Asia Resource Action Center.
Oakley, Anne. 1974. *The Sociology of Housework*. London: Robertson.
Okihiro, Gary Y. 1994. *Margins and Mainstreams: Asians in American History and Culture*. Seattle: University of Washington Press.

Omi, Michael, and Howard Winant. 1994. *Racial Formation in the United States*. New York: Routledge.

Ong, Aihwa. 1995. "Women Out of China: Traveling Tales and Traveling Theories in Postcolonial Feminism." Pp. 350–372 in *Women Writing Culture*, ed. Ruth Behar and Deborah A. Gordon. Berkeley: University of California Press.

———. 1996. "Cultural Citizenship as Subject-Making," *Current Anthropology* 37 (5): 737–762.

———. 2003. *Buddha Is Hiding: Refugees, Citizenship, the New America*. Berkeley: University of California Press.

Pantoja, Adrian D., Cecilia Menjívar, and Lisa Magaña. 2008. "The Spring Marches of 2006: Latinos, Immigration, and Political Mobilization in the 21st Century." *American Behavioral Scientist* 52 (4): 499–506.

Park, Lisa Sun-Hee. 2005. *Consuming Citizenship: Children of Asian Immigrant Entrepreneurs*. Stanford, CA: Stanford University Press.

Park, Robert E. 1950. *Race and Culture*. Glencoe, IL: Free Press.

Pateman, Carole. 1988. *The Sexual Contract*. Cambridge, MA: Polity.

Pellow, David N. 2002. *Garbage Wars: The Struggle for Environmental Justice in Chicago*. Cambridge, MA: MIT Press.

Pellow, David Naguib, and Lisa Sun-Hee Park. 2002. *Silicon Valley of Dreams: Environmental Injustice, Immigrant Workers, and the High-Tech Global Economy*. New York: New York University Press.

Perea, Juan F. 1998. "Am I an American or Not? Reflections on Citizenship, Americanization, and Race." Pp. 49–75 in *Immigration and Citizenship in the 21st Century*, ed. Noah M. J. Pickus. Lanham, MD: Rowman and Littlefield.

Petersen, William. 1966. "Success Story Japanese American Style." *New York Times Magazine* (9 January): 20–21, 33, 36, 38, 40–41, 43.

Piven, Frances Fox, and Richard A. Cloward. 1997. *The Breaking of the American Social Compact*. New York: New Press.

Platoni, Kara. 2007. "When Something's in the Air . . . Refinery Neighbors Damn Well Want to Know about It: Not Just Some of Them, and Not Just in English." *East Bay Express* (28 February–6 March). Available at http://www.eastbayexpress.com/news/when_something-s-in-the-air-/Content?oid=388057 (accessed 13 November 2008).

Pontecorvo, David. 2008. *East Bay Community Assessment: 2008 Update*. Oakland, CA: East Bay Community Foundation.

Portes, Alejandro. 2002. "English-Only Triumphs, but the Costs Are High." *Contexts* 1 (1): 10–15.

Portes, Alejandro, and Ruben G. Rumbaut. 1996. *Immigrant America: A Portrait*. Berkeley: University of California Press.

———. 2001. *Legacies: The Story of the Immigrant Second Generation*. Berkeley: University of California Press.

———. 2006. *Immigrant America: A Portrait*. 3rd ed. Berkeley: University of California Press.

Portes, Alejandro, and Min Zhou. 1993. "The New Second-Generation: Segmented Assimilation and Its Variants among Post-1965 Immigrant Youth." *Annals of the American Academy of Political and Social Science* 530: 74–96.

Prashad, Vijay. 2000. *The Karma of Brown Folk*. Minneapolis: University of Minnesota Press.

Puar, Jasbir K. 1996. "Resituating Discourses of 'Whiteness' and 'Asianness' in Northern England: Second-Generation Sikh Women and Construction of Identity." Pp. 127–150 in *New Frontiers in Women's Studies*, ed. Mary Maynard and June Purvis. London: Taylor & Francis.

Puar, Nirmal. 2004. *Space Invaders: Race, Gender and Bodies Out of Place*. Oxford: Berg.
Pulido, Laura. 1996. *Environmentalism and Economic Justice: Two Chicano Struggles in the Southwest*. Tucson: University of Arizona Press.
Purkayastha, Bandana. 2005. *Negotiating Ethnicity: Second-Generation South Asian Americans Traverse a Transnational World*. New Brunswick, NJ: Rutgers University Press.
Robles, Rowena. 2006. *Asian Americans and the Shifting Politics of Race: The Dismantling of Affirmative Action at an Elite Public High School*. New York: Routledge.
Rosaldo, Renato. 1994. "Cultural Citizenship and Educational Democracy." *Cultural Anthropology* 9 (3): 402–411.
Rumbaut, Ruben G. 1994. "The Crucible Within: Ethnic Identity, Self-Esteem, and Segmented Assimilation among Children of Immigrants." *International Migration Review* 28 (4): 748–794.
———. 1995. "The New Californians: Comparative Research Findings on the Educational Progress of Immigrant Children." Pp. 17–70 in *California's Immigrant Children: Theory, Research, and Implications for Educational Policy*, ed. Ruben Rumbaut and Wayne A. Cornelius. San Diego: Center for U.S.-Mexican Studies, University of California.
———. 1997. "Assimilation and Its Discontents: Between Rhetoric and Reality." *International Migration Review* 31 (4): 923–960.
———. 2000. "Vietnamese, Laotian and Cambodian Americans." Pp. 175–206 in *Contemporary Asian America: A Multidisciplinary Reader*, ed. Min Zhou and James V. Gatewood. New York: New York University Press.
Rumbaut, Ruben G., Nancy Foner, and Steven J. Gold. 1999. "Immigration and Immigration Research in the United States." *American Behavioral Scientist* 42 (9): 1258–1263.
Rumbaut, Ruben G., and Kenji Ima. 1988. *The Adaptation of Southeast Asian Refugee Youth: A Comparative Study*. Washington, DC: Office of Refugee Resettlement.
Rumbaut, Ruben G., and Alejandro Portes. 2001. *Ethnicities: Children of Immigrants in America*. Berkeley: University of California Press
Saechao, Fam Linh. 2001. "From War to Welfare??? An Immigrant Teenager Fears for Her Community." *Youth Outlook*. San Francisco: Pacific News Service. Available at http://www.youthoutlook.org/news/view_article.html?article_id=285 (accessed 30 November 2010).
Saetern, Moung Khoun. 1998. *Iu Mien in America: Who We Are*. Oakland, CA: Graphic House Press.
Sagar, Aparajita. 1997. "Homes and Postcoloniality." *Diaspora* 6 (2): 237–251.
Saito, Leland T., and Edward J. W. Park. 2000. "Multiracial Collaborations and Coalitions." Pp. 435–474 in *The State of Asian Pacific America: Transforming Race Relations; A Public Policy Report*, ed. Paul M. Ong. Los Angeles: LEAP Asian Pacific American Public Policy Institute and UCLA Asian American Studies Center.
Sakamoto, Arthur, and Hyeyoung Woo. 2007. "The Socioeconomic Attainments of Second-Generation Cambodian, Hmong, Laotian, and Vietnamese Americans." *Sociological Inquiry* 77 (1): 44–75.
Sanchez, George J. 1997. "Face the Nation: Race, Immigration, and the Rise of Nativism in Late Twentieth Century America." *International Migration Review* 31 (4): 1009–1030.
Sandosham, Renita. 1999. "Welfare Offices to Become Bilingual." *West County Times* (28 May).
Sandoval, Chela. 1991. "U.S. Third World Feminism: The Theory and Method of Oppositional Consciousness in the Postmodern World." *Genders* 10: 1–24.
Schafran, Alex, and Lisa Feldstein. 2009. "Racial Politics in a Changing Richmond: A New Progressive Agenda and the End of a Coalition." Paper presented at the conference "The Diverse Suburb: History, Politics and Prospects," Hofstra University, New York City, 22–24 October.

Schlesinger, Arthur. 1992. *The Disuniting of America.* New York: Norton.
Sewell, William H. 1992. "A Theory of Structure: Duality, Agency, and Transformation." *American Journal of Sociology* 98 (1): 1–29.
Shafer, Lisa. 2000. "How Safe Are California Schools?" *West County Times* (1 March): A3 and A7.
Shah, Bindi. 2007. "Being Young, Female and Laotian: Ethnicity as Social Capital at the Intersection of Gender, Generation, 'Race' and Age." *Ethnic and Racial Studies* 30 (1): 28–50.
———. 2008. "'Is Yellow Black or White?' Inter-minority Relations and the Prospects for Cross-racial Coalitions between Laotians and African Americans in the San Francisco Bay Area." *Ethnicities* 8 (4): 463–491.
Shire, Kara. 2001. "School, Educators Work toward Improvement." *West County Times* (3 November): 10.
Shohat, Ella. 1998. "Introduction." Pp. 1–62 in *Talking Visions: Multicultural Feminism in a Transnational Age,* ed. Ella Shohat. New York: New Museum of Contemporary Art; Cambridge, MA: MIT Press.
Sit, Jenny. 2000. "Refinery Warnings to Get New Voices." *West County Times* (4 August).
Smith, Michael Peter. 2001. *Transnational Urbanism: Locating Globalization.* Malden, MA: Blackwell.
Smith, Michael Peter, and Luis Eduardo Guarnizo, eds. 1998. *Transnationalism from Below.* New Brunswick, NJ: Transaction.
Smith, Michael Peter, and Bernadette Tarallo. 1993. *California's Changing Faces: New Immigrant Survival Strategies and State Policy.* Berkeley: California Policy Seminar, University of California.
Smith, Valerie. 1990. "Split Affinities: The Case of Interracial Rape." Pp. 271–287 in *Conflicts in Feminism,* ed. Marianne Hirsch and Evelyn Fox Keller. New York: Routledge.
Smith-Hefner, Nancy J. 1999. *Khmer American: Identity and Moral Education in a Diasporic Community.* Berkeley: University of California Press.
Solomos, John, and Liza K. Schuster. 2000. "Citizenship, Multiculturalism, and the Politics of Identity: Contemporary Dilemmas and Policy Agendas." Pp. 74–94 in *Challenging Immigration and Ethnic Relations Politics: Comparative European Perspectives,* ed. Ruud Koopmans and Paul Statham. Oxford: Oxford University Press.
Somekawa, Ellen. 1995. "On the Edge: Southeast Asians in Philadelphia and the Struggle for Space." Pp. 33–47 in *Reviewing Asian America, Locating Diversity,* ed. Soo-Young Chin, James S. Moy, Wendy L. Ng, and Gary Y. Okihiro. Pullman: Washington State University Press.
Squatriglia, Chuck. 1999. "Blast, Fire at Chevron Spark Calls for Tougher Regulations." *West County Times* (26 March): A1 and A18.
Stacey, J. 1988. "Can There Be a Feminist Ethnography?" *Women's Studies International Forum* 11 (1): 21–27.
Stepick, Alex, Carol Dutton Stepick, Emmanuel Eugene, Deborah Teed, and Yves Labissiere. 2001. "Shifting Identities and Intergenerational Conflict: Growing Up Haitian in Miami." Pp. 229–266 in *Ethnicities: Children of Immigrants in America,* ed. Ruben G. Rumbaut and Alejandro Portes. Berkeley: University of California Press.
Superintendent of Schools Fiscal Crisis and Management Assistance Team. 2001. "West Contra Costa Unified School District Assessment and Improvement Plan." Richmond, CA.
Sze, Julie. 2004. "Asian American Activism for Environmental Justice." *Peace Review* 16 (2): 149–156.
———. 2007. *Noxious New York: The Racial Politics of Urban Health and Environmental Justice.* Cambridge, MA: MIT Press.

Takacs, Stacy. 1999. "Alien-Nation: Immigration, National Identity and Transnationalism." *Cultural Studies* 13 (4): 591–620.

Tayanin, Damrong, and Lue Vang. 1992. "From the Village to the City: The Changing Life of the Kammu." Pp. 1–71 in *Minority Cultures of Laos*, ed. Judy Lewis. Rancho Cordova, CA: Southeast Asia Community Resource Center, Folsom Cordova Unified School District.

Taylor, Dorceta E. 2000. "The Rise of the Environmental Justice Paradigm: Injustice Framing and the Social Construction of Environmental Discourses." *American Behavioral Scientist* 43 (4): 508–580.

Taylor, Ula. 1999. "Proposition 209 and the Affirmative Action Debate on the University of California Campuses." *Feminist Studies* 25 (1): 95–103.

Teitz, Michael, and Philip Shapira. 1989. "Growth and Turbulence in the California Economy." Pp. 81–103 in *Deindustrialization and Regional Economic Transformation*, ed. Lloyd Rodwin and Hideniko Sazanami. Boston: Unwin Hyman.

Thapar-Bjorkert, S., and M. Henry. 2004. "Reassessing the Research Relationship: Location, Position and Power in Fieldwork Accounts." *International Journal of Social Research Methodology* 7 (5): 363–381.

Thomas, William I., and Florian Znaniecki. 1927. *The Polish Peasant in Europe and America*. New York: Alfred A. Knopf.

Time. 1993. "The New Face of America: How Immigrants Are Shaping the World's First Multicultural Society." Special issue (November 18).

Timmons Roberts, J., and Melissa Toffolon-Weiss. 2001. *Chronicles from the Environmental Justice Frontline*. New York: Cambridge University Press.

Toommaly, Bouapha. 2000. "AYA Victory at Richmond High School." *APEN Voices* 5 (1): 15–17.

Trueba, Henry T., Lila Jacobs, and Elizabeth Kirton. 1990. *Cultural Conflict and Adaptation: The Case of Hmong Children in American Society*. New York: Falmer Press.

Truong, Michael H. 2007. "Welfare Reform and Liberal Governance: Disciplining Cambodian-American Bodies." *International Journal of Social Welfare* 16: 258–268.

Tuan, Mia. 1998. *Forever Foreigners or Honorary Whites? The Asian Ethnic Experience Today*. New Brunswick, NJ: Rutgers University Press.

Um, Katarya. 2003. *A Dream Denied: Educational Experiences of Southeast Asian American Youth—Issues and Recommendations*. Washington, DC: Southeast Asian Resource Action Center.

United Church of Christ Commission for Racial Justice. 1987. *Toxic Wastes and Race in the United States: A National Report on the Racial and Socio-Economic Characteristics of Communities with Hazardous Waste Sites*. Available at http://www.ucc.org/about-us/archives/pdfs/toxwrace87.pdf (accessed 10 March 2002).

U.S. Census Bureau. 1990. Summary Tape File 1 (STF1)—100 Percent data, Table P007, Detailed Race. Available at http://factfinder.census.gov/servlet/DTTable?_bm=y&-state =dt&-context=dt&-ds_name=DEC_1990_STF1_&-mt_name=DEC_1990_STF1 _P007&-tree_id=100&-redoLog=true&-all_geo_types=N&-_caller=geoselect&-geo _id=01000US&-geo_id=04000US06&-geo_id=05000US06013&-geo_id =16000US062330&-search_results=16000US062330&-format=&-_lang=en (accessed 14 March 2002).

———. 2000a. File 1(SF1) 100-percent Data, Table PCT7. Available at http://factfinder .census.gov/servlet/DTTable?_bm=y&-state=dt&-context=dt&-ds_name=DEC_2000 _SF1_U&-mt_name=DEC_2000_SF1_U_PCT007&-tree_id=4001&-redoLog=true& -all_geo_types=N&-_caller=geoselect&-geo_id=01000US&-geo_id=04000US06&

-geo_id=05000US06013&-geo_id=16000US0660620&-geo_id=16000US0668294&-search_results=16000US0668294&-format=&-_lang=en (accessed 14 March 2002).

———. 2000b. Table DP-1, Profile of General Demographic Characteristics. Available at http://factfinder.census.gov/servlet/QTTable?_bm=y&-state=qt&-context=qt&-qr_name=DEC_2000_SF1_U_DP1&-ds_name=DEC_2000_SF1_U&-tree_id=4001&-redoLog=true&-all_geo_types=N&-_caller=geoselect&-geo_id=label&-geo_id=16000US0660620&-search_results=16000US0660620&-format=&-_lang=en (accessed 14 March 2002).

U.S. Commission on Immigration Reform. 1997. *Becoming an American: Immigration and Immigrant Policy*. Available at http://www.utexas.edu/lbj/uscir/becoming/full-report.pdf (accessed 20 March 2002).

U.S. News and World Report. 1966. "Success Story of One Minority in the U.S." December 26: 73–78.

Valenzuela, Angela. 1999. *Subtractive Schooling: US-Mexican Youth and the Politics of Caring*. Albany: State University of New York Press.

Võ, Linda Trinh. 2000. "Performing Ethnography in Asian American Communities: Beyond the Insider-versus-Outsider Perspective." Pp. 17–37 in *Cultural Compass: Ethnographic Explorations of Asian America*, ed. Martin F. Manalansan. Philadelphia: Temple University Press.

———. 2004. *Mobilizing an Asian American Community*. Philadelphia: Temple University Press.

Võ, L., and R. Torres. 2004. "Guest Editorial: Mapping Comparative Studies of Racialization in the US." *Ethnicities* 4 (3): 307–314.

Voderbrueggen, Lisa. 2001. "Racial and Ethnic Percent of Population." *West County Times* (3 November): 4.

Waldinger, Roger. 2001. "Strangers at the Gates." Pp. 1–29 in *Strangers at the Gates: New Immigrants in Urban America*, ed. Roger Waldinger. Berkeley: University of California Press.

Waldinger, Roger, and Jennifer Lee. 2001. "New Immigrants in Urban America." Pp. 30–79 in *Strangers at the Gates: New Immigrants in Urban America*, ed. Roger Waldinger. Berkeley: University of California Press.

Walker, Dick, and the Bay Area Study Group. 1990. "The Playground of US Capitalism? The Political Economy of the San Francisco Bay Area in the 1980s." Pp. 3–82 in *Fire in the Hearth: The Radical Politics of Place in America*, ed. Mike Davis, Steven Hialt, Marie Kennedy, Susan Ruddick, and Michael Sprinker. London: Verso.

Walker-Moffat, Wendy. 1995. *The Other Side of the Asian-American Success Story*. San Francisco: Jossey-Bass.

Wang, L. Ling-chi. 2000. "Race, Class, Citizenship, and Extraterritoriality: Asian Americans and the 1996 Campaign Finance Scandal." Pp. 518–534 in *Contemporary Asian America: A Multidisciplinary Reader*, ed. Min Zhou and James V. Gatewood. New York: New York University Press.

Warner, W. L., and L. Srole. 1945. *The Social Systems of American Ethnic Groups*. New Haven, CT: Yale University Press.

Waters, Mary C. 1996. "The Intersection of Gender, Race, and Ethnicity in Identity Development of Caribbean American Teens." Pp. 65–81 in *Urban Girls: Resisting Stereotypes, Creating Identities*, ed. Bonnie J. Ross Leadbeater and Niobe Way. New York: New York University Press.

———. 1999. *Black Identities: West Indian Immigrant Dreams and American Realities*. New York: Russell Sage Foundation.

Waters, Tony. 1990. "The Parameters of Refugeeism and Flight: The Case of Laos." *Disasters* 14 (3): 250–258.
Waters, Tony, and Lawrence E. Cohen. 1993. *Laotians in the Criminal Justice System*. Berkeley: Policy Research Program, California Policy Seminar.
Weitz, T. A., C. Harper, and A. P. Mohllajee. 2001. *Teen Pregnancy among Asians and Pacific Islanders in California: Final Report*. San Francisco: University of California–San Francisco Center for Reproductive Health Research and Policy.
West, Cornel. 1993. *Race Matters*. Boston: Beacon Press.
Wilson, William Julius. 1987. *The Truly Disadvantaged*. Chicago: University of Chicago Press.
Wolf, Diane Lauren. 1996a. "Situating Feminist Dilemmas in Fieldwork." Pp. 1–55 in *Feminist Dilemmas in Fieldwork*, ed. Diane L. Wolf. Boulder, CO: Westview Press.
———, ed. 1996b. *Feminist Dilemmas in Fieldwork*. Boulder, CO: Westview Press.
———. 1997. "Family Secrets: Transnational Struggles among Children of Filipino Immigrants." *Sociological Perspectives* 40 (3): 457–482.
Wong, Paul. 1999. "Race, Ethnicity, and Nationality in the United States: A Comparative Historical Perspective." Pp. 293–314 in *Race, Ethnicity, and Nationality in the United States: Toward the Twenty-First Century*, ed. Paul Wong. Boulder, CO: Westview Press.
Wyn, Johanna, and Rob White. 1997. *Rethinking Youth*. London: Sage.
Yang, Kou. 2001. "Research Note: The Hmong in America; Twenty-Five Years after the U.S. Secret War in Laos." *Journal of Asian American Studies* 4 (2): 165–174.
Yuval-Davis, Nira, Floya Anthias, and Eleonore Kofman. 2005. "Secure Borders and Safe Haven and the Gendered Politics of Belonging: Beyond Social Cohesion." *Ethnic and Racial Studies* 28 (3): 513–535.
Zhou, Min. 1997a. "Growing Up American: The Challenge Confronting Immigrant Children and Children of Immigrants." *American Review of Sociology* 23: 63–95.
———. 1997b. "Segmented Assimilation: Issues, Controversies, and Recent Research on the New Second Generation." *International Migration Review* 31 (4): 975–1008.
———. 2001. "Progress, Decline, Stagnation? The New Second Generation Comes of Age." Pp. 272–307 in *Strangers at the Gates: New Immigrants in Urban America*, ed. Roger Waldinger. Berkeley: University of California Press.
Zhou, Min, and Carl L. Bankston III. 1998. *Growing Up American: How Vietnamese Children Adapt to Life in the United States*. New York: Russell Sage Foundation.
Zhou, Min, and Jennifer Lee. 2004. "Introduction: The Making of Culture, Identity, and Ethnicity among Asian American Youth." Pp. 1–30 in *Asian American Youth: Culture, Identity, and Ethnicity*, ed. Jennifer Lee and Min Zhou. New York: Routledge.
Zhou, Min, and Yang Sao Xiong. 2005. "The Multifaceted American Experiences of the Children of Asian Immigrants: Lessons for Segmented Assimilation." *Ethnic and Racial Studies* 28 (6): 1119–1152.
Zia, H. 2006. "Why Privacy Matters—the Case of Wen Ho Lee." *San Francisco Chronicle* (6 June). Available at http://www.sfgate.com/cgi-bin/article.cgi?f=/c/a/2006/06/06/EDGDOILM0B1.DTL (accessed 14 June 2007).

INDEX

Acculturation, 39, 41, 47, 82, 126–128, 179; selective, 157. *See also* Adaptation
Activism, 7, 8, 46, 80, 99, 103; community, 5, 46, 127, 131, 163; environmental justice, 5, 6, 50, 85; social justice, 49, 153. *See also* Second-generation Laotians: and activism
Adaptation, 6, 39–41, 43, 51, 80, 134, 154; factors that shape, 14, 31, 40, 44, 52, 105; outcomes, 27, 38, 41, 94, 105, 134, 154, 178n3
African American(s), 52, 69, 78–79, 82–84, 90–91, 92, 108; and demographic trends in Contra Costa County, 9, 28, 30; and education, 27, 97–98, 104; and ghettos, 175n2; racial positioning of, 43, 98, 104–105, 149, 160; and social relations with Laotians, 31, 88, 90, 92, 98, 104, 114–115, 143, 164; stereotypes of, 43, 89–92, 99; and toxic exposure, 2–4, 29
Agency, 20, 46, 49–50, 128, 132, 148, 151
Alba, Richard, 40
Alliances. *See* Cross-race
American(s), 37–38, 42, 46, 150; becoming, 6, 8, 21, 38, 40, 43, 49, 53, 80, 93, 101–102, 109, 139–140, 149, 156, 159–160; culture, 17, 31, 38, 40–41, 82, 101, 119, 151, 158; dominant values, 8, 39–40, 47, 102, 104, 111, 115–116, 158; dream, 32, 44, 90, 92, 96, 174n14; nation (society), 41, 93, 149; national identity, 6, 8, 21, 34, 39, 42, 103, 107, 139, 148–149, 154, 158–159, 163; questions about nation, 34, 38, 62, 158
Americanization, 31, 40, 80, 128, 157, 171n19, 173n13
Ancheto, Angelo, 43, 83, 148
Anthias, Floya, 48, 111, 113, 130–132

Anti-immigrant sentiment, 31–34, 67, 171n20, 171nn22–23
APEN (Asian Pacific Environmental Network), 4–5, 14, 36, 79, 86, 116, 145, 152, 154–155, 159, 165, 172n12; as American space, 148; goals, 5, 36, 59, 75, 78, 79, 83–84, 123, 146, 162; political values, 5, 7–8, 50–51, 53, 69, 71, 75, 78–81, 84, 86–87, 93, 120–123, 160, 162–163; projects, 5, 9, 36; staff, 6, 9, 14, 36, 56, 99, 102–103, 160; strategy, 6–7, 36, 52–53, 61–63, 80–81, 154–155, 165 (*see also* Laotian Organizing Project); structure, 36
APIRH (Asian Pacific Islanders for Reproductive Health), 9, 121–122
Asian American(s): activism, 14, 99, 164; category, 18, 49, 99–103, 107, 176n14; community, 100; consciousness, 14, 99–101, 103, 145; culture, 101–102; in environmental justice movement, 6, 36, 102, 172n12; identity, 83, 99–103, 105, 176n16; leaders, 161–162; organizations, 49, 144–145
Asian gangs, 26–27, 170nn4–6
Asians and Asian Pacific Americans, 25, 43–44, 82; as aliens/foreigners, 31, 43, 83, 147–148, 151, 158, 172n7; as model minority, 46, 49, 83, 96–99, 155, 172n7, 176n11; and racial sameness, 108, 157; young people, 7, 27, 44, 46, 155
Assimilation, 32, 34, 39, 47, 92, 94, 105, 151, 157, 160; barriers to, 40–41, 158; inassimilability, 38, 149–151; linguistic, 62, 173n13, 174n18; theories of, 39–41, 94, 172n4
Authentic carers, 124, 140–141
AYA (Asian Youth Advocates), 4–6, 10, 50, 89, 116, 136–137, 141, 146, 157, 163, 169n6;

AYA (Asian Youth Advocates) (*continued*)
activities, 1, 5–6, 11–12, 55–58, 63–65, 67, 69–78, 86, 113, 117, 121–122, 126–127, 135–136, 144, 146–147, 150, 172n1, 174n16; funding, 9; leadership development, 5–7, 80, 127, 163; participants, 9–13, 164–165; strategy, 52–53, 63, 78, 140–141. *See also* Laotian Organizing Project

Belonging, 8, 11, 52, 62, 130, 134, 148, 150–152; facets of, 131–132; politics of, 6, 153; symbolic, 41, 43–44, 50, 151, 154. *See also* Home
Bilingual, 53, 58; and academic performance, 67, 174n20; education, 11, 32, 62–64, 66–67, 173n13, 174n22; second-generation, 5, 7, 11–13, 50, 131, 154; services, 63–64
Black(s). *See* African American(s)
Black English (Ebonics), 17, 88
Bloemraad, Irene, 8, 79, 159
Blunt, Alison, 132
Bonilla-Silva, Eduardo, 42–43, 83, 87, 160
Border space, 82, 87, 104–105
Brubaker, Rogers, 48, 83, 107
Brulle, Robert J., 155
Bryant, Bunyan, 9, 49
Bullard, Robert, 85

California, 25, 31–32, 62, 70, 171n1
Californians for Justice (CFJ), 63, 65, 67, 69
California Wellness Foundation, 9
Cambodian (Khmer), 18, 42–43, 176n6; young, 175n5, 177n16
CCCS (British Birmingham Centre for Contemporary Cultural Studies), 45–46
Chan, Sucheng, 13, 22, 47
Cheng, Lucie, 83, 92, 104, 160
Chevron, 1–3, 28–29, 35, 54–55, 165
Chinese/Chinese Americans, 43
Chung, Angie, 49, 79–80
Citizenship, 6, 123, 156, 160, 177n15; become subjects, 8, 44, 154 (*see also* Political: subjectivity); cultural, 158; legal, 8, 33–34, 42–44, 49, 60–61, 79, 153–154; substantive citizenship, 8, 34, 39, 42, 44, 49–50, 52, 58, 61, 69, 80, 92, 151, 153–156, 159–160, 163; and young people, 7, 54, 81, 155–156
Code-switching, 13, 113, 118
Cole, Luke, 4–5, 49, 169n1, 169n3
Collective action, 43, 50, 78, 80
Collective self-understanding, 48, 69, 78, 83, 85–87, 104–105, 129
Collins, Patricia Hill, 42, 48, 158
Commission on Immigration Reform, 171n19
Communities for a Better Environment, 2–3, 29, 35, 165

Community, 24, 41, 46, 132, 134, 150–153; activism, 5, 10, 46, 79, 127, 130–131, 137, 152, 163; building, 5, 7, 47, 119, 129, 163; new immigrant, 5, 35, 43, 48, 61, 84, 103, 154, 159; organizations, 9, 35, 48–49, 51, 53, 59, 102, 145, 160, 163, 173n12; organizing, 6, 36, 49, 77, 102, 126, 139–140, 162, 164; politics, 127; of resistance, 148
Cooper, Frederick, 48, 83, 107
CRHRP (UC–San Francisco Center for Reproductive Health Research and Policy), 9
Critical incorporation, 8, 36, 50–51, 80, 129, 155
Cross-race: coalitions (alliances), 9, 31, 44, 61, 71, 78, 82–84, 104–105; solidarity, 21, 31, 43, 87, 92, 99, 103, 105, 159–160
Cultural capital, 51, 88, 102, 124–125, 149
Cultural politics, 8, 51, 152, 155
Culture: American, 17, 31, 38, 40–41, 46, 82, 119, 158; conceptualization of, 39, 47, 107, 110, 128, 157–159; ghetto, 88–92, 96, 98, 160, 175n5; popular, 51, 115; white, 92–93

Danico, Mary Yu, 13
Dirlik, Arif, 159

Ehrkamp, Patricia, 8
English learner (EL) students, 27, 31, 63
Environment, 4–5
Environmental health, 7, 36; and reproductive health, 7, 120–121
Environmental justice, 4–5, 34, 53–54, 56, 60, 82, 85–86, 154; in new immigrant communities, 50, 130, 152; principles of, 4, 50, 61, 154, 159, 169n2; scholarship, 49–50, 155
Environmental justice movement, 4–5, 34, 49–50, 61–62, 85–86, 169n1, 169n3; Asian Pacific American face of, 6, 36, 59, 80, 102, 162, 172n12
Environmental Leadership Summit, First National, People of Color, 4, 36, 50
Environmental racism, 4, 49
Environmental toxins, 9, 55, 121, 165; impact of, 29, 55, 173n5
EPA (Environmental Protection Agency), 2–4, 29
Espiritu, Yen Le: Asian Americans, 47, 60, 99, 100, 152; Asian immigrants/Asian Pacific Americans, 43, 148, 177n10; assimilation, 41; differential inclusion, 132, 148; immigrant ideology, 83; immigrant women, 46, 111–113; national identity, 148; racialization, 52
Ethnic: boundaries, 40, 101, 104, 114, 120, 158; bridging organization, 49; community building, 40, 47; identity, 13, 31, 38, 40, 44, 47, 83, 100, 103, 107–109, 112, 119, 129, 132, 157–

158, 172n10; inter-ethnic relations, 14, 60, 79, 160–163; multiethnic, 39; patterns of ethnic self-identity, 100–101, 105, 107
Ethnicity, 38, 41, 47–48, 107, 109–110, 129, 156–159; and gender, 112–116, 120, 128, 177n5; reactive, 179n11
Ethnogenesis, 38
Exclusion, 8, 34, 43, 105, 130, 135, 148–149, 151, 171n22, 178nn5–6; and differential inclusion, 148–149, 150, 156

Family, importance of, 118–119, 177nn10–11; relations (*see* Second-generation Laotians: intergenerational relations)
Filipinos/Filipino Americans, 27, 36, 42, 107, 177n10, 178n3
Flores, William, 158
France, Alan, 7, 54, 81
Frankenberg, Ruth, 83

Gangs, 26, 94, 170n4
Gans, Herbert, 40
Gelder, Ken, 46
Gender: discrimination, 7; equality discourses, 8; inequality, 112, 120, 125; in policy, 33; relations, 120, 177n2 (*see also* Laotian: gender relations)
Generations, classification of, 13–14
George, Rosemary Marangoly, 132, 147
Ghetto, 88–91; culture of poverty, 90, 92, 175n2. *See also* Culture
Giroux, Henry, 7, 45, 155
Glenn, Evelyn Nakano, 8, 42, 119–120
Gotanda, Neil, 43, 83, 147

Hein, Jeremy, 22–23, 26, 47, 60–61, 127, 156
Hmong/Hmong American, 13, 22–26, 35, 38, 46–47, 107, 125, 170n4, 175n26, 176n6, 177n9, 177n16, 178n6, 179n10
Home, 41, 130–134, 138, 140, 143, 147, 148, 150–151, 172n11; conditions for inclusion, 140–143, 147; definition of, 132; and exclusion, 135–137, 146, 148; homelessness, 140, 142–143; and power, 132, 141–142, 148
HOPE (Health, Opportunities, Problem-solving, and Empowerment) for Girls Curriculum, 121–122
Horowitz, Ruth, 125, 177n13, 177n15
Hsu, Ruth, Y., 39, 41, 158

Identity: culture and, 7, 107, 109, 146, 148, 157, 179n11; fluidity, 47–48, 62, 102, 132, 138–140, 157, 159; formation, 19, 44–45, 48, 156; gender, 113; political, 19, 20, 51, 53, 62, 79, 83–85; racial, 19, 53, 158; as subjectivity, 48,

53. *See also* Laotian Organizing Project: collective identity, construction of
Immigrant(s), 4, 6, 8, 30, 33, 37–38, 44, 63, 68, 92, 154, 159, 171n22; children of, 6, 8, 13, 38, 45, 66–68, 79, 105, 107, 126, 153; and gender, 92, 175n3; and mobilization, 34, 153; representations of, 32–33, 42–43; women, 7, 16, 50–51, 120. *See also* Anti-immigrant sentiment
Immigrant ideology, 83, 92–93, 96, 104, 160
Immigration, post-1965, 37–38; settlement patterns, 37–38, 82
Incorporation into American society, 5–6, 14, 34, 36, 38–39, 44, 49, 50–51, 105, 154, 158, 160; mode of, 50, 139; politics of, 50; site for, 8, 14, 50, 154; sociopolitical (political incorporation), 8, 14, 49, 154, 160
Interracial, 9, 82–84, 87, 88 (*see also* Cross-race); tension, 84
Intersectionality, 7, 19, 44, 47–48, 53, 82, 105, 107. *See also* Relations of power
Isin, Engin F., 8

Kelly, Peter, 45, 70, 80
Khmu, 13, 22–25, 35, 47, 57, 59, 100, 147
Kibria, Nazli: Asian Americans, 83; Asians and Asian Pacific Americans, 107–108, 149, 156, 176n16; methodology, 17; second-generation, 40, 100, 103, 126
Kim, Claire Jean, 43, 83
Kim, Nadia, 42, 44, 156
Korean/Korean Americans, 42–43, 99–100

Lahu, 22, 47
Lao, 13, 22–23, 26; language proficiency, 11
Laos, 22–24, 26, 60–61, 93
Laotian: category, 47–48, 159; community organizations, 35, 174n17; culture, 27, 108–111, 117–120, 122, 138–139, 177n12; gender relations, 7, 23, 111–116, 120, 125–126, 128, 157–158, 177n16 (*see also* Gender: relations); invisibility of, 9, 58, 78, 145, 179n10; leadership, 7, 60, 127, 161; linguistic isolation, 3, 26, 33, 35, 57, 63; migration to the USA, 22–24, 118, 170n1; multiple dialects, 35, 173n4; racialization of, 42–43, 52, 83, 90, 134–135, 149; social life, 119; socio-demographic patterns, 3, 24–27, 33, 88, 91, 170nn2–3, 173n5; stereotypes of, 4, 135, 149; toxic exposure, sources, 3, 35, 55, 121
Laotian Organizing Project, 3, 5, 36, 62, 79, 131, 147, 150, 160, 164–165; as bridging organization, 80; collective identity, construction of, 36, 47–48, 62, 84–85, 143, 145–147, 151, 159, 173n12; elder activism, 56, 58, 59, 61;

Laotian Organizing Project (*continued*)
  multilingual emergency warning system campaign, 54–62, 159, 173n7, 173n11; Proposition 227 campaign, 62–69; school counselor campaign, 69–79; staff, 14, 162, 164; strategy, 5, 36, 56, 61, 62, 80, 164–165
Latino(s), 2, 3, 9, 27, 29–31, 42–43, 63, 78–79, 82, 84, 86, 91, 93, 95, 100, 115, 145, 171n17, 174n18; racialization of, 98, 171n18, 172n2; scholars, 158
Laws: Anti-Terrorism and Effective Death Penalty Act of 1996, 171n22; Border Protection, Anti-Terrorism, and Illegal Immigration control Act of 2005, 171n23; Gang Violence and Juvenile Crime Prevention Act of 2000, 172n8, 175n25; Hart-Cellar Immigration Reform Act, 37; Illegal Immigrant Reform and Immigrant Responsibility Act of 1995, 171n22; PRWORA (Personal Responsibility and Work Opportunity Act) of 1996 (*see* Welfare Reform Act of 1996); USA Patriot Act, 171n23
Lee, Jennifer, 46, 80
Lee, Robert, 42–43
Lee, Stacey, 33, 45–46, 96, 111, 135
Linguistic: equity, 57; isolation, 7, 26, 35, 54, 63
Lipsitz, George, 46
Lowe, Lisa, 6–7, 41–43, 51, 172n6
Lue, 13, 25

MacDonald, Jeffery, 35, 109, 117–120, 127
Maira, Sunaina, 46, 114
Massey, Doreen, 132, 148
May, Stephen, 158–159
Methodology, 13–16
Mien, 13, 22–25, 27, 35, 47, 59, 61, 88, 94–95, 106–107, 109, 112, 117–118, 120, 127; language proficiency, 11–13, 58
Model minority, 7, 80, 96, 99, 104, 149, 176n10. *See also* Asians and Asian Pacific Americans: as model minority; Second-generation Laotians: and model minority
Mohai, Paul, 9, 49
Mohanty, Chandra Talpade, 16, 42, 46, 48, 51, 125, 132
Moore-Howard, Patricia, 23, 177n7, 177n12
Ms. Foundation for Women, 9
Multiculturalism, 31, 158–159

Nativism, 31–32, 38, 62, 69, 159, 171n20, 174n14

Okihiro, Gary Y., 83–84, 172n7
Omi, Michael, 42, 99–100, 158
1.5-generation, 13–14

Ong, Aihwa, 8, 16, 42–44, 47, 50, 83, 107, 125, 128, 156, 172n10
Orientalism, 43, 172n6

Park, Lisa Sun-Hee, 41–44
Particularistic self-understanding, 48, 83, 107, 125–126, 157
Peer: counseling, 6, 117, 136; support, 10
Pellow, David Naguib, 49, 155
People of Color, First National Environmental Leadership Summit, 4, 36, 50
Peres Elementary School, 1–2, 35
Political: efficacy, 5, 50, 58, 60, 80, 102, 130–131, 139, 143, 154; socialization, 50, 79–80, 86–87, 139, 154; subjectivity, 49, 53, 65, 80, 139
Political process: access to, 60–61, 80, 102, 162; barriers to, 58, 60–61, 161, 173n11; participation in, 8, 36, 61, 69, 79, 151, 161; visibility, 58, 60
Portes, Alejandro: ethnicity, conceptualization of, 47; Laotian category, 48; post-1965 immigrants, 37; second-generation, 14, 38, 153, 179n11; segmented assimilation, 40, 94, 105, 157
Power, conceptualization of, 50–51
Privatization, 49, 59
Proposition 187, 32
Proposition 209, 32
Proposition 227, 32, 62, 65, 69, 174nn22–23

Racial caste system, 75, 98
Racial discrimination, 11, 32, 92, 103–105, 172n4, 179n11
Racial formation, 39, 41–42, 159
Racial hierarchy, 42–44, 83, 104, 160
Racialization: of African Americans, 98, 105, 160; of Asian Americans, 31, 43, 107, 172n2; of Laotians, 4, 44, 83, 103, 135; of Latinos, 98, 171n8, 172n2; processes, 6–7, 41–42, 46–47, 52–53, 83, 160; reaction to, 27, 62, 92, 105, 160; of social crises, 46, 53
Racial politics, 44, 74, 83–84, 104–105, 155
Racial positionality, 43, 83
Racial segregation, 175n2. *See also* Ghetto
Racial stereotypes, 89–90, 92, 96, 175n1. *See also* Model minority
Racism: anti-Asian, 52; avoidance strategies, 91, 93, 138; new scientific, 43
Reevaluation counseling, 136, 178n7
Reflexivity in research, 16–19, 125
Refugees, 8, 23–25, 33, 34, 37, 43, 83, 149
Relations of power, 8, 18–19, 41, 44–48, 50, 125–126, 132, 142, 157, 160; gender, 14, 42, 44, 110; negotiating, 50–51, 107, 128, 155, 157; racial, 83, 92, 128

Richmond, 1–3, 68, 90–91; demographic trends, 9, 25, 30, 91, 101; employment, 30; and gang violence, 26, 94, 170n4; industrial history, 28–29; Middle College High School, 89; Richmond High School, 11, 27, 70–72, 75–76, 78–79, 98, 136, 174n15, 176n7; toxic contamination, 2, 9, 28–29, 35, 54, 121
Richmond Equitable Development Initiative, 164
Rosaldo, Renato, 158
Rumbaut, Ruben G.: anti-immigrant sentiments, 38; English learners, 27; Laotian category, 48; Laotians, 24–26; post-1965 immigrants, 37; second-generation, 14, 38, 153, 176n6, 179n11; segmented assimilation, 40, 157

Sanchez, George, 31, 62, 171n18
San Pablo, 25–26, 55, 87, 91, 145
Second-generation, 13, 37–39
Second-generation Laotians, 8, 14, 40, 44, 48, 74, 80, 83, 93, 104, 128, 159, 164; academic performance, 27, 75–76, 94–95, 135–136, 176n6, 176n8; and activism, 7, 11–12, 14, 77, 79–80, 99, 127–128, 145, 148, 156, 163–164, 174n16; as cultural brokers, 68, 126–127, 163 (*see also* Bilingual: second-generation); and culture, 108–110, 119, 128, 146–147, 150, 157; and distancing strategies, 92, 104; and ethnic identity, 100–103, 105, 107–108, 129, 139–140, 156–157, 179n11; friendship patterns, 74, 89, 93, 98, 115, 143; gang activity, 26, 94, 170n4, 176n8; and gender, 92–93, 95, 104, 125 (*see also* Laotian: gender relations); intergenerational relations, 106–107, 110–120, 128–129, 134, 158; as leaders, 127; and model minority, 83, 90, 95, 96–99; representations of, 52, 67, 94, 106–107, 135, 175n26, 177n13; in school, 27, 63, 69, 71, 94, 136; and teenage pregnancy, 4, 27, 123–125, 177n16; and views on APEN/AYA (*see* Home). *See also* Young people
Self-understanding, collective, 48, 69, 78, 83, 85–87, 104–105, 129
Shelter-in-place, 54–56, 172n3
Shohat, Ella, 38
Smith, Michael Peter, 23, 49, 111
Social capital, 50, 79–80, 129, 131, 163, 178n17
Social geography of race, 83–84, 104
Social justice organizations, 7, 34, 48, 51, 63, 79, 151, 154–155, 163–164
South Asians: activism, 103; attitude toward, 176n15

Southeast Asians, 25, 33–34, 83, 94, 176n6 (*see also under specific groups*); gang activity, 170n5, 176n8
Space invaders, 38, 158
Subjectivity, 48, 151. *See also* Identity: fluidity
Superfund site, 2–3, 28–29
Sze, Julie, 4–5, 49

Taylor, Dorceta, 49–50
Teenage pregnancy, 7, 27, 120, 125, 177n13, 178n18
Teen births, 27
Thaidam, 22, 57
Toxic tour, 1–3, 86
Tuan, Mia, 43, 147

United Church of Christ Commission for Racial Justice, 4
United States foreign policy, 22–23

Varley, Ann, 132
Vietnamese/Vietnamese Americans, 26, 36, 38, 42, 107, 149, 176n6, 177n8
Võ, Linda Trinh, 16, 18–19, 49, 82, 102
Voter registration, 63

Waldinger, Roger, 24, 29, 41, 82
WCCUSD (West Contra Costa Unified School District), 63, 70, 72, 74, 170n7, 174n24
Welfare, discourses on, 42, 122, 124, 177n13
Welfare Reform Act of 1996, 33–34, 156; impact of, 33, 148, 172n1, 179n10
West County Toxics Coalition, 2, 34–35, 56, 165, 170n12
White(ness), 40, 42; and citizenship, 42, 92–93, 105, 160; culture, 92–93, 148; and power, 46, 83, 92, 105, 158, 160; suburbs as, 91
Winant, Howard, 40, 42, 99, 158
Wyn, Johanna, 45, 54

Young people, 45–46, 87, 125; as active agents, 7, 47, 53–54, 68–69, 76–81, 155; as "at risk," 45, 70, 80, 135, 155–156; of color, 46, 175n25; and policy, 172n8, 175n25; programs for, 10; representations of, 45–46, 67, 74, 79–80, 155
Youth: approaches to, 45; and gender, 46, 172n9; research on, 46; resistance, 46, 54; subcultures, 7, 45–46
Yuval-Davis, Nira, 111, 113, 130

Zhou, Min: Asian American young people, 45–47, 80; post-1965 immigrants, 38; second-generation, 14; segmented assimilation, 40, 105

Bindi V. Shah is Lecturer in Sociology at the University of Southampton, United Kingdom.

www.ingramcontent.com/pod-product-compliance
Lightning Source LLC
Chambersburg PA
CBHW031253230426
43670CB00005B/167